GOODNIGHT CHILDREN EVERYWHERE

MEMORIES OF EVACUATION
IN WORLD WAR II

EDITED BY PAM SCHWEITZER

WITH ANDY ANDREWS AND PAT FAWCETT

PHOTOGRAPHY BY ALEX SCHWEITZER

RESEARCH BY PAT FAWCETT, ANDY ANDREWS, GEMMA ⌐R,
PAM SCHWEITZER

FOREWORD BY DAVID JACOBS

AGE EXCHANGE GRATEFULLY ACKNOWLEDGES GENEROUS FINANCIAL SUPPORT
FROM THE INNER LONDON EDUCATION AUTHORITY WITH THIS PUBLICATION

CONTRIBUTORS

Thea Arnold
Howard Baker
Beryl Batten
June Biggs
Barbara Birchall
Jim Brittain
Rose Brittain
Allan Burnett
Lilian Burnett
Jean Carter
Bill Clapham
Joan Clarkson
Valerie Clayton
Harry Cole
Anne Conway
Rosemary Davis
Ivy Ellis
Paddy Evans
Pat Fawcett
Tony Fawcett

Margaret Gardiner
Milly Gardner
Dave Gelly
Alan Grant
Gervaise Du Bois Grout
Pola Haward
Valerie Hedges
Doreen Henry
Bill Herring
Joan Herring
Heather Hodge
Doris Hollands
Jim Hughes
Iris Humphreys
David Jacobs
Joan Jackaman
Joyce Kerr
Margaret Kippin
Doreen Knights
Pamela Lyne

Joan Marriott
Olive Martin
Marianne Mason
Ruby Maw
Joyce Milan
Stanley Miller
Josie Moir
Joan Morgan
Alan Morgan
Miss Gladys Mulhern
Lil Murrell
Yvonne Nicholls
Eileen Owen
Joan Pearce
Jane Pepper
Margaret Phair
Joy Plant
Dymphna Porter
Shirley Pugh
Lorna Pyke

Ethel Robinson
Iris Sharp
Sheila Shear
Renee Silverman
Eric Smidmore
Ena Smith
Peter Smith
Millie Squibb
Irene Swanton
Pat Taylor
Gladys Thomas
June Tillet
Anita Truman
Olive Tuck
Marjorie Walker
Michael Ward
Maureen Weller
Eileen Wells
Eileen Woods
Deirdre Wynne-Harley

Transcription by Andy Andrews, Christopher Downing, Pat Fawcett, Helen Gaynor, Farida Hughes, Bob Little, Melanie Mousley, Deborah Pearson, Clare Summerskill, Dora Schweitzer, Pam Schweitzer and Karen Venn.

For the loan of photographs and documentary material we wish to thank the Greater London Photographic Library, the Imperial War Museum, South East London Mercury, Patrick Cook, Jan Wright, Joan True and the Living Archive Project.

All other photographs have been loaned by the contributors, to whom we are extremely grateful.

Warmest thanks to all the volunteers at the Age Exchange Reminiscence Centre who took part in our schools project, GOODNIGHT CHILDREN EVERYWHERE, and who advised us during the creation of this book.

Picture Credits: Greater London Photographic Library: Front and back covers, pages 7, 19, 23, 30, 33, 45, 73, 109, 114, 115, 119, 153, 157, 194, 227, 231, 235, 245. Imperial War Museum: Pages 13, 21, 25, 29, 39, 51, 116, 133, 143, 146, 149, 151, 218, 222, 229, 239, 243, 254. Drawing on title page by Richard Pope, aged 11 of Rushey Green School, S.E. London.

Design and layout by Pam and Alex Schweitzer and Andy Andrews.

GOODNIGHT CHILDREN
EVERYWHERE

GOODNIGHT CHILDREN EVERYWHERE

Donald McCullough, (Uncle Mac) of Chidren's Hour fame, used to end the programme each night with the words 'Goodnight children everywhere.' And the programme was surely a link with home for all those children away from their familiar surroundings.

The song 'Goodnight Children Everywhere' was then written by Rogers and Phillips and published by Norris. It was sung and recorded by many artistes of the day.

'Goodnight Children, Everywhere.'

Goodnight children, everywhere
Your Mummy thinks of you tonight.
Lay your head upon your pillow,
Don't be a kid or a weeping willow.
Close your eyes and say a prayer
And surely you can find a kiss to spare.
Though you are far away
She's with you night and day.
Goodnight children everywhere.

Goodnight children everywhere.
Your Daddy thinks of you tonight.
And though you're far away
You'll go home one day.
Goodnight children, everywhere.

3

FOREWORD
DAVID JACOBS

If you were around in the days when when the saying "Goodnight Children Everywhere" was heard daily by listeners to the BBC's Children Hour, then this is the book for you. It's a book about memories, memories that are for sharing. You may find within its pages a story that is familiar. Indeed you may have been one of the people involved, for we were really all in the same boat, a boat that rocked from time to time but which now, for me at least, is in safe harbour.

School was never my favourite place. Looking back on it now across the years, I'm saddened by the fact that not one of my teachers inspired in me the wonders of learning. I'm sure if they'd tried, they would have found somewhere inside me that need, but they didn't. My mind was allowed to wander off into other worlds, none more frightening in that summer term of 1939 than the prospect of war. At the age of thirteen one's fear was laced with a certain sense of excitement, the whole of one's life would change and one hadn't the sense to know that it wouldn't be for the better for a very long time.

The masters at the Strand School in Tulse Hill, mid-way between Streatham Hill (where we lived) and Brixton Hill, talked at length about the prospect of our being moved lock, stock and barrel to the safer hills of Surrey. I viewed the move with mixed feelings. As it happened, though in due course my classmates were evacuated to a small village near Leatherhead, I didn't go with them. I was already in a comfortable and in many ways enviable situation. I was spending my summer holidays, as I had done the year before, with old friends of my parents, Mr and Mrs Massey, on their farm at Hoath, a small village some eight miles from Canterbury in Kent. Whilst there, I was convinced that to be a farmer's boy was more magical than anything I had known before. Certainly my memories of those days are vivid today.

At the back of my mind was the thought that, if war did come, I should not go back home and would stay there in Hoath and my dream would come true. And then, one Sunday morning, I sat beside the old battery wireless set in a front room of the farmhouse. I was alone, listening to the thin, sad voice of Mr Chamberlain.

When he had finished, I looked out of the window and saw Mr Massey walk past, still in his familiar tweed suit and turned down felt hat, but with a steel helmet slung over his shoulder, and on his arm a blue-and-white striped arm-band as head of the local special constabulary. The sirens were sounding the false alert that marked the opening of the phoney war. And I was guiltily conscious that my heart was leaping for joy because I was destined to be a farmer.

In the meantime there had to be an attempt to complete my formal education. The Masseys arranged for me to attend the local secondary school at Sturry. This entailed the excitement of being collected by the school bus and treated to a fascinating tour of the neighbouring villages every morning and afternoon. But at the school itself, which was co-educational, my reputation was somewhat mixed.

There were few enough subjects — English composition was one — in which I was equipped to show off. But my success in these, and the kindly attentions of the mistresses who made a great fuss of the little stranger in their midst, got me into ill-favour with the local boys. They also took considerable exception to what they regarded as my very affected Streatham accent. A certain amount of pushing, shoving and sly pinching occurred.

The girls, on the other hand, adopted the same friendly attitude as the mistresses and were most kind in their attentions. I was, alas, a backward lad in many respects and failed to respond with more than a shuffle and a blush. And by Christmas my dream was over. It looked as though the phoney war would continue for ever and there was no need for me to stay on at Hoath. Very reluctantly, I went back home.

INTRODUCTION

PAM SCHWEITZER

GOODNIGHT CHILDREN EVERYWHERE is a collection of memories taken from tape recordings and written accounts of evacuation in the Second World War. The stories have been collected over the last two years at the Age Exchange Reminiscence Centre in South East London. Many of the contributors have not previously thought through or recorded their wartime experience, with all the tremendous disruption it caused them, and for some of them the experience of recalling those years in some depth has been a painful one. At Age Exchange, where we mounted a special exhibition to mark the fiftieth anniversary of the massive exodus of London's children, evacuees have had the chance to meet each other and compare notes on their experiences. In addition to official photographs, documents and memorabilia of the period, we have been lent original letters and snapshots, some of which are reproduced in this book, poignantly re-evoking the long stretches of separation the evacuees endured from their loved ones.

Although plans for evacuation had been laid well before the war, and even practice marches out of the school gates had been conducted, the evacuation of hundreds of thousands of children in such a short space of time in September 1939 to often ill-prepared and even unwilling households led to considerable confusion for all and much unhappiness for some. The resilience and cheerfulness of the majority is impressive, given their sudden separation from everyone and everything familiar. There are some remarkable stories here of new friendships and lasting affections, where country people opened their homes and hearts to the London children. There is certainly a companion volume to this book to be written, exploring the situation from the point of view of those who received evacuees, and we have begun to collect memories in the West Country and East Anglia along these lines.

Many of the contributors live in the South East London area, near our Reminiscence Centre in Blackheath, and their memories are not of one, but of two great evacuations during the war. The first was in September 1939, mainly to the south coast and to rural areas of Kent, Sussex and Surrey, and the second was after the Battle of Britain and during the Blitz of 1940-41, when the children were moved to safety much further afield in Wales, the West Country and East Anglia. For this reason, many of our contributors tell of at least two billets, and of having to make double or treble adjustments to fit in with widely differing life styles and sets of expectations in each new home.

Of the vast army of children leaving London in September 1939, half had already returned by that Christmas, parents' fears having been assuaged by the continuation of the Phoney War. Parents and children had been missing each other so much that many preferred to risk possible danger rather than to extend their period of separation. It took the horrors of the Blitz to persuade these parents to part with their children a second time, and some resisted all government propaganda even then, so that schools had to remain open to cope with the fluctuating child population.

When so many children were staying in London and others were continually returning, those who stayed away had a tendency to feel unwanted, even where that was very far from the case. And it is true that many who were away for the duration of the war never found again that closeness within the family which they had known before it. The families to which the evacuees returned in 1945 were often much altered from those they had left in 1939 or even in 1941. Fathers did not always return, and often there were new brothers and sisters, and maybe a new step-parent to get used to. Furthermore, the children had often adjusted to a radically different way of life which made their London homes feel alien and, in many cases, rather poky and dirty after the great open

Tea in the garden. Iris, Ron, John and Joan Taylor of 7 St Alfege Passage,
London SE10, staying with Mrs Denham, 2nd Avenue, Torquay.

spaces of the countryside. Some children developed such strong country accents that it took a while for them even to make themselves understood back home. And many testify to missing the countryside and the people they had grown to love during the war years.

We have included in the book memories of children who evacuated with their parents and of mothers who evacuated with small children and often elderly relatives. Some of the experiences of these groups are almost as hair-raising as those of unaccompanied children. It was always the luck of the draw which determined whether one was billeted in a loving comfortable home with a good school nearby and proximity to long-standing friends and family, or if one spent the war years being pushed from pillar to post with people who showed little care or understanding for one's needs. All the contributors felt that their evacuation experience had marked them for life, for good or ill. Most of them have said to us that they would never agree to part with their own children if a similar situation were to arise again, since the emotional price of physical safety was quite simply too high.

At Age Exchange, we have mounted a Theatre in Education experience for primary schools, in which whole classes of London children aged between eight and twelve years old, have spent a day at our Reminiscence Centre taking part in a simulated evacuation, with professional actors playing key roles, such as teacher and billeting officer. During the programme, the children have met and worked with several people who were 'real' evacuees, and listened with fascination to their first hand experiences. Seeing the war through the eyes of these wartime evacuees has enabled today's children to make far more sense of those years than they might have achieved from the average history lesson. This meeting across the generations has been creative and productive for both age groups, and the original evacuees have been happy to see their experience put to good use. They have all found that the task of telling, writing down or tape-recording their experiences was worthwhile, partly so that their experience of that difficult period could be more widely understood by others, and partly for their own peace of mind.

We have not opted for a chronological approach to the stories, since each of the contributors covers a wide range of topics and a considerable stretch of time, and we have not been able to organise the pieces on a geographical basis, since so many people moved around a great deal in those years. Instead, we have arranged the contributors alphabetically, and it is our hope that readers will enjoy picking stories at random and finding for themselves the common threads. Some contributions are quite lengthy, and we have not edited savagely, since this book is intended to give scope to hitherto unexplored feelings and experiences. Many are told with great insight and humour by accomplished writers. Others are very straightforward expressions of gratitude or anger towards the 'host' community, and some are mere snatches of memory salvaged by the stimulus of the Age Exchange exhibition, or by some of the excellent footage put out on television in September 1989 to mark the fiftieth anniversary of the outbreak of war.

We very much hope that readers will derive pleasure and understanding from these stories and relish the wonderful photographs we have been lent by the contributors. We wish to thank them all for their splendid co-operation and commitment to this important reminiscence project.

Joyce Milan and our evacuation map showing where people stayed during the war.

Children taking part in the Age Exchange project, 'Goodnight Children Everywhere', trying out gas masks.

AN ANONYMOUS CONTRIBUTION

When the Doodlebugs began to cause such havoc, arrangements were made to evacuate the children from our area on the outskirts of London. My father was a soldier and he was away. My brother was seven and I was ten. We had to leave our sister at home, because she was only four, and at that time they did not take anyone under five. My mother said that she would have sent her away also if she had been older, for safety reasons.

Oddly I cannot recall any of the days leading up to our departure, but I recall that we had to assemble in the playground of a senior school, some way from our home. I can still visualise what seemed at the time to be dozens of red double-decker buses. These were to be used to transport us to a London mainline station. There were only a few tears. I can remember, even then, being surprised by that; none of us cried. I think we all just accepted the inevitable and were too weary from sleepless nights anyway, as the air raids were so bad.

The railway station teemed with hundreds of children all wearing their brown luggage labels with their names on. We had no idea where we were going; for security reasons our destination could not be told. We travelled in a corridor train which many of us had never done before. We ate our sandwiches and sang, 'We don't know where we're going 'til we're there'.

On reaching our destination we found we were in Wales and we were taken by buses again to various centres. We sat in classrooms in a school. It seemed as if we were there for hours. From time to time someone came and took one of us away and soon my brother went. No−one told me where he was going or if I would ever see him again. This was very worrying as my mother had asked me to look after him. I was too shy to ask about it. Eventually there were only a couple of us left. At the time I thought the people coming in must be choosing us and no−one wanted me, but in fact we had been allocated in advance.

When the lady of the house to which I was going arrived, she explained that they had had a delivery of coal. In that valley village, coal was dumped on the pavement outside your front door, and the householder was then responsible for seeing that it was taken indoors, or through to the back. She had been helping to move the coal and that was why she was late to collect me.

The father of the house was a sailor and he was based in Portsmouth. There was a boy of thirteen and a girl of nine, so I, at ten, fitted in between. I was made to feel welcome, but I can remember telling my first recognisable lie there, for on being asked what time I went to bed, I said half past eight, when in reality I had had to go to bed at half past seven. Aunt, as I called her, said I could go to bed at eight o'clock, so I gained a bit!

It was not strange sleeping in a bed with the other girl, as we had all slept together in the Morrison shelter in London, me at the top, with my small sister and my brother at the bottom. When the warning went my mother and grandmother used to come down from upstairs and join us.

My brother, I discovered, had been billeted next door to me and was with a family that had many children. I secretly hoped that when I got to know that family, they would let me take the baby out. However, my brother was moved from there quite quickly to a family of all grown-ups. The little children and the baby reminded him of our sister and he had cried all the time. I felt cheated, and also embarrassed by his blatant display of homesickness. I too was homesick but determined no one should know about it.

The early school days were a misery; in fact they were a lasting misery. It must have been a nightmare for the authorities and teachers involved, to have to cope with this great unflux of pupils. There were insufficient seats and desks and for the first week. They did not know what to do with us and it took a long time for them to sort us out. I spent a short while at one school where several classes were held at the same time in the assembly hall. We had to sit on the floor. Later we sat three to a desk. Then I was transferred to another school which was more senior.

The whole school period was a disappointment. I early discovered they were far behind the one I had come from in England. Any given work I accomplished in the first five minutes. I then sat and did nothing or read my library book under the desk. I usually read through most of the

1940. London children leave for West Country.

Welsh lesson as they did not really bother much to teach us and there were too many of us, although I can remember writing some of the language down. I felt very frustrated at that time and worried constantly about the things I was missing and how I would ever catch up again when I went home.

Meanwhile, my brother was thoroughly enjoying himself. He was filthy, allowed to stay up until about midnight, played out in the street until all hours and spent a great deal of time at the pictures. Apart from the layer of grime, his hair permanently looked as if it needed to be cut. He lived with a mining family. The father and a couple of sons went down the mine. They took him down and each gave him pocket money every week. As they gave him half a crown, he was very wealthy, or he would have been if he had not smoked.

If we met in the street one of us would say, 'I've had a letter from my mother'. It was difficult to believe we had the same mother. Our mother would send us a one shilling postal order each week. Out of that we had to buy a stamp to write home and thank her for it and to let her know that it had arrived. It seemed to go quite a long way; we could perhaps buy a birthday card or go to the pictures and sit up in the gods for twopence and then buy potato scallops from the fish and chip shop on the way home, all for inside the shilling.

My brother was very bad about writing home and my mother used to ask me if he was all right. I felt very old and responsible about the issue as I knew she would be very worried and upset if she knew how dirty and unkempt he was. So I told her only the things I thought she would want to know! I felt quite guilty about this but I felt it to be better than the truth.

A girl who was evacuated with me caused her mother a lot of anxiety as she had not written home. So my mother wrote to me and asked me to tell her to write to her mother right away. This she did and apparently the letter consisted of:– 'Dear Mum, I bought you a peach. On the way home I sat on it so I ate it. Love Rosemary.' From this, I assume, the mother gathered that her child was all right and had thought about her.

The winter snows were very severe and my legs were chapped from my ankles to my knees. I can still feel the agony, especially when they were washed. You could only get up the mountain to the school by holding on to the railings of people's gardens. This was a new experience for me.

There were many good points about the experience of being evacuated. We played in and near the river, sitting on stepping stones in the middle, eating freshly baked bread and raw swede. We spent hours on the mountainside hiding in the long ferns and I still remember those days as soon as I smell ferns. We played dangerously on the railway line and slid, on our bottoms or on planks, down the slag heaps and must have been filthy in consequence. I loved the countryside and exploring the disused entries to the mines, where we played often, especially when it rained, for they remained dry.

Then my life changed. My first family went to live somewhere near Portsmouth and I was moved to a family higher up the mountainside. The parents were quite kind but I was unhappy in that house. There was an older boy, of seventeen, whose shoes I had to clean. He was all right. Then there was a small boy of six for whom I soon did everything. I can especially remember scrubbing his knees and caring for him. I suppose he was a substitute for my brother whom I only saw infrequently. But the thirteen year old girl, 'M', obviously resented me and was particularly spiteful to me.

In that house I did a great deal of housework, which I did not really mind, as I liked it and was happy to please. Unfortunately, this made M more resentful of me. We would go to the river to look for the flat white stones which were so good for whitening the front doorstep. On a Sunday it was our job to wash up. M always dried so she was finished ages before me, as I was left with all the pots and pans to do.

The dad, in that place, worked down the mine and had his bath in front of the kitchen fire when he came home. They did not have pit head baths then. We used to get everything ready with all the kettles on and then had to get out of the kitchen until the ritual was over!

M had a whole bookcase of books which she looked at on a Sunday, but she would not let me look at them. This girl would take my library book, when she could, and lock it in her drawer until it was overdue and then I would have to pay when I took it back.

Boys from Stanley Street School, Deptford take their morning dip in a Pembrokeshire lake.

In the coldest weather I would wake in the bed, which M and I shared, to find that I had no bedclothes. M would declare that I had had them all night and it was now her turn. As I had been asleep I could not dispute it. This was a time when I was miserable with the cold, for I was growing rapidly and my nightwear was getting shorter all the time.

In that house we went to church and I did enjoy the singing of the choir. Each week, M and I went to the church youth club. The club leader kept the room in virtual darkness and then proceeded to sexually abuse us to differing degrees. Sometimes we were kept in whilst the others were sent to play in the churchyard amongst the tombstónes and sometimes it was the other way round. Looking back, I suppose I was fortunate personally, as I was not subjected to too much, other than the man fondling me. But some of the others experienced much more. I knew it was wrong but there was no−one to tell and I was always afraid of getting other people into trouble. I suspect too, that it was a comfort to think somewhat misguidedly, that someone liked me when no one else seemed to. I was also sworn to secrecy, by the bully, M, who used to pinch me to enforce the point.

However, at no time either then or at any point during the time I was away from home did I cry, either in private or in public. I hurt too much inside and could not talk about it. I desperately tried at all times to pretend that I did not care about anything, being away from home, and all the events and upsets.

The family started to ask me questions such as, 'How would you like a brother or sister?' From the beginning I thought this charade quite ridiculous. It was obvious that my mother was expecting a baby. I suppose she thought we would feel usurped, and so she hesitated to tell us. I felt resentful that she considered me too young for such news. Howéver, I did not tell my brother, as I thought he was too young and might get upset, but the burden seemed quite heavy. I knew about the baby but I could not talk about it. I was worried my mother might die, and if the baby lived but she did not, I could not see how I could bring up three children. I felt that I would never be able to understand the ration books.

When we were able to return home to London I was very afraid that my brother would look as he had been. But when we met at the station I was relieved to see they had cleaned him up and had had his hair cut. I did not want my mother to see him looking like that. I have discovered, since I have been an adult, that the authorities had apparently intervened where that family were concerned and my brother was to have been removed from them because he was neglected and running wild. However, as he was happy, they let him stay there but visited regularly.

We were taken to a church hall where our mothers were to collect us. I was very shy and did not speak much. My mother was heavily pregnant. Both my brother and I had very marked Welsh accents, my brother's being stronger than mine, as he had been with a Welsh speaking family. My mother could hardly understand anything he said and I had to interpret for her.

On return I attended the senior school where I discovered that I was nearly two years behind in everything. The English was not so bad because I had read a great deal but I never understood or caught up with the Arithmetic. All the evacuees were given the opportunity to take the eleven plus exam twice, somewhat belatedly, if we failed the first time. Generally speaking, the rest of my school days were a disaster.

Overall, physically, I did not suffer unduly. I enjoyed the countryside and the new experiences. I loved the sound and the feel of the Welsh language and especially the male voice singing. However, I did not fare so well emotionally, as I was already a very nervous and anxious child. I think the fact that I never felt able to talk to anybody about my fears did not help. Also, although very immature in many ways, I also felt like a premature adult, as I worried about my brother. This was probably made worse by my strong maternal instinct. I still cannot understand why no one checked to see if we were all right. But then, perhaps they did, when we were at school. Or maybe I was too shy to speak if they spoke to me. I certainly cannot recall seeing anyone, even when I had to move from the happy home to the hurtful one. I do not think it would happen like that today, people are more aware of psychological damage done to children one way or another and try to avoid it.

It took a long time to adjust to home life again, because I had held myself tightly in rein whilst away. I seemed to regress, dissolving into tears if only looked at, a development which infuriated my mother. She said, if, as I said, I had not cried whilst away, why did I have to do it now? Once bottled up again I did not cry for many, many years.

THEA ARNOLD

Just before the war started, I was down on the south coast with the children, staying with some friends. The atmosphere was getting very alarming, so I brought them home to Mallards, my parents' house in Moulsford, a little village in Oxfordshire. They'd dug an air raid shelter, and were all busy getting braced up for war there. Then my son Andrew had another of his awful chest attacks, and I thought to myself, 'My God, if I have to get this child out of bed and take him down into that air raid shelter, I shall lose him with pneumonia, much more likely than bombs.'

My brother, Dick, was working as a Chartered Accountant in America at the time, and so when I heard that his wife, Dorothy, was taking her little girl, Sally, out there, I thought I'd see if I could go out with them. They were leaving in ten days, so there was very little time to get things organised. Dorothy's sister, Elaine, said she thought she could help me with the paperwork, so she and I went up to London. There was a lot of fuss about who could go and who couldn't, and of course I couldn't take my nanny. I had an excellent girl, Nurse Polgate, and I had to leave her behind, because they wouldn't let her out of the country. Anyone who was useful to the war, or could do anything, they wouldn't let them go. I could, because I had two children to take. Thanks to Elaine and her contacts and persistence, I got everything that was necessary by the end of that day, and in ten days time, we were off to Southampton.

The ship was in an awful mess. It had brought a whole lot of troops over, and they were very short of staff. Things had been broken, bits of the plumbing were damaged, all sorts of things had been lost, or thrown over board. We all piled on to this boat, luggage was just rammed on deck. We were all civilians, and I think there were about a hundred unaccompanied children on board. They'd just been pushed on to the boat and someone was supposed to take care of them. There weren't nearly enough people to look after them, so the poor little kids spent all their time tied in cots.

It was a very alarming voyage. We kept having these emergency drills, when the iron doors came down and you found that where you wanted to go you couldn't. It was very frightening. I had to carry these two small children from the bowels of the boat to get them up on the deck. They were about five and three, and they were very seasick, poor dears, terribly ill. I also had Dorothy's daughter, Sally, to look after, and she was an absolute pestilence.

I had an awful row with the Captain, because I hadn't put my smallest child into one of the lifejackets — he'd have fallen out of it! And then I wanted blankets, and there weren't any. We had to queue for food and manage for ourselves, and help each other as best we could. It was real rough going, I can tell you. Everybody was a bit panicky. As far as I can remember, most people were just like me, they were going to get out of England, to join people they knew over in Canada. But there were also all these children who had just been dumped on the boat by their parents to get them away.

It was an anxious journey, and we had to put up with some very tiresome people. I don't remember any serious trouble on board, but one Canadian man had a fight with some of the sailors and came to me for help with a knife in his back — but that was just a personal thing. Another poor lady had collapsed lungs and couldn't get her lungs blown up, so we had quite a job to help her.

Then there was this submarine scare, so we switched to a much more Northerly course, where it was cold and we were among the icebergs — we were told we very nearly hit one, and I certainly saw them going by.

Eventually, after what seemed an awfully long time, we arrived in Montreal, where, as far as I remember, it was very hot. We were met by my brother's agent, who had an office in Montreal. He took us to a hotel and we spent a night there. Then, after much discussion, we were whisked off to a hotel out in Como, which is about an hour's train ride out of Montreal. It was a little tiny village, right on the lake. There was practically nothing there. There was just this hotel, one or two houses and a French Canadian boarding house.

First of all, we went to the big hotel, because it was summer, and it was open, but it closed down for the winter. So, when the winter was coming on, I had to think what to do, and we got ourselves into this boarding house, which was very rough, but the Legers, who ran it with their son Fred, were awfully nice people. It wasn't very big. There were about three guest rooms, and I had the end of a passage. I made one of the rooms into a sitting room, and we all slept together in another room. We were all right there, they were very kind to us, we were well fed, and it was warm. There were some very tiresome occupants of the house, and there were quite a number of problems with people who drank too much. Even people you knew quite well, you never knew what sort of a state they'd be in. I did have some very unfortunate experiences.

Later on, Dorothy and Sally came to stay there as well. Dorothy was all over the place, she'd met a boyfriend on the boat out, a pilot who flew planes to and from England, a very risky job. He was an awfully nice man, and he fell for her, and she fell for him. She was always sprinting about with him, which caused quite a bit of scandal because she came to the boarding house and the other residents didn't like it.

The children enjoyed themselves, I think. They went to school in Hudson, which was the next town up, there were a few more people

Felicity and Andrew Arnold in Canada where they learnt to skate and ski.

there. They made great friends with the man who was known as the ice man. He had his horse and cart, and they used to go out with him for miles on to the middle of the lake where he cut huge blocks of ice and used to bring it back loaded on the cart and put it in Fred's outhouse, where it was all packed with straw, and that's what kept them going all the summer. And they learnt to skate and they learnt to ski. I tried skiing and damaged myself twice badly, once on my back and once on my front, so I had to give that up.

I had several friends who were awfully good when I became very ill. At one stage I was in hospital for weeks and they took the children. When I came out, I had to have a nurse with me. I was in a dark room with my head packed down in ice and when that was removed, I couldn't manage my head, I couldn't pick it up! If I sat up, my head just rolled around, I had no control over it at all. My neck had been frozen, you see. The doctor said I really ought to come back to England, because they couldn't guarantee that I'd live through another do of that sort, and the children would have been left on their own, which would have been terrible. I couldn't face that, so I had to pull myself together and make arrangements to get home. I did get better, but I wasn't at all well.

We had been there about three years, so when I came back it was the middle of the war, 1943, just in time for the flying bombs! We had a terrible trip back. We were to set sail from Philadelphia, so we had to get there by train. This time we were in convoy, so we had other ships with us to guard us. Once on the way back, we got out of line and a battleship came rushing out towards us with guns pointing at us. It went round and round, trying to make contact with the Captain, because we were right in the way of a convoy route coming the other way. We shouldn't have been there at all. Finally, the Captain was found and the crisis passed, but really we had wondered what was going to happen to us! Another time, there was an air scare. The children were terribly seasick, absolutely green, so I thought, 'I must get them out in the air.' So I got two deck chairs, and sat right in the front with the children. Then there was this air raid warning. Well, I was right away from everybody else, and I knew I couldn't carry them both, I couldn't do anything about it. We saw this plane in the distance, and the men rushed to guns, because they thought it was attacking us. All I know now is that if you're actually faced with what I thought was death, you just think, 'Well, that's it.' All I could do was to shove the children close together

Thea Arnold with her two children, Felicity and Andrew in Canada.

17

and lay on top of them, and wait for the worst. After all that, it turned out that it was one of ours.

We were supposed to be safe, because we weren't carrying anybody of military age; but when we got to the Azores, we were landed with an army of soldiers who filled the boat, and they were all over the decks, looking through our windows. Of course we became a sitting target.

When we got to Portugal, we were landed at Lisbon, from where we were supposed to be getting a flight the next day, but it was just after a plane had been brought down, so they stopped the traffic. We arrived in the summer and didn't get home until just before Christmas, so we must have been there about six months.

There had been two scares when we were told a flight was going and we all rushed back to pack. The first time we got as far as the station to go out to the flying boat before we were turned back. The next time, we got on to the train and got as far as Lisbon before we were sent back. After that, the next time there was a scare, I said I wasn't going to take a blind bit of notice of it, so we stayed down on the beach. But at about six o' clock, I thought, perhaps I'd better go up and see if there was anything happening. When I got up there, it was a fact, they were going! So I had to bustle round, pack the children up, and off we went on this flying boat.

We were told what to do if we were attacked - we'd got to jump out, more or less, which didn't sound too good. It was very frightening, I can tell you. We left in the dark so of course when we got back, it was pitch black, and we weren't used to blackouts. I remember going into the station, you couldn't see a thing. I couldn't see where the train was, I'd got baggage and children hanging on to me as I struggled down tunnels and up steps on to the platform. We were told a train was coming, but I couldn't see a train. It came in with all the blinds down, you just couldn't see it. There was a very occasional chink of light, but that was all. I got in a bit of a muddle and finally opened a carriage door, found there was room, and got in but I was desperately worried about my luggage. Then, a very nice Naval officer got in and sat opposite me, and I don't know how we started talking, but I told him I was worried and he took charge of us completely, saw to our luggage and helped us to change trains at Basingstoke. I was so grateful.

When we got to Reading, the family came to meet me and I got out of the train with this smart Naval officer - I think they began to wonder what was going on! He was so nice. I was sorry to see the back of him.

I couldn't say it had been a very happy time in Canada, because my marriage was falling apart and my husband was still in Bagdad. Of course, I was also very worried about my family over in England. Every time I heard the news, I was absolutely terrified. However, I moved back into Mallards, my home which had been left empty while I was away, and that was really that.

NORTH BUCKS WELCOME FOR LONDON EVACUEES

Boys and Girls Settling Down to Country Life

HAPPY IN THEIR NEW HOMES

MORE THAN 4,000 OF THE CHILDREN FROM THE LONDON AREA, WHO WERE EVACUATED UNDER THE GOVERNMENT PLAN FOR THEIR GREATER SAFETY DURING THE WAR ARRIVED IN NORTH BUCKS LAST WEEK-END, AND IN TOWNS AND VILLAGES THEY HAVE BEEN GIVEN A FRIENDLY WELCOME. THEY ARE RAPIDLY SETTLING DOWN TO THE NEW AND STRANGE CONDITIONS IN WHICH THEY FIND THEMSELVES, AND ALREADY THEY ARE ENJOYING THEMSELVES THOROUGHLY, AND WE HOPE THAT NOT ONLY THE FOSTER PARENTS BUT THE PUBLIC GENERALLY WILL DO EVERYTHING IN THEIR POWER TO MAKE THE STAY OF THE CHILDREN IN THIS DISTRICT AS HAPPY AS POSSIBLE.

Bucks Standard, 9th September 1939.

HOWARD BAKER

I don't think the worries of grown-ups during 1939 had reached my five year old mind when we assembled at Cecil Road School, Gravesend, to be evacuated.

I remember sitting on my father's shoulders walking to the High Street to join the boat. I've learnt since it was West Street and also that my father, a policemen, had put me there so that I could not see him crying his eyes out.

When we boarded a vast boat called the Royal Sovereign we went to the upper deck where paper bags were handed out just in case. I was disappointed when I didn't have to use mine. Mr Schrimmins, of St Georges School, was dragging a large crate of apples round the deck and we sang a bit to pass the time. It was then I discovered war was declared, although we were oblivious at the time.

My next memory is of Yarmouth Racecourse where our bed for the night was straw, and the sky was clearly visible through a stable door. The next day we wandered around the racecourse while everyone else was assembled in a queue at the parade ring.

My next home was Brick Kiln Farm with Alf and Rod Slapp. I was very homesick, but life on the farm was wonderful for a town boy. And I was very lucky that the people I stayed with were lovely and treated me like a son. There were cows, pigs, chickens and steam tractor engines driving threshing machines in the yard.

The house was lit by oil lamps and candles and water was drawn up by an iron hand pump. The toilet was a small shed at the bottom of the garden with a bucket under a hole in wooden seat.

I learned to make butter by hand in the dairy. Up to then, I had thought milk came from bottles not dirty old cows.

School was a two-mile walk away and was held in the church hall which seemed vast. I envied friends in the village who were living in a sweet shop. That first winter was very cold with huge snow drifts.

I returned to Gravesend in time to see the arrival of the doodlebugs.

To be a farmer's boy.

Boys from St. Georges C. of E. School, Battersea, dig potatoes in Pembrokeshire.

BERYL BATTEN

I was nearly six when the second mass evacuation began in 1940. Dad had received his call up papers for the army, so it was only a matter of weeks before he would be leaving home for God only knew where and for how long. With my mother, my sister and my little brother, I boarded a train for Penzance in Cornwall. Sennen Cove was a beautiful place about ten miles from Penzance. There were golden beaches, picturesque cottages and a quaint little cove. In the background there was a landscape of wooded areas and shrubs and flowers.

We were billeted with many other evacuated families at a hotel overlooking the cove, perched high on a hill. The interior of the hotel was quite smart. The dining room facilities were excellent and the views from the windows were breath-taking.

The woman who owned the hotel had five large dogs all of different breeds. We had a fright one day when one of these dogs, a Chow, jumped onto my sister's back whilst she was pushing my brother in his push chair. It would not budge and she was holding onto the push chair for dear life. The Chow being so heavy was pushing her towards the sea wall. It was quite a drop below and it was a frightening experience for my sister and toddler brother. The locals beat the dog with sticks and threw stones at it but still it would not budge. Finally someone had the sense to throw a bucket of cold water over it and that did the trick. It jumped off with shock. The cold water soon dampened his ardour!

Things went smoothly for a while, but bickering began among some of the mothers, usually the trouble was over children, and gradually the families began to disperse. Some were sent to other billets and others went back home.

When the evacuees left the hotel, rumours abounded that cutlery, linen and other items had mysteriously disappeared. The evacuees were suspected of course. Whether these things had been stolen will never be known, but the people staying there certainly were a mixed bunch. Fortunately my mother was very popular at Sennen, which was just as well, as most evacuees had a bad name down there. To some extent I could understand it as I grew up. After all, it must have been nerve shattering to have hoards of people descending on you, disturbing the tranquility of the place. I think there was overwhelming relief felt when the majority of the townies went back home.

We were allocated the top part of a house further from the cove. It consisted of three rooms, if you included the tiny kitchen, and they were clean and functional. Our access to the rooms was through an outside metal staircase. There was a mesh-covered larder for perishable foods attached to the wall on the way up. Downstairs was the home of the owner, a Miss Pender. Her parents owned several properties at Sennen and Miss Pender remained a spinster due to the fact that her R.A.F. boyfriend had been shot down during a raid. A wife and child of a serving officer lodged downstairs with Miss Pender, and also two boy evacuees.

Miss Pender had an old car and once a week she went to Penzance, the nearest town, to do her shopping. She would also purchase items for other people as far as money would allow. It was quite an event in those days. We were fortunate that we had access to Miss Pender's own private toilet. All the local cottages had to use the primitive types.

My sister and I went to the local village school in Sennen, which was quite a long, uphill climb away. The only real excitement we got at school was when a farmer's goat broke loose from its rope and went beserk in the school. The goat ate everything within reach; chalks, pencils, papers all got chomped up and the mess and damage it created..... it was as though all hell was let loose. The children were

London children evacuated to Chalfont St. Giles, Bucks, going to village school.

running in all directions, both frightened and gleeful at the same time. It was the farmer who managed to control the goat in the end, because no one else could. It was butting all and sundry.

The locals' first taste of war was when a mine blew up and blasted the roofs and windows of some of the buildings. Some of them were only of a wooden structure. We were all cowering under tables and at first thought we were being attacked. The locals were petrified. They had never encountered anything like that, unlike us city dwellers. A lot of the beaches were mined and were secured with barbed wire to keep people out, though at Sennen this was not so. Where the mine actually went off no-one seemed to know.

Another incident I recall is walking across a field with some school pals and hearing planes droning overhead. When we glanced upwards there were two planes diving very low. To our horror we realised they were German. We flattened ourselves in the grass, which fortunately for us was long, because the pilots began to machine-gun us. They obviously could not get close enough and flew off higher, but we stayed there for some time, fearful in case they should return. A farmer's wife who had flung herself on the ground, jumped up as soon as the planes disappeared and started running across the field, hell for leather. I remember screaming out, 'Lady, lady, save us!' Thankfully the planes did not return.

On another occasion, an evacuee picked up a metal object from the ground and it blew two of his fingers off. One day I saw a crowd gathering by the sea wall and curiosity got the better of me. I saw men dragging up bloated dead bodies which had drifted in from the sea. Whether they were allies or foes I do not know. The authorities used a local fire station as a temporary mortuary until they disposed of the bodies. We used to hear the distant sounds of convoys being bombarded even from where we were. On one occasion, a shoal of mackerel was swept up to the beach, probably blasted out of the sea. Much of it was encased in ice to save it from rotting and most of the inhabitants helped themselves to it.

Our one weekly pleasure was visiting the local cafe, 'Georgina's'. How she managed to make a living I do not know, but she did. We used to eat egg and chips listening to singers of the time in the background. I particularly remember sitting at the table listening to George Formby singing 'When a Certain Little Lady Goes By.'

Sennen Cove was not without its scandal. A London evacuee, who I must admit seemed to get on well with my mother in spite of their different life styles, began to associate with a local fisherman. He was renowned for being a drunkard and one night he came storming to our door, banging the knocker hard and waking us up. It frightened my mother and she would not open the door. It appeared that he had mistakenly thought his lady friend, Leonora, was there. My mother was disgusted and the next day told them in no uncertain terms what she thought of them. Leonora had three children and previously she had made a couple of trips up to London and Mum had cared for her children. What we did not know was that she was in the process of getting a divorce from her husband. After the incident of knocking on our door late at night, Mum refused to have any more to do with her. It always puzzled me how smartly dressed she was considering they were austere times and money was tight!

My mum had a bad fright one evening when a policeman knocked on the door and, without first asking her name, informed her that her husband had been killed in action. As Mum had not heard from Dad for some time, for he was in the Middle East, she collapsed. There we were clinging to her and sobbing. Then the policeman verified her surname and it appeared that a Mrs Williams had resided there prior to us and it was her husband who had been killed.

We stayed at Sennen for over two years and probably would have stayed longer, had it not been for complications back home. My grandmother had written to say that the house we rented in London had been bombed and hardly anything had been salvaged. There was a strong possibility of our being able to rent a modern flat in the dockland area where Grandmother lived, as there were so many places deserted. My mother tended to worry about my grandmother a lot because she knew she was lonely. Grandmother did go to stay with some relatives in the Lake District from time to time but her visits were always short ones. Mum decided to go back home. It was an attractive idea for us as we were feeling a little homesick, but it was not a sensible thing to do.

George Formby entertains shelterers. George Formby entertained 2,000 people in underground shelters in concerts organised by ENSA. 28th November 1940.

Back home we went, and we were allocated a flat next door but one to my grandmother's. There we stayed for some time until the air raids became heavy again. Then Mum decided we should return to Cornwall, but it was not that simple. The second time around it meant that Mum would have to pay our fares, and also she assumed Miss Pender would be able to accommodate us. Unfortunately Miss Pender was fully booked. She had been opposed to us returning to London in the first place and did not expect us to return to Cornwall. However, Miss Pender wrote and suggested we contact an old fisherman whose name, I recall, was John George. He owned a cottage near where we lived before and John agreed that we could lodge with him.

When we arrived at Sennen the cottage was deserted. The fisherman had left a note stating that he would be absent for a while and to make ourselves at home. I remember Mum preparing a meal for us from Spam and American dried egg. We had not even got round to unpacking and we sat and ate our meal in silence. Mum had inspected the kitchen, which had a typical stone flagged floor, and also the dining room. The cutlery and table linen was very clean but the thick cobwebs and spittle on the kitchen floor turned our stomachs.

Mum consulted us, asking if we would be happy to stay there, and my sister and I just dissolved into tears. Without any further hesitation Mum wrote an apologetic note to John George, saying it was not to our liking and we were going to seek alternative accommodation. Off we went again. We had to trudge up a hill with bags and baggage to the nearest bus stop. Whilst we were waiting for the bus to take us to Penzance, Mum realised she had left the large framed photograph of my father in army uniform, on the table. My sister ran down the hill back to the cottage and picked up the precious photo. Fortunately John George had not returned.

Eventually we arrived in Penzance and made for the police station. Mum explained the situation but the police thought my mother had acted very irresponsibly and she should have been grateful for the offered accommodation. Anyway by then we were all feeling exhausted and were thankful when a police officer offered us mugs of cocoa and some toast. They helped us as much as they could, but as it was short notice the only place they could find for us to stay the night was in a church mission hall at a place called Marazion. We slept on camp beds,

EVACUATION

THE GOVERNMENT HAVE DECIDED THAT IF THERE ARE AIR RAIDS YOU WILL HAVE ANOTHER CHANCE OF SENDING YOUR CHILDREN AWAY.

THIS TIME THE CHILDREN WILL NOT GO UNTIL AIR RAIDS MAKE IT NECESSARY.

THE NEW SCHEME WILL BE FOR SCHOOL CHILDREN WHO WERE AT SCHOOL LAST JULY, OR WHO HAVE REACHED THE AGE OF FIVE SINCE. IT APPLIES TO NO OTHERS.

NOW IS YOUR OPPORTUNITY TO REGISTER YOUR CHILDREN FOR EVACUATION. FILL UP THIS PAPER AND RETURN IT AT ONCE.

You are free to make up your mind, but you must MAKE UP YOUR MIND NOW. It is your duty to do so for the sake of your children. The authorities cannot make their plans at all if they do not know how many they have got to provide for.

If you want any help or there is anything you do not understand go to the nearest school, where you will either be able to get help or you will be told where you can.

for lighting we used a parraffin lamp, and we were so worn out we slept like logs. We remained there for three days but we did not mind because it was more like an adventure for us children.

Our next venture was being sent to a hostel at a place called Lilant. It was only a temporary arrangement and there were several other evacuees also staying there. The kitchen facilities were communal and the food was pooled. Everyone had to share their resources. Although the evacuees mostly consisted of mothers and children there was one exception, a man was present with his wife and child. He wore a Petty Officer's uniform, and what he was doing there was anyone's guess. Also in their party was a friend and her child. After a time it was noticed that food was going missing and women began to suspect the 'Petty Officer'. For some reason he was not popular, and all sorts of wild tales were spread. One of the tales was that he had been seen being over-familiar on numerous occasions with his wife's friend. Someone must have complained and made enquiries about his presence there, for he disappeared soon afterwards with his family.

We stayed at the hostel for a couple of months until we were all sent to a large house in the next town called Hayle. The house was surrounded by woodland and again we were fortunate that we were close to a lovely beach. Also at Marazion, close by, there was an old castle out at sea called St. Michael's Mount. When the tide was out it could be reached by walking over the stones and rocks. We were forbidden to enter the grounds however and I think some soldiers were billeted there.

American Air Force personnel were based not far away and they used to entertain us with concerts from time to time. They were a friendly crowd and even brought urns of pineapple juice and hot dogs on to the beaches for us to enjoy. The usual chewing gum and candy was plentiful and we enjoyed their company. We were sorry when they moved out.

Again, after a time, the evacuees became restless. Some of the women had their differences. More often than not, children were the cause of the rifts. Even so, in times of trouble there was a comradeship. There was a lake nearby and the boys made makeshift rafts, which we used to sit on and push out from the bank. One day a little boy, about four years old, slipped off a raft and nearly drowned. Fortunately a woman, who had had first aid experience, managed to resuscitate him. But for her efforts he would have died.

Beryl at Barnehurst in Kent with her parents at the time of her father's demob.

The second accident affected my own family, my sister was the victim. It happened that my mother asked my sister to get my little brother from the outside garden. We were going to the beach for a picnic. This was quite a frequent trip when we were not at school. On the staircase was a large window and below, a sort of lean-to construction attached to the wall. My sister thought she heard young voices coming from that direction and was afraid my brother had climbed out of the window. There was a small skylight on the roof of the building obscuring her view, so she stepped out of the window on to the flat roof, thinking it was made of slate. It was not, and the glass caved in under her weight with horrific results. I was the first one to encounter her plight; she had managed to drag herself out of the shattered roof and staggered up the stairs to our bedroom. All I could see was a bloodied leg, with slivers of glass protruding from it and she was shaking with shock. I ran screaming out of the room to find my mother and by the time I reached her I was laughing hysterically. The woman who had saved the little boy from drowning tied a makeshift tourniquet around my sister's thigh, whilst someone ran to get help. I remember Mum pacing up and down the lane waiting for the ambulance to arrive. It seemed like hours. My sister was lucky because the accident could have been far worse. She was taken to a hospital run by medical nuns and she had fifty odd stitches in her leg. After a long stay in hospital, she was sent to convalesce at the home of a lady who was a retired nurse. We used to visit her there once a week, and I remember feeling a bit jealous of all the attention she was getting. I was not old enough to realise that she could have bled to death. When she was fully recovered and had been sent home, our life was soon back to its normal routine. We were sitting on the beach one day and my sister was idly looking out at the shore line. The waves were choppy and she suddenly noticed that a toddler had paddled out near some rocks. A large roller knocked him over and without hesitating my sister ran into the sea and pulled him to safety. The salt water seemed to do more good than harm to her wound.

A few months later my mother decided to chance her luck and go back to London again. She was warned about returning to the dangers awaiting us there but to no avail, her mind was made up. My sister and I could have stayed and lodged with a family but we wanted to stay together. By then there were only two families left at Riviera House, everyone else had gone back home to face the consequences. It was another year or so before the war finally ended and we never left London again. We survived to tell of our experiences as did many more evacuees.

JUNE BIGGS

I had two sisters and one brother, and we were evacuated from Brockley in south east London to Oxted in Surrey. My mum told us we were going on holiday to the seaside. Armed with our pillowcases, hundreds of us kids walked down the road. Mostly we enjoyed it, coming from a poor family we enjoyed the things we never had.

We had two other girls billeted with us who were very posh and went to the Central School. As they were older, they sometimes minded us while the lady went out to play whist. Once they frightened us by playing ghosts. Next morning they got into trouble, but I decided to run away.

I walked to Oxted Station, and got a train to Brockley Cross. I only had my gas mask and a yellow purse with 2/6d. I still had it when I arrived in London, as I told a really hard luck story to the passengers, who kindly fed me with sandwiches. When I arrived, I forgot where I lived. After asking a few people, I got to our flats and saw my mum crying with a neighbour. She was over the moon to see me, as the police were searching for me. I went to the police station with my parents. The policeman was very kind, explaining what trouble I had caused. I went back to Oxted to be re-united with my sister. That was a big day out for me.

People queuing for shelters in London, 21st Sept 1940.

Children boarding buses for the country. 1st September 1939.

BARBARA BIRCHALL

I was evacuated with my sister when I was aged three to Reading, Berkshire, and we can remember being on the train and seeing big barrage balloons in the sky. Then being on the platform, waiting for someone to pick us to go to stay with them. We went to a lady and her husband who had one daughter. They owned a shoe mender's shop.

They were very nice people, we thought. But after a couple of years they were very cruel to us. They never fed us much. If one of us was naughty, she used to make us stand and watch the family eat, and give us nothing, only the crusts of bread which her daughter left. We were always locked in our bedroom. She had a big double bed which my sister and I slept in, and we used to cuddle up to each other. But one day she came into the room and said, 'I will have none of that soppy stuff.' So she used to pin the sheet in the middle with a big Scotch kilt pin to stop us getting near each other.

Outside our bedroom window there was a cherry tree, and my sister used to lean out of the window and I used to hold her legs and she used to get the cherries in. We used to eat them, wrap the stones in newspaper and stick them up the chimney on a ledge. One day she had the chimney sweep, and down came all the stones. She hit my sister with a one sided hand mirror till her little backside was raw, and I used to have to watch. I would be shouting, 'leave her alone.' Then it would be my turn but I would always escape and run out.

My father was in Alamein as a cook. He used to send us jars of sweets but we never got any. One night we were so hungry and thirsty that we crept downstairs to find something to eat and drink. We couldn't find anything. We were desperate, so I saw the tap was dripping and it had made a pool of water in the bottom of the bowl, my sister pulled up a chair to the sink and helped me up. She was one year older than me. Then I bent my head down and got some of the water in my hand to drink. Then we heard footsteps coming and the woman caught us. She opened the coal cupboard and pushed us in and locked the door. We had to stay there till the morning and it was very dark, cold and spiders! Horrible, we were very scared.

Bathtime used to be four inches of COLD water in front of the fire. If she was cross with us, she used to lock us in the garden shed at the bottom of the garden all night. It was really a nightmare. Today I suffer with agoraphobia which I am sure came from my childhood in the war. When the billet worker used to come to see if we were well and happy the woman and her husband used to put on a big spread of cakes and sandwiches, and always cuddled us in front of her to make it look good. But our time there was very unhappy. Very.

My sister had irons up her legs and couldn't walk very well, so I used to take her to school and we were so hungry and sick that we used to sit by the pig swill bins and wait for the rubbish to be thrown away. Then we used to eat as much as we could out of the bins. One day we had a big harvest festival and in the front row was fruit and vegetables and these big tomatoes. We were all sitting on the floor quiet when my sister made a mad dash and took a big bite out of the tomato. The teacher took her and spanked her on the knuckles with a ruler. When I explained that we were very hungry she called us liars and got the woman round who looked after us and she denied that we were not fed. When we got home she beat us and her husband beat us and we were very afraid that we would die if we didn't get out of there.

When the end of the war came I was glad, even though I didn't understand if it was going to be a good thing or bad. I remember big bonfires in the street, spuds and sausages or corned beef, and a man dancing on the hot coal.

I am not very sure of what happened after that, but I suppose we went home. Our experience of the war time was definitely not a happy one, and has caused me a lot of unhappiness in my later years.

JIM BRITTAIN

For some reason my brothers and I missed the initial evacuation, possibly because we were at different schools and our parents wished us to be kept together. I was thirteen, Roy was ten and Raymond was seven. In the event we were included in the evacuation that took place on Sunday, 3rd September, 1939 which embraced a large contingent of expectant mothers and school children from Blackstock Road School, Tottenham. I had been attending Haringay Senior School for Boys, whilst my brothers were at Campsbourne Road School.

On the train journey we stopped at various stations where we seemed to be unhitching carriages, thus making the train shorter on its journey north. As we were halted at Sandy station, Bedfordshire, the declaration was made about the existence of a state of war with Germany. Our journey continued and our carriage was de−trained at Somersham, while the train continued on its way to Chatteris, March and beyond.

We left the station and made our way to the centre of the village, about six hundred yards away where we were received in the Village Hall known as 'The Palace', even though it was clad in corrugated iron. In 'The Palace' we all stood around and I held on to my two brothers, as prospective 'fosterers' looked over the evacuees and decided which to take into their households. There was little enthusiasm in taking on a whole family of three boys, and I had made it clear that we were to remain as one unit. 'The Palace' was therefore starting to get rather empty, when at last someone decided to take us all. In fact we did not have far to go, for our new home was to be at 'The Grange' in High Street, Somersham, less than 50 yards away on the other side of the road.

What we did not know was that our Foster Parents, Mr Clarence and Mrs Sarah Rowe, had a family of six children of their own, aged between three and eighteen years old. And they had a maid, who I believe, was about seventeen years old.

The Grange had large cellars and ground floor, first floor and an attic where we slept. There was an indoor toilet, but no bathroom. Baths were taken in a galvanised bath in the scullery. There were also outside toilets in the garden. Outside there were outbuildings and barns where chickens and a pig were kept, as well as some cows. The land embraced a kitchen garden, lawned garden (including a tennis court) a field and a paddock.

Meals were taken together in the kitchen−dining room around a massive pine farmhouse table, big enough to accommodate the eleven of us. Mrs Rowe used to serve the vegetables whilst Mr Rowe carved and served the meat. Leading off the kitchen was a large walk−in pantry. Mrs Rowe was a very good cook and the kitchen garden ensured a plentiful supply of vegetables and fruit, the latter providing the ingredients for many a tasty pie.

As regards school, the village Primary/Infants school did not have the necessary spare capacity and all the evacuees were educated in a Wesleyan Chapel in Park Road, Somersham. This meant that there was only one classroom, with pupils whose ages ranged from five to thirteen years and the older ones were, of necessity left very much to their own devices. I had two years French behind me and the local Vicar, Rev Sheppard gave me some tuition at the Rectory from time to time.

Soon after we arrived, Mr Rowe took us in his car to Wyton Airfield, some eight miles away where we had our first glimpse of Blenheim bombers which were tuned up on the runways and at dispersal points. There were other RAF airfields nearby at Warboys and Upwood, near Ramsey. We were, therefore, fairly close to some action. The occasional German aircraft had strafed in the vicinity and we appeared to be on their flight path for bombing runs to the Midlands industrial centres.

Evacuee boys doing drill on the beach in Wales.

Following the British Expeditionary Forces' evacuation from Dunkirk, Infantry troops arrived by train in the village and were refreshed at 'The Palace'. I have forgotten where they were permanently barracked but recollect them marching in and recall that they seemed to be understandably somewhat disillusioned. Then there were several liaisons between them and the local lasses.

So far as life at 'The Grange' was concerned, we were accepted fully into the family. I subsequently acquired a bicycle and with David, one of the sons who was about my age, I was able to visit St. Ives, which boasted a cinema, Chatteris and other villages. In the summer of 1940 I earned some pocket money picking fruit, mainly plums, in orchards around Bluntisham.

Jim Brittain with one of his model aeroplanes.

David Rowe, Jim's cycling companion.

Otherwise, spare time was spent in the garden, fields and around the adjoining 'Ballast Hole' lake, which derived its name from the finished gravel extraction. I managed to collect quite a few birds' eggs to add to a collection that I already possesed. Having obtained my roller skates from London I started roller skating around the village, which encouraged others to take up the activity. During the winter the Rowes lent me a pair of 'Fen Runner' ice skates (wooden bodied with inset metal blades) and I joined in the ice skating on the Fen dykes and on the 'Ballast Hole'. The 1940/41 winter was particularly severe and I remember skating until March, eventually having to jump onto the ice after the edges along the banks had thawed. The ice was extremely thick, possibly fifteen inches, and the fish had died because of the lack of oxygen.

Having started aero modelling in London I continued this hobby at 'The Grange' and often spent evening hours in my bedroom making aeroplanes. It was at 'The Grange' that I had my introduction to tennis, with the occasional game on the court in the garden. Mr Rowe was the keenest player in the family. The family opposite also had a court but I believe that theirs was a hard court. I also managed to get hold of my camera, a box Brownie, which I had bought for sixpence from a cobblers in Boyton Road. With the camera, when in funds, I took some pictures of the Rowe family, which I still have. The pictures were developed and printed by the local chemist.

Despite the rationing, food was not too much of a problem as there were plenty of vegetables, fruit and eggs. We each had our own allocation of cheese and preserves set aside in the pantry and I seemed to be able to manage much better than the others by rationing my rations so that they lasted until they were due for renewal. I think that it was permissible to keep, and kill, one pig for the household and this was, of course, a great help.

My two brothers returned home fairly early, whereas I remained for about eighteen months. Eventually the time came when I realised that I was not obtaining any benefit from attending school and I therefore returned home to Boyton Road, Hornsey in April, 1941, beginning work as a clerk with Hornsey Highways Depot at Highgate, on 1st May, 1941. I have kept in contact with the Rowe family ever since.

ROSE BRITTAIN

I had three children who were evacuated with the school. I did not see them off because I was too upset. For the first two days after they went I could not eat I was so upset about them going. My eldest boy, James, was nearly thirteen, and the others were ten and seven. He would not be parted from the other two and so they were left until last to be chosen.

The lady who had them was a marvellous lady and she looked after them very well. She was in the W.V.S. and they were in charge of the billeting. She was called Mrs Rowe, and she was the Lady of the Manor in a small place called Somersham in Cambridgeshire. She had six children of her own and her husband was a farmer.

My youngest son, Raymond, was not used to going to bed on his own in the dark and he did not like it. My middle son was all right, he was having the time of his life, but he did object to having to learn to knit. He said 'I'm not a girl, and I am not going to knit scarves!' But I had a little talk with him and told him he had got to be a good boy. Mrs Brewer had told the children to help themselves to the apples and she said, 'I have never seen a child eat so many apples as he does!' In the winter the ponds froze over and they learned ice skating. They were very lucky.

After about six months my youngest boy was fretting for me and he got bronchitis. When I went to see him he wanted to come home and because he wanted to come home so did the middle boy. So we took them home with us. My eldest boy wanted to stay there and the family wanted to keep him. They thought a lot of him. So he stayed there until it was time for him to come home and get a job when he was fifteen. We still keep in touch with the family. There could not have been a better family and I do not regret having to let the children go on evacuation.

Rose Brittain with her sons, Jim, Roy and Raymond, in 1939 at Jaywick Sands.

ALLAN BURNETT

Soon after the Battle of Britain began, my father, on arriving home from work one day said, 'I think you had better go, they're getting nearer.' There was a strange superstition about at the time that you would only suffer a direct hit 'if the bomb had your name on it', a curious, and impossible to disprove, fatalism. One of my father's duties was to follow up every incident in the Borough and it seemed to him that the German bombs were landing in ever-decreasing circles, and getting nearer to our tenement each day. Sure enough, one week after our departure, a bomb landed two doors away, rendering our house unfit for habitation.

The previous week saw my mother, then aged thirty, me (a nine year old) and my three month old sister amongst the hurley burley of St. Pancras Station. We felt a strange mixture of excitement, anticipation, and apprehension as we waited for the train that was to speed us to an unknown destination 'somewhere in England', as the saying was. The journey seemed endless. Unlike the prosaic joyless rail experiences of today, journeys of yesterday were memorable experiences of giant, noisy, hissing whistling steam locomotives, attended to by diligent crews with oil cans and wheel tappers. Guards had peaked caps, waistcoats, pocket watches, whistles and red and green flags; the very stuff of drama to a very small boy.

The journey seemed endless. It took all day, although it was only a little over a hundred miles. Perhaps the coal was not of the required quality, or the threat of enemy action could bring the train to an untimely halt.

cent attendance, could not fill one row, and nothing else. There was nothing else. No school, shops, pub, post office, library, hall, clinic or any amenities whatsoever. There were two buses a week with standing room only, and a weekly delivery of groceries. One day we walked five miles, and queued all Saturday for a haircut. The culture shock was complete.

Our hosts had never seen a tramcar, escalator, department store or even a lavatory chain. The privy was at the end of the garden, and designed for two, so at least there was no waiting, but in inclement weather constipation had its compensations! Contrary to popular opinion, us Townies did recognise a cow when we saw one and we did know that a cluster of milk bottles was not a cow's nest. We had exchanged electric light, a gas stove, a modern fireplace, a vacuum cleaner, and flush toilets for oil lamps, a smoky kitchen range, filthy brooms, and bucket sanitation in the middle of nowhere reminiscent of Hansel and Gretel.

Allan Burnett in the late 1930s.

At our destination we were herded, hundreds of us, into a school. We were tired, hungry, and irritable, and nobody seemed to know what was happening or who was responsible for what. After a while, we were aware that our numbers were shrinking as people gradually disappeared. There was a touch of the Noah's Ark about it, and it would have provided a marvellous script for a farce, except that it wasn't funny. St. Pancras seemed so distant, millennia away in time and space. Eventually we were shepherded on to a Stone Age single decker omnibus, a wheezing coughing contraption protesting volubly at the late night passengers. I presume the bossy lady with the clipboard and Joyce Grenfell accent was the billeting officer.

We were deposited in a seventeenth century farmhouse with as much livestock inside as out. We were hardly welcome, but none of us had any choice in the matter. London met Leicestershire head on. Chalk and cheese.

The hamlet consisted of a crossroads, a hall made derelict by the military, and a huge church which, if it commanded one hundred per

We co-existed in mutual misunderstanding. Having experienced some of the blitz, we were quite blasé about bombs. When Nottingham, only twenty miles away, 'copped it', our hosts fled into the fields to watch the distant inferno, but we stayed in our beds, as we had seen it all before.

At school, the teachers could not give out detentions because we had to catch the bus to get back to our billet. We got the cane instead! One World War One veteran was reckoned to have more power in his remaining right arm than most people had in two. It is funny the things that stick out in your mind. I remember the headmaster bursting into the classroom, and whilst we all wondered what was coming (including Miss) he announced jubilantly, 'Benghazi has fallen'.

After only a few months, mother decided that enough was enough. The whole tiresome journey had to be made in reverse. The train into London was so late that Father had given up and gone home. With no money, Mother persuaded a taxi driver to take us the three miles on a promise. Such was the spirit of the times that this was cheerfully done, except that Father was not at home and I was despatched to his usual haunts to try and track him down. I was not successful, the taxi driver departed sans fare until some time later when he returned to meet the breadwinner whose welcome when he did appear was somewhat muted.

That night, May 10th 1941, London suffered one of its worst air raids. I spent the night under the kitchen table, while father took a garden roller to the incendiaries landing on the tram lines outside in the road. We were home!

LILIAN BURNETT

My daughter was born in June 1938, so when the war began in 1939 she was just fifteen months old. It was obvious there was going to be a war and the 'powers that be' had begun preparations, if rather slowly as it seemed to us.

By the summer, we had to go and collect our gas masks. There were ordinary ones for the adults and older children, but for the toddlers they were slightly different. These were red and had a kind of little flap where the nose would be and as the child breathed in and out it moved. They were called Mickey Mouse gas masks. For babies they were different again, you had to lay the baby on a table or some flat surface and put her in a kind of large bag. What a palaver it was! I never knew one single person who found that it worked - and when you think that it was the child's life at stake!

At this time every householder was advised to dig a deep hole in their garden and install an air raid shelter. You put this galvanised iron shelter as deep as possible in the ground, then covered it with lots of earth. It was thought it would be safe if a bomb dropped very near and in any case you would be out of the house.

If you did not have a garden then you had a kind of reinforced cage with a very heavy top, which you could use as your table in your living room. If a bomb dropped on the house, this shelter would at least prevent some of the debris from falling on you and prevent you from being crushed.

During this time the government were putting forward plans to evacuate the children. Under five year olds were to be evacuated with the mother and over fives to go without the mother. I thought to myself, 'I'm not going anywhere,' and at the time I really meant it. Over the next few weeks, day after day, on the wireless was this chap Dr Hill. He kept on about the selfish mothers who would not consider the offer of safety for their children. Day after day he kept on and on, and in the end I put my name down to go with Pam.

We were told to meet on Saturday, September 2nd at half past eight in the morning at the school, and we were told to take with us only what we could carry. As I had a small child to carry, I just could not take very much in the way of luggage. I was very pleased that Pam was potty trained because I could not have taken nappies - especially as they were made of terry towelling in those days, there were no disposable ones known then.

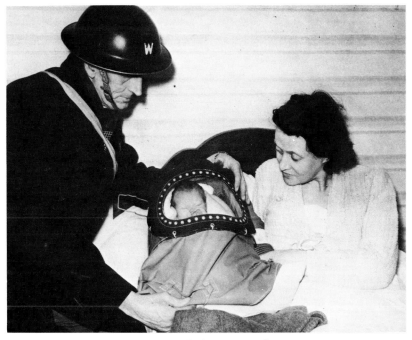

Trying out a baby gas mask.

For some reason we were not told where we were going, so you can imagine the rumours that were going around the hall. We were still there at the school at half past eleven, and you can imagine the noise of the children, and babies crying, everyone wanting something to eat or drink. Many had not bothered to have any breakfast and quite a lot of mothers were thinking of going back home if we did not get going soon!

At noon we made a move and we were on our way to Queens Road station. We had to walk about half a mile with all our belongings. What a pathetic sight we must have looked, like a lot of waifs and strays! We got on the train and soon realised we were going towards the south coast. Worthing was our destination. As with most government projects it was utter chaos. Previously, householders in Worthing had been approached about taking in a mother and child from London. As long as there was a room, or even a bed, it was to be a kind of bed and breakfast arrangement, the mother looking after herself and her children, and having to be out all day. Of course there were not enough people willing to do this for complete strangers, bearing in mind that the war had not yet started.

We were taken to a hall and given a cup of tea and a large carrier bag, one for each person, so I had two. The bags contained a tin of corned beef, some very large and hard biscuits, sugar, tea and some powdered milk. This was to last you till the shops opened on Monday morning, as it was then eight o'clock on Saturday night. I could have done without these carrier bags for it was all extra weight for my aching arms.

As there was nowhere for the majority of us to go, we were taken from the hall in a lorry, stopping at the end of each street. The welfare workers went knocking on doors asking if anyone could take us in, even for a night.

It was nearly ten o'clock by the time I got into a house with Pam. The family consisted of a man and wife and two girls, aged four and six. They all had to sleep in the same bed so that Pam and I could have the other bed. It was not very nice for them because they were already in bed when we got there. Of course the children were well awake and were arguing and kicking each other half the night.

I was so tired that I did eventually get to sleep. I think that September 2nd, 1939 was a bit of a nightmare.

On Sunday, September 3rd, at about half past ten, a few of us, who had been taken in along the same street, decided to go to the hall. We were hoping to find out if anything had been sorted out for us. It was eleven o'clock and suddenly the air raid warning sounded. It meant take cover, enemy planes coming. It was such a shock we did not know what to do, so we started to run back to the house where we were staying. All the time the siren was sounding.

I felt I was not getting along very fast as I was carrying Pam, so I put her down. Then I picked her up again and, by this time, she had become very frightened. My sense of direction was never very good and I was quite surprised to actually get back to the right house.

The rest of the family were listening to the wireless and we had been told that a state of war now existed with Germany. The next thing that we heard was the Air Raid Wardens dashing round the streets waving these things that made a kind of clacking noise. It was sort of wood against wood going round in a ratchet making a rattle. It meant danger of gas so we all started to put our gas masks on, but they had made a mistake, it should have been the All Clear sounding.

What a Sunday morning that was! I felt so exhausted and I needed a stiff drink but no one gave me one. The rest of the day was spent indoors because everyone was afraid to move outside the house.

JEAN CARTER

My school was evacuated in September 1939, I believe they went to Kent. My mother wouldn't let me go, I stayed in London. I was nine years old. They closed the schools to use them as rest centres, and of course a lot of teachers had gone with the children who were evacuated. I went to school in a big house that had been taken over. I only went for half an hour a day so as soon as you'd got there and taken off your coat, it was time to leave again! I virtually had no schooling at all.

I was getting bored, and wanted to go away. I think one of the reasons for this was because I enjoyed being with other children, and a lot of my friends had already gone. I was an only child and had always wanted brothers and sisters. I can't blame my parents for not wanting any more, they both came from large families, and had been poor. When my father had come back from the First World War, he couldn't get a job, and my mother said she wasn't going to be poor and so I was the only one.

I begged my parents to let me go, and at last they agreed, but they warned me, 'You make your bed, you lie in it!' We assembled at Greenwich High School. There were quite a few of us from all different schools that hadn't gone the first time round. We had no idea where we were going, and I can't remember the journey at all except that it felt like I was going to the moon.

We got on the train in the morning, and we didn't reach Devon until the evening. When we got to our destination, they put us in a big church hall, and the local people came and chose you. Eventually there were just three of us left, me and another little boy and girl, a brother and sister. We were right at the back. They took us to a village called Wythercombe in Devon.

It was a cottage with a thatched roof, which I'd never seen before, and they took us up the stairs, right up to the attic. I can't remember a bed being there, I think we slept on the floor. The next day we climbed out of the window and slid down the thatched roof. It came right down, almost to the ground. We had no proper bedroom and after a month I got fed up with it, so I went to the billeting officer, and asked to be transferred.

I was sent to a new estate at the back of Exmouth. The road was called Featherbed Lane, and there were fields opposite. She was a school-teacher and he was a violinist and they obviously hadn't been married very long. I was the only one there, and to get a friend for me, the woman asked for another evacuee. I think the blitz must have been on in London by now because this evacuee had come straight from Poplar. When I was evacuated, I'd had to have a medical and have my hair cut short, but when this evacuee came, they hadn't had time to give her a medical at all. She had nits and scabies, and, of course, when she arrived I contracted them too. We were sent off to isolation.

We were put in an old hotel on the seafront in Exmouth. They bathed us and put this foul smelling cream, like marzipan, all over us, and we had to wear itchy combs. Everything in our billet including the furniture had to be baked, because scabies is very contagious. It must have been awful for the people I'd been billeted with. We had to stay in isolation for a whole fortnight. I was supposed to be taking my scholarship at that time but couldn't, so when I did take it, I was all on my own in a room in Exmouth. I got sent to the Central school, and that was also in a hotel on the seafront. By this time, I'd been in Featherbed Lane for about a year, and of course after all the business of the scabies, I think the family were rather fed up with me. The other girl had gone back to London.

I was ten, getting on for eleven then. I hadn't seen my mother or father

for a whole year because my father was in the air force, and my mother wouldn't come down unless my father got leave, and anyway Devon was such a long way to come. I used to write, of course, but all I ever said was, 'Send money,' or, 'Send sweets.' I also kept asking to be allowed to come home. I'd wanted to go because it was an adventure, but then the gilt had worn off the gingerbread, and I wanted to go back. My mother wouldn't let me because the blitz was at its height.

PRINTED MATTER

Pictorial
Folding
LETTER CARD
of

CEMAES BAY

Mrs. L. Cooper.
124, Lewisham Road.
Lewisham.
London·
S.E.13.

England.

Photographed & Published by F. FRITH & CO., LTD., REIGATE   Entirely British Production

Llanbadrig Church. Where we are going.

where we live.

Coast Line, Cemaes Bay.

My Dear Mum
            Some more pictures
of where we are. Please send
some ~~must~~ money and some sweets
if you can. Give my love to all at
home. tons of love and kisses.

        Sean.
X X X X X X X † X †
X X X X X X

We are having a lovely time,
   and getting lovely food.
   Plenty of flowers.
You'd love it when we go for a walk
along the rocks and beaches.

I got myself another billet, and at last my father came down to see me, on his own. By this time I think they had bombed Exmouth itself, and I said I didn't want to stay. I think he must have given me some money because I can remember sending my mother a telegram saying, 'Meet me at Waterloo.' She was furious, but I came home and wouldn't go away again.

I was sent to Sandhurst Road School, and I'd only been there three months when it was bombed on January 20th. 1943. We had a direct hit. I wasn't injured, but unfortunately a lot of the youngsters were killed, about forty-six of them. When the school was bombed we were all sent off to convalesce.

I was sent to Anglesey. Everyone had to go even if they weren't injured, perhaps because they thought we were suffering from stress. We were right at the tip of Anglesey, and it was a convalescence home and hospital unit. The place was full of ATS. WAAFs and WRENs. It was where they went when they had to convalesce. They were really wonderful to us, they taught us how to make beds and all sorts of things. I had to stay there for three weeks. I was fed up with it by then because there was nothing much to do.

When we were sent home, we couldn't go back to Sandhurst Road School, so we were sent to a school in Catford. I didn't like this much either, some of our teachers had been killed and nothing seemed to be stable anymore. My mother said if you can find yourself a job then you can leave, so I did, and left school aged fifteen.

Looking back on my experiences as an evacuee, I suppose it taught me to stand on my own two feet. I was an only child and a bit spoilt, particularly by my grand parents. As an evacuee, you were on your own, the billeting officer didn't come round to see if you were all right, so if you didn't look after yourself no one did. I think it did alter me; I don't think I ever really got close to my parents after I came back because of that break. When I came back I felt I could look after myself. As an example, nobody ever told me about periods or anything like that, and the people I was billeted with hadn't got children of my age, and didn't really know how to look after a twelve year old.

The people were very kind to me in a way, but there was always something awkward about it. I don't think there was anything wrong on their part, it was just that the situation was forced on all of us. I got fed up with everything falling apart all the time. Nothing was ever stable, you'd just get used to something, and it'd be gone. The main thing I missed out on was my education. When I hear of girls not finishing their schooling or messing up their education, I think it's such a pity because a missed education is something you can never replace. I felt I had to grow up far too quickly.

> My dear mummy
> Just a few pictures to show you what the place is like. We have have been too most of these places. Every morning we go for a long walk all along the beaches and climb cliffs. There are plenty of primroses. We have smashing food.
> tons of love and kisses.
> Jean.
>
> One A.T.S. is making us laugh she trying to play the piano. I can't write for laughing
>
> Send Money Please.

BILL CLAPHAM

In 1939 I was eight years old and was attending Rotherhithe New Road London County Council Junior School. I was an only child and lived with my parents in part of a typical terraced house with a small back garden, my grandfather and two aunts living in the remainder of the house. My father worked at Deptford Power Station and he continued to do so throughout the war.

War was in the air in the late 1930s and I had seen cinema newsreels of the bombing of Chinese cities by the Japanese. I also knew that my grandfather's two sons had been killed in the 1914–18 war and that my father had been in the army.

In September, 1938, at the time of the 'Munich Crisis', my parents had attended a meeting at my school about the evacuation of children in the event of war and signed a consent for me to go (evacuation was voluntary). A practice was held at the school which involved taking the kit that would be needed to school with us. Also, at this time, communal air raid shelters were built on the allotment ground at the back of our house. Later, in April, 1939, individual 'Anderson' shelters were delivered in sections and erected in our back gardens. These were then covered with earth and later strengthened and made more habitable.

As war loomed nearer, more meetings and rehearsals were held at the school on 26th and 28th August, 1939 and the evacuation actually went ahead on Friday, 1st September. The 'Blackout' started that evening and war was declared on the 3rd September.

Those children being evacuated met at the school. Some parents had decided they would rather risk the bombing. I had a haversack with some spare clothes, some food and chocolate for the journey, a small amount of pocket money and some writing materials and stamps. We wore identifying labels and carried our gas masks in cardboard boxes. Some, but not all, of our teachers went with us and we walked to Surrey Docks Underground station and started our journey from there. Our mothers saw us off but I cannot remember whether that was at the school or later.

We travelled to the small town of Hailsham in Sussex, about six miles inland from Eastbourne. In those days Hailsham had a railway station and I assume we travelled all the way by that means but I have no memory of the journey except that we seemed to have to stand around waiting for a long time. Other children were travelling, but we kept in our own school party. At Hailsham we were taken to Hailsham parish church hall, where we had to wait until collected by the families with whom we were to be billeted. I went with a family who lived on the edge of the town in Battle Road. The husband was a postman and the rest of the family consisted of his wife, two grown up sons and a son, rather older than me, still at school.

On Saturday, 2nd September, my mother got a letter from the lady to say I had arrived. The Postal Services were usually very efficient during the war.

Almost immediately after the declaration of war the air raid sirens sounded and I needed reassuring by one of the older sons, that we were not about to be bombed. My parents paid six shillings per week towards my keep. This was by an arrangement through the LCC and did not involve any negotiation with the householder.

The following week, school began. We remained as our own school group using the Methodist church hall in the mornings, then walking some way to a local school where we had dinner and our own classes there in the afternoon. We tended to play in our own group too, climbing trees, going fishing or playing cricket at the recreation ground. We did not have much contact with the local children, although I cannot remember there being much antipathy.

I wrote to my parents regularly and they came down to see me, travelling by Southdown coach. By the end of September, however, I was ill with a skin infection which, before the days of antibiotics, needed a month in Heathfield Hospital where I was pretty miserable, although my parents came and visited me there. After leaving hospital, the family said they could not keep me any longer because they had to care for an elderly relative. Whether this was just an excuse to the billeting officer I do not know; changing billets was a common occurence.

In November I moved to North Street in the middle of the town, where I shared with another evacuee from my school. The husband worked at an antique shop and they had two sons, both already away with the forces. My parents continued to visit me from time to time and a hall, the Liberal Hall, was made available as a place where parents of evacuees could meet their children.

There was one cinema in the town with the programme changing twice a week and, apart from radio, this was the main source of information and entertainment. The weather became very cold, and the pond near the station was frozen over so that we could walk out to the island in the middle.

A regiment, I think the Devonshire, was stationed nearby and they used to parade with their band on Sundays. Local buildings, such as the council offices were protected with sand bags and, at the school, a row of old pigsties had been pointed out as air raid shelters, but otherwise there was no tangible sign of war, so much so that I was able to go home for a fortnight at Easter 1940.

This all changed by the early summer and, with the threat of invasion, it was considered that Hailsham was too close to the coast to be safe and that we should move further — to Wales. Although the people in Hailsham had looked after me well enough, in spite of food rationing and shortages, I was unhappy away from my home and parents, and even more so at the prospect of going to Wales. I had only the vaguest idea where it was but it sounded a long way away. However, after taking advice from our teachers and a lot of heart searching, it was decided that I should go. During the stay at Hailsham, many children had returned to London and for many parents, Wales was the last straw, so it was only a

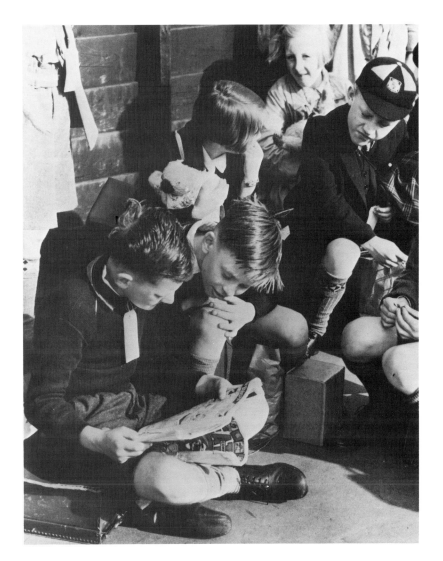

remnant of the original evacuees who left for Wales on Sunday, 23rd June, 1940. My mother had travelled down from London by coach to see us off.

Not until we were on the train did we hear that our destination was Carmarthen, which I had never heard of. Again there seemed to be a lot of waiting around on platforms and the journey seemed interminable. At Carmarthen we waited, I think at a school, for our final destination and eventually the boys travelled on six miles to the village of Llanddarog, while other groups from our school, the girls, went to other villages. The village was on the road from Carmarthen to Swansea and consisted of a single street, with a church, a chapel, a general shop, kept by Jones—the—shop, a post office, two pubs and about twenty houses.

Bill Clapham in Cub's uniform at Rotherhithe just before evacuation.

JOAN CLARKSON

I was away on holiday with my mother and sister in Kent when the war started. We returned home and found that my school had already been evacuated. Because my parents and sister were at work and there was no school open, my parents were worried about leaving me in the house alone during the day. They were expecting bombing raids and so they tried to get me evacuated but the council was not interested in evacuating a single child.

I had been on holiday with the school the previous summer and stayed with some people. As I had found it quite pleasant there, my mother wrote to them asking if they knew anyone who would be willing to take a child privately. The woman wrote back to say that her mother was willing to have me. She lived in a village just outside Kettering in Northampton.

My parents took me up on the train and the people made us quite welcome. She was a lady of about fifty, and although fifty is not all that old these days, she had worked hard and fifty was old then. I think she took me for the money, my parents were paying privately, but she was not interested a great deal in me as a child. I wrote and told my parents that I was unhappy and I wanted to come home but of course, they were too worried to let me. The woman was very cross because I had written and said that I was unhappy and wanted to go home.

Nothing had prepared me for that sort of life. The water was a tap in the garden. The loo was at the end of the garden and it had never been connected to sewerage, so you went there with a bucket of water. The cooking was always done on the fire so you always had a fire, summer and winter. Although it was a thatched cottage it was very cold in the winter and I did suffer with extreme cold. I was given a stone hot water bottle at night, wrapped in flannel, and when I got up in the morning the water was still luke warm and I had to pour it in the bowl and wash with it. Nothing was wasted.

I had been a cherished little girl with an older sister and two parents to look after me. They had lost a son, so they cherished us girls, and for me to go to someone who merely tolerated me was very hard. If you were seen you were not to be heard. You must always be busy, the Devil made work for idle hands! You went to church or chapel three times on a Sunday because it got you out of the house. The lady's husband was not a nice person and she worked to keep him. She had been in service when she was younger, and now she took in washing.

There was a barn built on to the side of the cottage and in there was a big copper where you lit the fire underneath and that was where she did all the washing. She had a great big bath and a scrubbing board. There were times that I helped her, but I think that was just to pass the time. She would wash, dry and iron, and she would send me with great big bales of washing to collect the money. She would say "Mind your manners and tell no−one my business."

In the end I became so depressed I did not talk. I was fed and looked after but I was not wanted. My mother used to buy me dainty clothes and nice things, but the lady did not think any of them was serviceable. She told my mother what I was to wear. I had to wear thick lisle stockings and have elastic to make garters with. I just about knew which end was up with a needle, but she never sewed a button on for me or anything. I had to do that and make my own garters. She taught me to darn so that I could mend my own stockings. My mother could not believe it when she came back and saw me. I had these dreadful lisle stockings on and I was wearing those great big thick soles that she had had put on to my shoes. She walked everywhere and I had to too.

When my parents came to see me, the people were surprised that they were so smart. They thought Londoners were not clean, they did not think we ate properly, they thought we were not very well nourished and that a good meal would do you good.

The village school was not too bad but Londoners were barely tolerated there. There were two other girl evacuees there who lived with their aunt, and there was the niece of the billeting officer. There used to be things going on in the village, like concert parties and fetes in the summer. On May day, in the school there was a May Queen picked and we made garlands of flowers. We used to go all round the villages collecting money for Comforts for the Forces. Everyone used to knit and sew for them.

I suppose they were lucky really, in that village, they had hardly anyone billeted on them in the early stages of the war, but during the Battle of Britain, they brought there a lot of young women with small children and babies. For these evacuees it was like being in a cattle market. They were taken to the village hall and then the local people would go along and choose those they liked the look of. Whoever was left was waltzed around the village by the billeting officer, and wherever there was room they had to be taken in. There was a young woman, about twenty six, with a baby about eighteen months or two years old, and they came to stay where I was.

She had two little boys who had been evacuated to Devon and her husband was in the army. She was very frightened on her own in London and she was billeted with us. She was not chosen. She used to sit and hold the little girl all day as she was not allowed to put her down on the floor in case she touched anything. The little child was still in nappies, and nothing was done to make life easy for this young mother. She was not made welcome, she was barely tolerated. She stayed about six weeks and then she made friends with another young woman with a baby. They got a small cottage in another village two or three miles away. They slept on mattresses on the floor and they only had boxes to sit on, but they were vastly better off there on their own. These two young women's husbands were away abroad fighting, but the village people seemed to have no compassion.

People never stayed in the village for very long. Within a few weeks all the children and everyone had all gone back home. I was there in that place for about three years, and it never got better. All children make a noise when they play but people used to say 'Bloody Londoners, you're a nuisance, go back to London and have the bombs drop on you'. They did not understand. I don't know how people could be so unkind, especially to children. The lady's daughter was a very spiteful woman, but I had not realised that before when I had only stayed for a few weeks holiday. There was frequent verbal abuse and a child cannot defend itself. If my parents had known, they would have been horrified. I can remember the people being very unkind to me and I was very unhappy.

When my parents came to visit me, a very nice front was put on, but although they knew I was unhappy, they could not have me home. My Father worked in the docks, my Mother was doing war work, she had to do a full day on Monday, and Tuesday to Friday she used to work from 7.30am to 1.00pm. and when she finished queueing up for food and whatever was available, she had to do her work at home. I do not know what would have happened to me if they had got killed, my hostess would not have wanted to keep me.

The village school children after a display of country dancing.
Joan was the only evacuee.

During the very bad raids my mother, my sister and my grandmother went to stay for a few weeks with my hostess's daughter, the lady I had stayed with before the war. The raids were getting very bad in London and no-one was getting any sleep. It was all right for about two weeks but then the lady really did not want them after that. She began to find fault with my sister and said that her husband was spending too much time with the young girl. There was nothing in it at all, he was just a very nice man and a lot of fun. With my mother and my grandmother there, they would not have allowed anything wrong.

Whilst they were there I used to see my mother every weekend and go and stay with them, but that was only for a little while. My father became ill and my mother had to go home.

On a Saturday morning, I had to get up very early and get the bus into Wellingborough and queue up for about an hour before the shop opened to get sausages and things that you could buy off ration. I would then have to go round to another shop and queue up again and that way I got some food for the lady I lived with and some for her daughter. On the way back I would have to go to her village first and drop off one lot of shopping and then get another bus back to the village where I lived. Thinking about it now it was done to get me out of the house.

Sometimes, when there was a lull in the raids, occasionally, I went home to London for a holiday. My parents would always have me home and then I was happier. They would come every two months to see that I was all right. They would bring me whatever I needed, or whatever they thought I might like. They used to save all their sweet ration and bring me all their sweets, send me pocket money and write to me every week. I was a bad letter writer, I got tired of asking them to take me home and I think they got just as tired reading it. It must have been very difficult for them, I was so unhappy.

After one visit home early in 1942 I came back and the lady had actually left her husband. She arranged for me to stay with her son and his wife and of course they were much younger. I stayed with them for a year and I did have a nice time with them. Whilst I was there, in the last year, I wore nicer clothes. The daughter-in-law was young, she was about thirty and she arranged for me to have my hair permed. I went to school in Kettering from that village and there was a school bus. It was a far better school with more facilities.

There were a lot of American soldiers there and they would give the children sweets, it was great. It was altogether a nicer, friendlier place.

Apart from when I went home I think I lived in that period totally without affection. It made a big mark on me. There was no one I could actually talk to, no one I could confide in. I had friends but I did not talk to them about it, because I was told not to talk. I just bottled it up inside, and although no one had ill-treated me physically, I was not loved. As I've got older I think I understand it more, but as a child I was withdrawn. It was a very hostile place to be.

When I came home eventually, although I had enjoyed the last year, I did not trust anybody for a long time. I never ever confided in my parents again. It was something, a barrier, that was there. I think it was because I kept asking to come home and they would not let me. I was unhappy, and although they explained it to me in their letters and when I came home on holidays, it was something that I, as a child, could not understand. I think I lost confidence in them. I learned to trust again with my husband and I gave lots of affection to him, as I do to my children and my grandchildren.

EVACUEES UNAWARE OF DESTINATION

When they left their London districts, the evacuees were unaware as to the stopping place of their train, even the leaders of the parties not having been given this information. Even when the train pulled up in the Wolverton railway station many were still unaware of their ultimate destination seeing they had ahead of them a bus journey into the surrounding villages.

Upon arrival at their billets, children posted a card to their parents informing them of their safe arrival and with information as to their new address.

Wolverton Express, 8th September 1939.

VALERIE CLAYTON

I was an evacuee aged about four, when I went with my gas mask, long dress and short brown coat and hat to a little place called Bennington in Hertfordshire to stay with a Mrs Pearman and her two boys, John and Nigel, my first boyfriend. He gave me a pincushion in the shape of a shoe. I still have it. Mrs Pearman was a teacher and very busy so my mother came to look after us all. When my mother died eight years ago, Mrs Pearman sent a wreath with the words, 'To a loving friend and courageous wartime comrade.'

I can remember the children calling out to me, 'We don't want you Londoners down here!' They used to hold me and put dead frogs and snails down my back on the way from school, which was about three and a half miles away. I walked there and back by my self, just aged four and a half. On my first day at school, it was winter, I had not got very far when I came back to tell my mother I could not go as there were big things in the road coming towards me that I had never seen before. They turned out to be cows.

My mother had to go into hospital to have my brother, so she took me along a lane to a farm to ask if they could look after me until she came home. All I can remember is, they gave me a big steel bucket, bigger than me, to get soft fruit. I went under nets all day and did not come in until evening. My bucket was only half full, I had eaten the rest.

After that we went to live in the big manor house with Mr and Mrs Bracy. Rainwater collected in a tub outside the house for shaving and washing hair. Mr Bracy got very cross when my brother threw things in Christmas 1944, when I was seven and my brother was three, we came down in the morning to a white scrubbed kitchen table. On it were two oranges, half a pound of sausages, and two bible books. I still have my one. I will never forget it, and remind my children of it every year. If only time would stand still.

I fell in love with everything we saw in the woods and fields in our adopted home. The smell of wood burning and primroses, violets and cowslips always make me think of those blissful days. Now I have to make a special trip just to see a few cowslips. I am going back this year to recapture old memories.

HARRY COLE

With the exception of my friends Rosie and Charlie, all my class of fellow ten year olds had been evacuated by the time the blitz had peaked in October 1940. We beleaguered three would meet each morning to discuss the previous night's bombing. Accurate details of these raids were never given on the radio. The announcer would merely say something nondescript such as, 'Enemy planes last night attempted to attack targets in the London area. They were repulsed with heavy losses, and bombs were dropped at random.'

I pointed out to Charlie how lucky we were to live in London, and not in 'Random'. That unfortunate town seemed to be raided about five times each day. The thing that puzzled me most, however, was just where 'Random' was. I assumed it must have been near London, but, until the blitz, I had never heard of it. Charlie, who was quite knowledgeable about these things, said he was quite sure it was a town in Essex. Rosie didn't think it could have been much of a town, because by then it would have been blown to bits. We weighed up the evidence, and decided that perhaps 'Random' was, after all, a much bigger town than we had given it credit for.

In mid October, after 'Random' had suffered yet another day-long raid, my dad called a family meeting of my mum, brother, grandparents, Aunt Eliza, Aunt Liz, Cousin Stella and Cousin Renee. He said the women and children should leave for the country. He pointed out that the raids had become both daily and nightly. This had been going on for two long months, and showed no sign of abating. If anything, they were becoming worse. 'To my mind,' he said prophetically, 'time is running out for us.'

It certainly seemed like Dad had a direct line to Hitler, because that night was the worst attack we had yet experienced. In spite of the heavy bombardment, I finally fell asleep, but was suddenly woken by the light of the ceiling bulb shining directly into my eyes. 'Come on,' Mum was saying, 'Move over.' I slowly assembled my wits and was surprised to see, in addition to the room's usual complement, three other familiar looking people. There standing just behind Mum, was Uncle George, Aunt Nell and six year old cousin 'Georgie-boy'.

Rubbing my eyes, I looked up at the clock. It was five past one. "Wassamarra?" The six of us, who were already in the bed, were to make room for yet one more cousin and an aunt. 'Georgie-boy' joined my brother and me at the foot of the bed, while Aunt Nell slipped into the top. The whole bed seemed to bubble with feet.

It transpired that forty-five minutes earlier, the newcomers had been blasted out of their Kennington flat. They had then walked two miles, through cascading bombs and exploding shrapnel, to reach us. Slowly thirteen of us settled down in that small kitchen. Someone turned off the light, and I turned gingerly away from Aunt Nell's left foot.

Around that moment on the brewery roof at the end of the street, a fire-watcher scanned the turbulent sky. Everywhere were exploding bombs and shells. Suddenly, he perked appreciably. It seemed like the guns had achieved one success after all. There, caught momentarily in a searchlight, was a parachute. The route it was taking should deposit the pilot squarely onto the roof of our crumbling tenement. Sadly there was no German pilot dangling anxiously on the end of that parachute; instead, there was an eight foot long sea-mine, packed with high explosives, and designed to blow battleships out of the sea.

Dad had been right, time had finally run out. It had run out not simply for the old buildings, but for half the folks who lived there. The explosion came in two stages. The first woke me instantly, but was all over in a moment. The second seemed to be within my head. I was aware of a great roaring noise and felt an enormous pressure inside my

Small children try on footwear sent to the English Speaking Union for distribution to children in bombed out areas. 51

skull. Once the effects subsided, it seemed to take an age but lasted, I suppose, just a few seconds, I began to take stock of the situation.

My first reaction was that everyone in the room was dead. In fact, other than some glass lacerations, they were completely unscathed. But there was total silence in the room. Then I realised the silence was not confined to the room. Everywhere else was deathly quiet. Huge clouds of dust billowed, but not a sound to be heard. Not a cough, not a sigh, not a moan.

Suddenly, noise began to gather momentum as parts of the building began to disintegrate. The first of many screams began to cut through the still night air, and slowly our room began to come to life. Urgent voices began to call across the darkened room. 'Georgie, are you alright?' 'How's Stella?' 'Is everyone okay?' 'I think my hand's cut!'. Suddenly, a more dramatic voice could be heard yelling from the communal staircase, 'Everyone outside as quickly as possible, the building is collapsing!'

The distant screams grew louder, as the old tenements began to fall apart. Each fall of masonry was followed by another great cloud of choking dust. 'Quick, outside,' ordered Dad curtly, 'and don't bother to dress.' This decree was all very well for the grown-ups, who always slept fully dressed, but all of us children were in night attire. Groping our way through the pitch black towards the door, we discovered a terrifying problem. The explosion had twisted the frame and the door was immovable. Yet it could well be that the door and its frame, twisted though it was, may have been keeping the four floors above from crashing down on us.

'Are you all right in there?' called another unfamiliar voice from the staircase. 'No, we can't move the door! Can you push on it?' replied Dad. 'It's a risk,' said the voice, 'but we'll have to take it. Stand back!' This was followed by several great thuds and suddenly the door splintered open. Standing in the doorway was a giant of a soldier, whom none of us had seen before.

'Quick!' he commanded, 'The buildings are falling apart.' He shone a small pocket torch around the room. 'Get down that staircase as quickly as you can. Come here you two.' With that, he bent forward and gathered my brother and me under each arm and led the whole party down twenty-eight stairs to the comparative safety of the shrapnel racked street. He then handed Stan to my father and placed me down gently on a small section of glass-free pavement. I looked up, but before I could thank him, he had returned into the dark crumbling block. To this day I wonder if he survived, for we never saw him again.

Dad and Uncle George stayed behind to help with the rescue, and the rest of us shuffled our way to the local rest centre, which also happened to be my own primary school. Amazingly, I made the journey through four glass-covered streets without so much as a scratch to my bare feet.

'Hello luvs,' smiled a rotund lady with a huge brown teapot. 'Have a cup of tea, then we'll find you some blankets and you can bed down.' 'Bed down!' echoed Aunt Liz, looking wide eyed all around the room. We were surrounded by glass, there were three huge windows and a glass partition between us and the next classroom. 'If a bomb goes off here, it'll be like sleeping in a box of razor blades.'

In spite of these fears, we huddled together and I soon fell asleep. My last clear recollection was of my mother sobbing quietly into her blanket. Next morning, I stood in front of a great pile of ill-assorted clothing, while my mother endeavoured to find something better than pyjamas with which to clad her two sons. Amongst all the uncertainty, one thing was sure, we could not sleep on the school floor for the rest of the war. It was, as even mum finally agreed, time for us to leave London.

As a result of that decision, we found ourselves, a week later, on a smoky platform at Liverpool Street station. Together with scores of other blitz victims, we were bound for an unknown destination. As the train rattled its way across the wet and ravaged London roof tops, word was passed from carriage to carriage. 'It's a top secret, so don't tell anyone else but we are bound for Norfolk.'

We were told to stand in line, and zombie-like we complied. Then, several people who had been sitting around the sides of the hall came forward and stared at us. One by one they then approached a tweed-suited lady who sat at a desk with a register in front of her. They would point at one of the families in the line and whisper in the lady's ear.

Harry Cole

Each time, the tweed suited lady would nod and ask the name of the family that had been pointed at.

'Brown.' 'Very well Mrs Brown, you and your daughter have been billeted with Mrs Dawson here. Off you go.' We had actually been put on display and offered for selection! It was like a slave market. It was a wonder they didn't look at our teeth. In twos and threes our numbers gradually diminished until there was only my mum, my brother, and me left. No one, it seemed, wanted a frightened woman with two cockney boys.

We looked anxiously at the last of the choosers. She was an elderly, silver haired, lady with a remote air of elegance about her. At first glance she appeared strict, yet this impression was not borne out by the kindly twinkling eyes. She was accompanied by her unmarried daughter Polly. 'I am very sorry my dear,' said the old lady to my mother, 'but we only have room for a mother and baby. We did make this quite clear at the beginning.' She turned a reproachful glance at the billeting officer.

'Oh please, please take us in,' begged mum, 'I promise you we'll be no trouble.' 'I would willingly do so my dear, but we only have one spare bed and it's not very big. I can't see how you could possibly manage.'

'Please, please,' sobbed mum, 'just give us one chance.' The old lady stared at us for a few seconds, then dropping a hand to my brother's head, she ruffled his hair. 'Oh come on,' she relented, 'If you don't all mind sharing the same bed, you are more than welcome.' 'Thank you Mrs Robinson,' said the tweed-suited lady, 'it's all worked out rather well really. That concludes the billeting for today.' Granny Robinson, as she came to be known, took hold of my brother's hand and led us out of the hall.

My mother was to stay until my father found another flat, some six months later. I remained for three years, until October 1943. My brother was so happy that he did not return until May 1945, two weeks after the war ended. Granny Robinson survived the war for just a short time, and since then my mother too has died. My brother emigrated to Australia many years ago, but I am delighted to say that Polly, now in her late eighties, is still in good health and, even after fifty years, we keep in regular touch and visit from time to time.

Whenever I hear horror stories told by evacuees, I realise just how fortunate one distraught mum and her two bewildered children were, those fifty years ago.

One difficulty, which neither the Reception committee nor those responsible for the welfare of the London children during their stay with us, had anticipated, is that of adequate clothing. A number of the boys and girls came into the district with no change of clothing and with shoes badly worn.

Many foster parents have made great sacrifices in this direction and have shown a sympathy and kindness which, to say the least, is remarkable, though it is characteristic of what Newport Pagnell people are always ready to do when consideration for the comfort of others is demanded.

Bucks Standard, 9th September 1939.

ANNE CONWAY

The school was on the Eastern Avenue, and had a long driveway. One drive led to the Infants School and one to the Juniors. The buses were parked just outside and we all bundled in with our cardboard gas mask boxes, hung on string, round our necks. I remember Mum walking back down the drive, she had on a straight black skirt and a hat tilted on one side of her head. She did not look back again and she had told me not to cry. Somehow I obeyed, though everyone else was bawling their eyes out. I was only four and a half years old, but this scene is as clear now as it was then.

My sister and brother are younger than me, so they did not go on this evacuation. I was sent to a village in Devon, where I was billeted with two other girls with an old couple and their two unmarried daughters. I think we were well looked after at this house. I remember summer time and wandering down the garden path by the tennis court. The bees were buzzing and the lavender bushes were as tall as I was. I watched, fascinated, while the old man painted watercolours and he gave me my first painting brush. The house was a pink—washed, thatched cottage and the two sisters, whom we called Auntie Kitty and Auntie Mary were the Brown Owl and Tawny Owl of the village Brownie Pack. We were taught how to clean our teeth properly and to wear a pinafore when helping with household chores, and we were taught how to wash our dolls' clothes.

Anne plays washing day. 1940.

I do not know how long I was there before returning to London. In London my 'Auntie' from across the road looked after us while Mum went to work at Plessey's. We had an Anderson shelter in the garden and I hated the spiders and the cold. We all used to go down there together, my Aunt, her three children, my mum and us three. I can remember running down there, with incendiaries dropping all around and the sky being lit up with them. In the back room downstairs we had a Morrison shelter. It was like a huge iron table and my sister and I were put to bed there and if the siren sounded I waited and waited and waited for Mum and baby brother to come under with us. It was a bit of a squeeze and Mum did not always come in, but I think there were only one or two bombs round our way in Chadwell Heath.

On the second evacuation, my brother, sister and I were all sent back to the same house in the same village. I think they had a problem dealing with us because we used to argue all the time. At least, I thought it was our fault that we were rebilleted. I remember on one occasion I was sent outside, my sister sent to a downstairs room and my brother to an upstairs room!

My brother and I were sent to a tiny terraced house in the village, with an old couple who had a grown up, retarded, son. Our parents must have been in touch with the people, because they knew that my brother was not happy. He used to cry a lot and did not want to go to bed, which he shared with the retarded man. We were not there for very long. My brother was taken home, he was pining, we were told. Later, I remember Mum talking to other grown ups about it in guarded tones, and it sounded pretty sinister.

I was sent to a newish detached bungalow by the river where my sister was staying. The time in the bungalow by the river must have been an idyllic time for a child. I hardly remember being indoors. We caught minnows in a jam jar with string tied around it, and we swung, dangerously, on willow branches overhanging the river. We played with the village children in a hay−loft and made a slide from wood.

One of the older girls, stocky, with red cheeks and a mop of thick curly blonde hair, told us how babies came! I remember soon after that playing with Auntie's make up and brush and comb, and wondering when my breasts would come.

Anne with the Charlesworth family.

The bungalow had a long orchard and an outhouse, where there were a couple of pigs. I do remember it was winter when they decided to kill one of the pigs. They tied it up and cut its throat and it squealed until it bled to death! I can hear that squealing yet.

The village school was a mile or so away in the village itself. We had to walk through two cow fields along by the river to get there. The classes had about eighty children in them, all different ages, and the school was run by a red−faced brute of a headmaster. If we went in the gate as the bell was ringing, that was counted as late, and everyone who was late was caned in front of the whole school. Every morning there was a long stream of children, mostly boys, lining up waiting for the cane. Once I got caught in this line. I was terrified of the cane, but that morning there were so many that the head gave up before he got to me.

There was an American Camp in the village. Instead of walking home through the fields, we used to go along the village road, past the camp and hang around asking for gum and sweets. The Americans were kind to us kids and let us in when they had a film show. One of the soldiers was black. He was fat and he smiled and patted our heads. After a film show we were quite scared, going home through the pitch black lanes, with owls hooting and bats flittering past.

At one spot in the river there was a small waterfall and just above this the river was calm, like a little lake, and we used to swim there. The Americans used to sit on the bank and watch us playing. I had a punctured swimming ring and one American told me to try to swim without the ring because he did not think it was holding me up. So I did, and found out that I had been swimming all the time.

I do not know if the couple who looked after us had any children or how old they were. She was plump, had curly brown hair and glasses. He was tall, bony and had dark red hair and large hands. He worked on a farm and he moved very slowly and deliberately. He did not say much but he seemed kind enough.

It was an Italian Prisoner of War who worked on the farm who got on my nerves. Paul, his name was, and he always seemed to be in the house when it was time to come in. He always bounced my sister on his knee and cuddled her. She looked like a little doll with her short blond hair,

The rubber ring with a hole in it.

blue eyes and plump red cheeks. I warned her that he was a Prisoner of War and should be locked up, not coming round the house playing his damned Opera records. There was one incident that I never forgot. We had few possessions, but I had managed to get hold of an HB pencil. I had always liked drawing, I am an art teacher now. He asked me to give it to him because he also liked to draw. I refused and he argued and I continued to refuse. He did not give up and in the end I broke the pencil in half and threw half of it to him. He was very angry, put me over his knee and spanked my bottom with a slipper, then I was sent to bed. I was fuming with rage, I never forgave him. I managed to get my sister on my side and we followed him around, plotting revenge, a trip wire, or shoving him into the river. Actually it was not because he was a prisoner that I did not like him. There was another Italian, called Peter, who used to cross the bridge by the house every day, but he was very quiet and gentle. He did not speak much, but he always smiled at us and we offered him a sweet some times.

I do not know how long we had been there, about eighteen months I think, when a man in a blue−grey uniform turned up at the bungalow. They said it was my dad, but I was not sure, until after the meal, when the man fell asleep in the chair in front of the range. So then I knew it must be my dad because he always fell asleep after a meal, and at home we had had a job trying to keep quiet, while he was sleeping!

The family and a few others having tea in the garden. 1940.

Anne and Aunty Kitty in the garden.

Dad, my sister and I went on a train journey, a very long, slow one; it must have been about a night and a day and then I was up in Scotland with Mum and my brother and sister. I do not think I liked Scotland very much. We lived in one room at a dentist's house. Mum cooked for him and we had to behave and keep quiet all the time. It was always cold and grey outside. I was afraid of the local kids and I hated the school and the teachers. They had the tawse (a leather strap) there. But we saw more of Dad because he used to visit us on a bicycle.

We were back in London when the doodlebugs and V2 rockets were dropping. There did not seem to be a lot of damage near us. I remember Mum and I were in Newbury Park and people were running to the station. I looked up and saw this cross in the sky, passing by, overhead. I was transfixed and stood watching it and Mum dragged me along by the arm. I went back to my old school and we used to collect satchels full of shrapnel, especially along the Eastern Avenue, but we had to be careful not to touch a Butterfly bomb. We were told that this was a bomb that looked like a butterfly, especially dropped by the Germans to kill the children.

Twenty five years later, with two children of my own, I visited the village and there was the bungalow, the river and the fields, just as before, except that the river was polluted by a chemical factory. And

there were Auntie Mary and Auntie Kitty walking through the fields to the village just as they had always done. I ran up to them and explained who I was. They nodded and smiled and said 'That's nice' or some other pleasantry, but they did not show any real interest, so we just walked away from each other and kept the memories locked away.

Anne, Joan, and Aunty May in front of the house.

ROSEMARY DAVIS

I came out of church with my mother, aunt and two girl cousins into the warm sunshine of that day in September 1939. We were coming to the end of a carefree holiday in a small farming and fishing community on the Essex coast, staying in our grandparents' summer chalet. The prayers in church had been particularly ponderous for three little girls of five, seven and nine. However, there was light relief for us during the hymns and canticles watching a village lad labouring to pump air into the ancient organ where the equally ancient organist appeared (and indeed sounded) to be playing with his elbows.

As we strolled down the lane towards Church Farm we could see the farmer and his wife at their gate, she with handkerchief to her eyes. My mother and aunt exchanged a few anxious words and hurried towards her. 'We're at war. We've just heard it on the wireless,' she said. We children picked out references to sons and husbands in the grown-ups' conversation, whose seriousness was not lost on us.

We did not go back to London. Instead, the family rented a farm cottage about a mile inland (our chalet was commandeered by the army for the duration of the war) and the five of us moved in. The cottage comprised one room up (crudely subdivided) and one room down, with a walk-in larder. Incredibly old, the front door was only five foot high and the beamed ceiling imposed a permanent crouch on all persons taller than five foot six inches.

Somehow, we all managed to fit into these cramped quarters and adapt to life without running water and electricity and gas supplies. Our water — wonderfully cool and clear — was hauled from the well in the garden; evenings were lit by the soft light of candles and oil lamps and a kitchen range served for cooking and heating. The 'lavy' was luxuriously spacious by contrast. Under a greengage tree at the end of the garden was our two-seater hay box privy, cleaned out nightly and hay renewed by our landlord farmer. The nearest school was four miles away and the nearest town ten miles — 'too far' ever to be visited by our ninety year-old neighbours who had never seen a railway train.

We three girls got to school on the school bus; journeys fraught with trepidation due to the boisterousness and rich rural language of the native children. My experience of school in the kindergarten of a refined girls school was poor preparation for the basic physical stridency of the village school. My class shared a large room with another. Each morning the partition which divided us would be folded back and several other classes would file in and stand around the sides. The headmaster (stout and stern) conducted prayers and reading in a pious manner. I can only recollect singing two hymns — 'Eternal Father, Strong To Save' (very appropriate to the seafaring locality) and 'Jesus, Good Above All Other' sung on alternate days. Neither was a suitable prelude for the scenes to follow. As soon as the Amen had been sung the headmaster would seize a boy by the back of his collar and haul him up onto the teacher's platform.

He then grasped the child by his shoulders and, lifting his feet clear of the ground, shook him like a rag doll all the while stertorously bellowing a catalogue of his misdemeanours. Quite often several boys would receive this treatment and I came to recognise those who got it regularly. I dreaded this daily ritual, and remember wondering why the headmaster didn't notice that this punishment was not doing any good as most of the boys continued their delinquencies.

Despite the remoteness of our geographical position, enemy aircraft would often pass overhead, and in those days, slowly and low enough to identify their markings. Many's the time we had to jump from our bicycles, throw them into a hedge and lie down in a ditch until possible danger had passed. The potential danger of invasion also began to loom

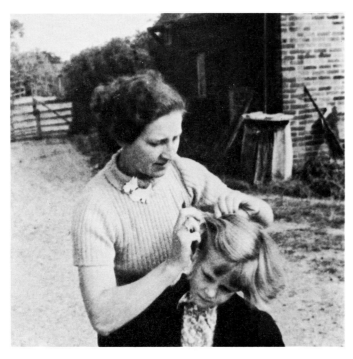

Rosemary down in the country with her mother.

standing but with all the windows out. The sound of the sweeping of broken glass was usual after the 'all clear' siren.

Every house with a garden large enough had its own Anderson air-raid shelter. Our shop yard was too small to take one so we took refuge in our cellar. Because of the incessant night raids most people slept in their shelters, and we in our cellar, although a direct hit would have buried us under the rubble from three storeys above us. In time, a public air-raid shelter was built on the pavement outside our shop with built-in bunks for mother and me to sleep on. This brought us out of the cellar into the world of East London night life. Being a public shelter anyone could drop in, and did, usually just after the pubs had closed. With the sounds of air-raid warnings, aircraft, gunfire, exploding bombs and boozy visitors, a good night's sleep was hard to come by.

Nevertheless, it was rats which finally drove us to abandon our shelter — probably they themselves had been bombed out. The local rector, aware of our predicament, offered us the use of two spare bunks in the rectory shelter during raids. For these quarter mile nocturnal excursions we had siren suits made to measure by a local Jewish tailor. I was so proud of mine, designed to pull on over pyjamas; it had massive pop-stud fastenings up the front and at wrists and ankles, and a back flap which unbuttoned from the waist 'for convenience'.

Each night as my bed time approached we would turn on the wireless. If the reception was being interrupted by a characteristic crackling sound we would know that an air-raid was imminent. Rather than go to bed, I would climb into my siren suit and await the warning siren. By walking and running ten steps alternately we could get halfway to the rectory by the time the first gunfire was heard and flashes appeared in the sky. With knees turning to jelly we could just about make the gate as the throb of approaching aircrafts' engines came near. On one of these nights, when the raids were in such quick succession that we couldn't return home to our beds, we emerged at dawn after the final 'all clear'. It had been the worst night we had experienced for aircraft and gunfire noise, and yet there had been very few local exploding bombs. An awesome sight greeted us. The entire horizon glowed red where the City of London was on fire.

Being burnt out was as much of a worry as being bombed out, but at least we had a better chance of diminishing the effects. Groups of

large so that London appeared safer than the Essex coast. So our country education came to an end. Having learned to glean corn, pick potatoes and lead a carthorse pulling loads of sugar beet, we returned to London . . . and to the blitz!

My father was soon called up for active service as were all the other male assistants in the family shop. My mother and I lived over the shop which she ran with the help of my aunt and grandfather. My own school had by now evacuated to Somerset, so I attended the local primary school. Daytime raids frequently interrupted our lessons. As soon as the air-raid warning sounded we would make for the cloakrooms which had been reinforced as shelters. In these confined spaces we would chant our tables, recite poems and sing national folk songs against a background noise of anti-aircraft guns firing from their base in the park nearby. An exploding bomb might cause dust and plaster to shower on us. 'That was a near one' we'd say, and then everyone would guess which road it had fallen in, hoping it wasn't one's own. Often we'd go home to find it still volunteer fire-fighters on rota guarded every street and block. Even we children were shown how to use the stirrup pump and bucket of water kept by our front and back doors with the buckets of sand. We also knew the distinctive whistling whine of a falling incendiary bomb or fragment of shrapnel. A newly dropped piece of shrapnel could be hot enough to start a fire, or be lying there on the ground before you. Many young collectors got their hands badly burned this way, and it was not unusual to see children spitting on shrapnel to see if it sizzled!

I think it was during my eleventh birthday party that we heard the heavy throbbing sound of an aircraft overhead, yet there had been no air-raid warning siren. It was unlike the sound of any aeroplane already familiar to us — very loud with a heavy pulse to it. It continued to get closer, but uncannily slowly. We all instinctively hid under the table as the sound reached us over head, and then total silence. After the deafening engine noise the silence was petrifying. It lasted for a good many seconds and then came the explosion which rattled the windows and shook the floorboards beneath us. We had experienced our first 'doodlebug' — the V1. From then on death and destruction could confront us at any time without warning. We were often able to watch a doodlebug approach, flying quite low above trees and houses, and selfishly we prayed it would keep on going until out of sight. The moment the engine noise cut out our hearts stood still, and if in school we all scrambled under our desks and waited for the explosion.

These weapons of terror were later followed by the V2 rockets which approached swiftly and silently and exploded where they landed, at random. In retrospect, it was quite astonishing how tenaciously we clung to normal life and routines. At school there was the Save Paper campaign alongside our one-third of a pint of milk for a ha'penny; cookery lessons demonstrated how to make the most of our rationed food, and parcels of sweets from America were distributed among us. Otherwise, and as far as circumstances would permit, lessons and homework proceeded as normal and so did our sport, music and drama.

When the war ended and the evacuated children rejoined us in London I recollect fearing that they would be superior to us because of their nurtured safety and lack of disruption. It was years later that I discovered that they feared *we* would claim superiority due to the maturing effects of having 'been here' and involvement in all the major experiences they missed. In the event there was remarkably little curiosity expressed by either group about the others' wartime existences; instead much energy went into rebuilding school life innovatively. Perhaps this is how children survive crises.

Rosemary at school in London.

IVY ELLIS

I wasn't evacuated until 1941. Until then my husband was at home, working in the Arsenal. I couldn't do war work because of my young children, twin two year old girls. We were a family unit, and also one of my twins had a certain kind of fit, and we had to have medical advice all the time, with a nurse nearby. Fortunately when I was evacuated, we had a nurse living just around the corner.

My husband was drafted into the Army, and he knew that he was going to be sent abroad, because the unit he was joining was already there. I had the offer of being evacuated with the children, so I decided to go. I think I would've have gone anyway once the land mines started. We lived in Ann Street, Plumstead, and next door got a land mine dropped right on it.

The evacuation itself was like hell let loose! I was trying to decide what to take for the children. It was April and still quite cold. We hadn't lived in the country at all, so we didn't know what it was going to be like. Summer was coming, so I packed night clothes, day clothes, summer clothes and a few woollies. We were only allowed to take what we could carry. I had the twins, so it was one case for me and one case for the twins. We had to take our gas masks with us, but the authorities did take the kids' ones for me because they were the cradle type, and I couldn't carry them and two cases.

We went by train from Plumstead station to London. I don't know how we got to Liverpool Street, but once there, we boarded a special evacuees train. It seemed like the whole of Plumstead, and very likely Woolwich too, were being evacuated at the same time.

I can't really remember much about the journey, but it was fairly difficult travelling ninety miles with two children who had never been on a train before. We'd taken sandwiches, and I think they supplied drinks on the train.

Our destination was Attleborough, about fifteen miles south of Norwich. We were met at the station by billeting officers, and they loaded us into two or three coaches. As we passed through various villages, some people would be dropped off with one of the billeting officers. We were taken about five miles to Rockland All Saints.

Charles and Ivy Ellis with twin daughters Pat and Sheila at Rocklands, near Attleborough, Norfolk.

Clarke family, where Ivy and family were billeted 1941 — 1945.

At first we were taken to a house about three miles from the school. There was a beautiful tea all laid out, and other evacuees sitting there waiting, but not eating or drinking. The billeting officer said, 'I think you'll be alright here.' But as soon as she'd walked out the door, the table was completely cleared of everything. The woman asked me if I'd brought my own food! I had left London at nine o'clock in the morning, travelled a hundred miles, and that was my welcome. It was then about seven o'clock, and the twins were irritable and ready for bed. We only stayed the one night!

They moved us on the next morning to a house a bit nearer to the village. The woman's name was Dolly. Her husband was in India. She had seven children of her own, her niece with two boys, her grandmother, and a Jewish family consisting of mother and two fairly grown up girls. With me and the twins, there were eighteen of us in the house!

When the twins got older, they went to the village school, and I took over running the house, because Dolly went out to work. We used to go down together, and meet the children from school pushing the twin pram I'd had sent down from London. Two of Dolly's children were more or less the same age as mine, two were younger, and three just a bit older. We worked very well together, and became very good friends. She even gave me back the billeting money she received, in return for running the home.

We had a lot of good times although we were evacuees. All the food was naturally fresh, because the house had two acres of land with it. We grew our own vegetables and also kept pigs. We had plenty of fresh milk, the baker came every day and the butcher three times a week. We did very well really.

I stayed there about four years. I did come home for two months, but the doodlebugs started again, and we were sent back again, fortunately to the same billet. I finally came home at the end of the war, and eventually my husband came back to join us. At last, we were a family again.

PADDY EVANS

It was the first Saturday in September 1939 and I was twelve. I left my house in Plumstead without saying goodbye to my mother. I couldn't bear to see her cry. I had a small case in my hand and a small square box filled with a gas mask slung around my back. We met at school, walked crocodile fashion to the station and were herded on a train - destination unknown. I remember little of the journey but arrived at Maidstone, hardly far enough away to be safe from a misguided bomb, but certainly far enough away to miss my Mum and Dad.

My friend, her name was Vera, and I, were ages being 'fostered', we just stood waiting our turn. Then, as a temporary measure, we were billeted with a married couple just for one night. We were famished, but as I had some curled up corned beef sandwiches left, I was made to finish them up. I have never liked corned beef sandwiches since! Then to bed, at least an air-bed. Mine had far too much air in it, and I kept rolling off. I don't think I slept at all. Next day Vera and I were placed with a couple of spinsters, a bit like Hinge and Bracket, though not so funny. The two things I can remember are that they were very kind and that we had tomatoes every day for tea.

We amused ourselves around the area. A farmer made over an orchard for us to play in, and apples disappeared with great rapidity. Education was hardly at a premium, and classes were held at odd times in a church hall. I don't think I learned very much except the pain of being away from home and family. Vera and I didn't stay long with 'the ladies'. I think we were too much trouble.

From then on I was on my own, again with a married couple, no children, but a Scottie dog called Jock! It wasn't bad there, but I was never really happy. The only nice thing I can recall Mrs Taylor doing was to take me to the pictures to see Robert Donat in 'The Citadel'. She had a crush on Robert. Mr Taylor was a large man and used to spit in the fire, which seemed very much out of character.

Nothing was happening at home war-wise, no bombs, no Germans landing by parachute, and when it came to the time for me to keep a dental appointment, on this occasion I was delighted to keep it. I was taken home, only to return to Maidstone to collect my belongings, say goodbye to Mr and Mrs Taylor, and then settle down to the normality of love, comfort and confidence in being with one's own family, whatever the war years might bring.....but that's another story!

Paddy is wearing her Kings Warren school blazer.

Paddy with her grandmother, mother, father and brother Dick.

Paddy with her grandmother, mother and father at Maidstone.

PAT FAWCETT

I knew there was going to be a war because I had heard about it on the wireless but I did not really know what war was. I had seen pictures of knights in armour in story books and I had seen Cowboys and Indians fighting at the 'pictures', but just how these were connected I had no idea, except that 'war' meant fighting.

My Father had been in the Navy ever since I could remember, and so after being a civilian for a year he had been called up in the 'Reserve' and had gone back to his ship, wearing his uniform. One of my aunts had married a man in the Royal Air Force but I thought his uniform was not as nice as my Dad's.

Now we had all been given identity cards and gas masks and there was going to be a war, but I could not think how it would affect me. I was evacuated with my mother and small sister. Janet was only eighteen months old. I was seven years old and I had been attending Woodhill School, Woolwich.

We had to go to the school on Sunday morning, 3rd September, 1939. My Auntie Eva and cousin Marie, who was five, were also with us. We were given labels with our names and the name of the school on them and these labels had to be tied to the children and not the luggage as I had thought. Luckily my mother had already labelled our suitcases.

We waited around for what seemed a long time, until there was a dreadful wailing noise and people began to panic! It was the siren. People began shouting and I heard the word 'gas'. I was very frightened. We were all hurriedly taken into a shirt factory, which was next door to the school but why, I have never been able to fathom out. Some women began to cry and say that they did not have gas masks for their babies. My sister Janet had a blue and red 'Mickey Mouse' gas mask, of which I was rather envious, as mine was only an ordinary dark grey one. We carried these gas masks in buff cardboard boxes on strings around our necks.

Bakers, the grocery shop in Wateringbury where Pat Fawcett (nee Ashton) was billeted with her mother and sister in September 1939.

The small babies were supposed to have great big gas masks, which they had to be laced inside, and the mother, or whoever was in charge, had to pump air into it. However there had not been enough of these to go round at the beginning of the war. One of the officials told the women to tear up pieces of shirting material, these were in large rolls on the work benches, and dip them into the fire buckets full of water, which were all around the walls. They did this and were prepared to hold these wet cloths over the babies' faces if gas was detected. I do not know whether these cloths would have been any good or not. It was very quiet in there and then someone began to sing 'Onward, Christian Soldiers' and we all joined in. Whenever I hear that hymn it takes me back to the shirt factory on that September morning.

After the all clear sounded we were taken out of the shirt factory back to the school, and then we had to walk to Woolwich Dockyard station. We were all put on to trains but we had no idea where we were going. When the train got to Snodland station, in Kent, we all had to get out. Ladies of the W.V.S. gave everyone a brown paper carrier bag with all kinds of things inside, including a tin of corned beef, a tin of milk, a packet of nuts and raisins. These were to take with us to wherever we had to go.

We were put into charabancs and taken to a small village called Wateringbury. I remember going into the school hall and just waiting around whilst people who seemed to be in charge kept coming and looking at us.

Eventually my mother, sister and I were taken to a grocery shop and there we were given two rooms upstairs. The shop was on the corner of a crossroads in the centre of Wateringbury. I do not remember much about the owners of the shop, the Bakers, but my mother told me to keep out of their way and not to bother them or else we would be sent home. There seemed to be a lot of mice there because I remember lying on my tummy on a horsehair sofa waiting for a mouse to come out of a hole and run from under the sofa. Then I would catch it by its tail and swing it in the air. My mother hated this because she was terrified of mice but to me it was a good game to play.

My aunt and cousin were also billeted in a shop further up the village and their hosts had given us a loft where all the evacuee families could meet. It was fun 'up the loft' and we had some chairs, card tables and games like Snakes and Ladders and Ludo to play there.

Pat, aged seven, with her doll's pram.

We went to school for only half a day. The village children went in the morning and the evacuees went in the afternoon. The next week we changed over. This seemed quite a good arrangement because it gave us children a lot more time to explore.

Whilst we were in Wateringbury we used to go hop-picking. This was particularly boring for me, but I used to help pick some of the hops to go into the bin. If I put in too many leaves I was told to run away and play and this was more fun, for we used to chase each other in and out of the hop vines and round and round the canvas bins. The hops stained your fingers orangey brown and it was difficult to wash it off. They also made the fingers smell very pungently and I did not like the smell at all.

All seemed to be quiet at home. There did not seem to be any danger. There had been no air raids in London and so my uncle, who worked as a driver, borrowed a van and brought us all back to Woolwich to spend Christmas. Everything looked the same, but different somehow. We did not go back to Wateringbury again.

In 1940, my grown-up cousin, whom I called Auntie Gladys, and her husband Fred were now living in Bridgend, South Wales, where Fred worked in the Bridgend Arsenal. It was proposed that I should be sent away from London again, for safety, so I was to stay with them. My Auntie Lou was to visit her daughter and she took me along, together with a small black puppy called Nicky. We sat facing each other in the train, my Aunt Lou and I, a long journey ahead of us. I nursed Nicky on my lap and now and again he licked my hand as if to reassure me, for we were on the way to Wales and both going to a new home. The journey seemed never ending and I dozed, cuddled the puppy, flicked over comics idly, without paying much interest, or just gazed out of the window. I had never been away from home on my own before and I was a little apprehensive.

At last the train drew into Bridgend station and we unfolded ourselves from it with much relief. My cousin and her husband were there to meet us and we drove in a taxi for what seemed miles through green countryside, finally stopping outside a small block of modern flats high on a hill near the edge of a village.

My Auntie Gladys suggested that the puppy would probably like to stretch his legs and Uncle Fred offered to walk with us up the lane to the farm where we could fetch some milk. We set off and I wondered why my uncle carried a large jug, but I was too shy to ask. We walked along a rutted cart−track between meadows where, Uncle said, the cows spent all day, but there were none there now. I could hear the clank and hum of machinery and snatches of conversation coming from a huge shed, and when we entered there were the cows, each in a small pen, attached by rubber tubes and shining steel to a long snaking pipe line. I was absolutely amazed. The farmer spoke to Uncle Fred in a queer sing−song voice. He spoke to me too, but I did not answer, for I was not sure what he had said. Both men laughed and it was explained that Nicky and I had just arrived from London. Soon I saw the reason for the jug, it was filled almost to the brim with frothing creamy milk and I thought that milk bottles could not have been invented yet in Wales.

We returned to the flat and I felt too tired to eat much supper. Besides, I was anxious to have another look at the small bedroom which was to be mine. My aunt had unpacked my suitcase and placed my new pyjamas on the bed. I undressed, but the exciting day had not yet finished. There was another surprise in store, for I was to have a bath in a real bathroom. At home we had an old galvanised bath which hung on the wall in the yard and had to be carefully inspected for spiders before being filled from the copper in the corner of the scullery. But this bathroom was something out of fairyland, a fantasy of pink, the walls, the towels, the soap, even the bath mat was pink and, wonder of wonders, so was the water! My aunt had tossed a handful of crystals into the bath and the swishing water slowly turned rosy too.

Drowsy from my bath I snuggled into my new bed. Nicky had been comfortably installed in a cardboard box in the kitchen, my aunts and uncle now kissed me goodnight, put out the light and I was alone for the first time that day. The room looked strange, unfamiliar and not altogether friendly, although I knew the grown-ups were not far away, as I could hear their mumbled voices in the living room. I wondered what my mother was doing in London and what my father was doing. I imagined him under the sea in his submarine but the picture was hazy, for I had no clear idea then of life in a submarine. My little sister would be fast asleep in her cot, I knew, with her teddy bear beside her, and I was glad I had my own teddy beside me. I had never been away from home completely on my own before and now I wished I had not come. London seemed so far away.

When I awoke, I heard a cheerful whistling and a chink of bottle on crate. I opened my eyes, realising that it was the milkman who had just called. Bottles did exist in Wales after all, for I had just heard the unmistakable 'clunk' of a milk bottle being placed on a doorstep.

That small bedroom became as familiar as my own at home and the fascinating Welsh voices as understandable as the London ones I was used to. Indeed it was not long before I too spoke in that sing—song way, punctuating my sentences with an occasional 'aye', 'isn't it', or 'over by there'.

I soon grew used to the Welsh way of life and attended Laleston village school, where I found to my surprise that the standard of work was below what I had been doing in London and I was considered 'clever for my age.' I was put into a class with children a year to eighteen months older than me and I found that I could keep up with the work quite easily. I was behind with my multiplication tables, which they learned by rote, but I soon caught up with those, they were 'sing—songed' every morning!

The village school had an asphalted playground at the front, and there was also a large playing field behind, which I thought was a marvellous place. I had never seen a grass playground in London. There was plenty of room for everyone to play without getting into each other's way.

Boys had enough space to play cricket or football and we girls could gather up the cut grass, which was turning into hay, and make houses to play in. This needed a lot of hay and an equal amount of imagination! The hay was laid on the grass in straight lines to outline the shape of the house. The house could be simple with two rooms or quite elaborate with four rooms, including kitchen and bathroom, and an entrance hall. The doors were indicated by spaces in the 'walls'. Although the walls were only in outline we never jumped over them or walked 'through' them, we always went through the 'doors'.

After the very bad air raid on London Docks on 7th and 8th September 1940, my mother left London with my sister Janet and came to Bridgend to stay. They had been to visit me only the previous week, and I had bid them a tearful farewell at the station when they left me. Imagine my surprise when I awoke a few mornings later, to find Mum and Janet sharing my bed. They had arrived suddenly in the night.

There was not enough room in my cousin's flat for us all to live there

Model figures made by Pat of her family. The boy evacuee whom she has included is her husband, Tony.

69

and so my Mother found us two rooms with a family called Phillips. Mr and Mrs Phillips had four children, Margaret, who was twelve, Jean who was ten, Walter, eight and Marlene, five. Walter was my special friend because he was the same age as I was.

I now went to Penybont school in Bridgend which was bigger and different from the village school in Laleston. I found myself learning the Welsh language as well as speaking with a Welsh accent. I enjoyed school very much and settled in easily.

At the weekends and during the school holidays we used to roam the fields and woods around Bridgend having all kinds of adventures. The River Ogmore runs through the town and the local park and playing fields. It was a source of delight to play beside that river, paddling and sailing paper boats. In the summer months when the water level was low it was fun to play on the stony edges of the river, collecting shiny stones, and bits of glass, washed smooth by the water. The river could rise quite high during the wetter season and became quite dangerous, but it was always very attractive to children.

In the spring we picked primroses and violets, and later on bluebells in the woods. In the summer there were wood anemones and wild strawberries to look for on the railway banks. In the summer months, it was lovely to take a bus trip to nearby Porthcawl and spend the day on the beach. Although some coastal areas were cordoned off with barbed wire, there were some places left where access to the beach was easy. Porthcawl has lovely sandy beaches. I was bought a red painted metal spade and a bucket with Mickey Mouse on it to dig sand castles. I had only ever had wooden spades up until then.

In autumn there were nuts and conkers to be found and in the winter we painted the hazel nut husks and fir cones that we had collected and turned them into Christmas decorations. I learned to identify many trees and plants in the country; what was edible and what was to be avoided.

We stayed in Wales for some time, but when the raids in London had quietened down we came back to Woolwich, where we stayed for the rest of the war. I learned to love the countryside and I wonder if I would know as much about nature now, if I had never been evacuated.

TONY FAWCETT

On Friday 1st September 1939, together with many other children from Mulgrave Place and Powis Street schools, I walked to the Woolwich Dockyard station, to begin our big adventure. My parents had told me that I would be home by Christmas, so I went quite happily. With the school label attached to my lapel, carrying my gas mask in a blue and white checked linen covered case, and my knapsack containing all the clothes thought necessary on my back, I might have been going on a somewhat bewildering day trip to Margate. The train journey, seeming to take hours and hours, eventually ended at a place called Snodland in Kent.

On arrival we were kept in groups, and were given carrier bags containing an assortment of food. I particularly remember a tin of Ovaltine tablets. When some charabancs arrived, some groups, mainly senior girls, were taken to Wateringbury, and we junior children were taken to the Village Hall at Wrotham in Kent. We ate our food and were given drinks, and local people chose which children would be billeted with them. I and another lad, ended up with a Mr and Miss Wickens, brother and sister, living in a little cottage called 'Roseneath' on the outskirts of the village.

The cottage had three bedrooms, the one we 'vaccies' had was the attic room. There was a large kitchen, a small sitting room, where the wireless was, a large parlour, and below that a cellar. Of course there was an outside toilet and no bathroom, and there was also a little

'Scotty' dog named 'Diana'. The biggest change from home, was that all the light came from paraffin lamps, and the cooking was either done on the kitchen range or on a 'Valor' paraffin stove. The Wickens's were of farming stock, Mr Wickens being a milkman who worked for his cousin who owned the local dairy.

Within a couple of weeks, the lad who was billeted with me became so homesick that his parents took him back to Woolwich.

My first real memory was listening to the broadcast by Neville Chamberlain on Sunday 3rd September 1939, when he announced that we were at war with Germany, sitting in that small room at Wrotham. It didn't mean much to me at the age of nine years. I was still thinking that I was really having a proper holiday, the sort that only rich people had.

The weather at that time was exceptional, an Indian summer. We did not go to school but were taken to see farms, hops being picked, a paper mill, even a button making factory at nearby Ightham. The Italian owners of that factory were later interned as aliens. Eventually we started school lessons again, using the village school in the afternoon, the local children having been there in the mornings. This didn't last too long as Mulgrave started to use the Freemasons Hall as a full time school. School life at Wrotham with Mr Froome the headmaster, Mr Atkins (Stan), and Mrs Ducker (Quack−quack), became as normal as it had been at Woolwich.

In no time at all I had settled into my new life. I laboriously wrote to my parents each week, seated at the bureau in the small sitting room, just to keep in touch. I could not forget my brothers, much older than I, nor my parents, but there was so much more to do, see and learn in my new environment. I joined the choir at St. George's Church, as I had before the war, at St. Michael's in Woolwich. The monthly payment of two shillings and sixpence came in very useful for pocket money!

Another evacuee, Stanley Kane, and I explored the whole area around Wrotham, and got to know it like the back of our hand. Together we joined the boys club in the village hall, and met a man who did much to welcome us to Wrotham, and taught us much of country life, Reg Palmer. He was a gardener to the Magistrate for Wrotham, and a part time fireman. At the boys club, he showed silent films of Charlie Chaplin, Felix the Cat and other favourites. Before returning the films, he would take them out to a large estate house at Kemsing, to show them to the several vaccies billeted there. Stan and I used to go to Kemsing with Reg on these occasions, and it was in the kitchens of that house that I learned that not all crisps came out of a packet. The cook used to give us all sorts of nice things. From my association with Reg I learned how to distinguish trees, birds, wildflowers, where to see rabbits, foxes and other wildlife, and our friendship continued until long after the war.

The Wickens's were very good to me. I remember them taking me to their Uncle's farm at Trotiscliffe (Trotsley) for our Christmas dinner. I was told to say 'chicken' when asked what I would like to have, as goose would be too rich for me. I had never eaten so well in all my life. Rationing didn't mean much to me, except for 'Personal Points', that is the sweet ration. I was a popular evacuee, as I did not like butter or margarine on my bread. I still don't. Miss Wickens desperately tried to get me to eat it, by giving me wholesome things like lettuce sandwiches. But all I did was to feed them under the table to the dog.

On the occasions when my foster parents went out in the evening, a little old lady who lived next door looked after me. I can't recall her name, but she typed manuscripts for authors. She told me many stories, including 'Oliver Twist', 'David Copperfield' and such classics. She had a big tabby tom cat with torn ears. These he got by chasing rabbits through the brambles in the woods. He was often successful on these hunting expeditions, and would bring young rabbits home.

One group of the British Expeditionary Forces on their way to France stopped over night outside 'Roseneath'. All the neighbours made tea and provided sandwiches for the troops. I was allowed to sit at the driving wheel of a fifteen hundredweight truck, and one of the soldiers gave me a live .303 round. I have often wondered how many of those men managed to escape from Dunkirk. The war started in earnest for me when in 1940 we were bombed. The roof was damaged, ceilings were down, and windows blown out. It seems ironic that we were sent to the country for safety, and one of the first bombs damages the cottage where I lived. Unexploded bombs nearby caused us to have more people share the house, until the bombs had been exploded or dug out.

Tony Fawcett in 1940.

The Battle of Britain I will never forget, as it took place above my head. The Bull Inn at Wrotham was the mess for the RAF officers stationed at Malling Aerodrome. It was to here that German airmen were taken after being shot down. We used to watch over the church wall to see if we could see any of the enemy. All schoolboys could identify all the aircraft. There was always a race to get to the scene of a crashed plane, to see what souvenirs could be had. But somehow it always seemed that a big RAF man with a rifle got there first.

Many times we saw 'dog-fights' taking place over head, planes being shot out of the sky, and airmen dangling on the ends of their parachute lines hoping to land safely. Many didn't. The night that the Luftwaffe came over in waves, and set the Thames on fire, the woods on the top of the Downs behind us were set alight. All the able bodied adults, and what firemen could be spared, set to and saved the woods from total destruction.

At the end of a year, my mother took me out for the day, back to my home in Woolwich. Everything looked so small and dingy. The windows with their crosses of sticky tape, an Anderson shelter completely occupying my father's garden of roses, and neighbouring friends saying 'Cor! Hasn't he grown'. I think I was glad to return to Wrotham.

Life at school with the other children from Mulgrave was pleasant enough. The numbers were such that the teachers gave us more attention than in peacetime Woolwich. I feel that I may not have succeeded in passing a scholarship exam, had it not been for their individual tuition. And so in July 1941 I moved from Wrotham, all the way to Sevenoaks, to start at my new school, Shooters Hill.

I was, at first, billeted with a widowed minister's wife and her two elderly spinster daughters. I think they wanted to be seen to be doing their bit, by taking in a poor London evacuee. If they had visitors, I was packed off to bed after I had completed my homework, at half past six. Tea was a case of wheeling the tea trolley into the parlour, and balancing a plate on one knee with a cup and saucer on the other. I suppose they had never had to deal with eleven year old boys before, and I didn't feel at all comfortable in that house.

Not long after, the headmaster of Shooters Hill school and the chemistry master and his wife, opened a large unoccupied house as a hostel for the pupils of the school. Luckily I was able to move from my billet into Hill House. There were about thirty-five boys of all ages living there, with a cook and a maid, it was like being in boarding school.

We had great fun. By this time I was in the Scouts, and we went on hikes and camping at the weekends. Knole Park was our hunting ground, and I learned to stalk with ease through the ferns, to spy on unsuspecting courting couples! The bombing by this time had eased off, and we Shooters Hill schoolboys then started to go home at the weekends to visit our families. Invariably, those of us returning on Sunday evening would bring all manner of consumable goodies with us. On one occasion we kept the headmaster awake (he slept in a room beneath our dormitory) practically all through the night. We were of course having a bun fight, but no one owned up to being out of bed when he stormed into the room. All of us ended up with sore bums at the end of the following day, the result of two swift strokes of the cane delivered in his study at school.

The school building was about two miles away, in a large house called Kippington Grange. It belonged to a Lord Hawke. Nearby another large house was being used by an anti-aircraft battery. The Sergeant Physical Training Instructor arranged to take us for PT, on the assault course that he had constructed in nearby woods. That was great fun, climbing ropes and ladders into the tallest trees, jumping off platforms which seemed about thirty feet off the ground, but in reality were nearer to eight feet. I thoroughly enjoyed being made to act like Tarzan!

There were no facilities for Physics, Chemistry or Woodwork at Kippington Grange, or playing fields for that matter. We were lucky to be able to share with Sevenoaks School, the large public school for boys, at the end of the High Street. The corridors in Sevenoaks School had rows of hooks, from which hung the boaters worn by the boys. It was always tempting to tug on the hats, to see the hook appear through the straw!

Lessons were all quite normal. But there was a war on. I remember sixth formers leaving, to return on a visit to the school a little later, dressed as

Outdoor classes at desks for boys.

subalterns in the Army, or Sub-Lieutenants in the Navy. One young man went to Rhodesia to learn to fly, and I saw him in the methodist church that I used to attend in the uniform of a Pilot-Officer. He had trained to be a fighter pilot. It seems only weeks later that a memorial service was being held for him − he had been shot down over France.

When in 1944 the Germans started to use 'Doodle-bugs' to bomb the south eastern corner of Britain, it was decided that Sevenoaks was no longer safe for us Shootershillians. At the Kent coast, anti-aircraft guns attempted to shoot down these 'Buzz' bombs. Over Kent, the fighters did their best to knock them out of the sky. One Tempest pilot, actually flew alongside the 'Buzz' bomb and used his own wings to tip the bomb's wing to send it down into open fields. All along the North Downs were placed barrage balloons, in the hope to stop the bombs reaching their destination, London. They were frightening days.

And so I went to Devon, to the small town of Ottery St Mary, with about half the number that were at Sevenoaks. I think the remainder returned to Woolwich. I was billeted with a lovely family in the Central Garage. Their own children were grown up. The eldest boy had been lost at sea, the next boy was already at sea as a Merchant Navy radio officer, and the youngest was training to be a radio officer at the Marconi college at Colwyn Bay. There was also a daughter who was serving in the WRAF. Certainly a family doing their bit!

In Devon the war was so very far away. They still spoke of the fifty pound bomb that blew some windows out at the jam factory half a mile away, early on in the war. Of course Exeter was very severely blitzed. The food rationing seemed to be able to provide such things as clotted cream, and there was never a shortage of meat. Maybe the fact that the garage sold petrol may have helped. Other than the continual concern that I had, whether my parents and brothers were safe with the 'Doodle−Bugs' and the new menace of the V2s, my stay in Ottery was idyllic.

For two months that summer of 1944, we had no schooling. The weather was superb, we played cricket, we taught the local girls to play rugby, I cycled around the countryside, visiting Sidmouth, Budleigh Salterton, Beer, Seaton and Lyme Regis. It was wonderful. And then a school was found for us. We attended Westminster City School, where even the Prefects wore gowns. They had been evacuated to Exmouth. We even

Central Garage
15 Broad Street
Ottery St Mary
Devon
7.10.1944.

Dear Mum,
I haven't been to school this morning. Instead I went and saw the doctor about a terrible cold etc that I have got therefore I must stop in today tomorrow and maybe Monday. But I'll soon get well again Keith my companion went home to Plumstead today as his mother thinks he doesn't do enough work at school None of us do hardly any work at school. Will you please send my rugger but down and also a pair of plimsolls if you can and my knife with them. Clothing coupons enclosed with bill for shoes.
Well I'll close now
Tony XXXXX

attended on Saturday mornings. A coach took us from Ottery, each day, and what a coach that was! It was probably built in the late '20s, petrol driven, with a rollback canvas roof. It was always breaking down, usually on the moors, miles from any human habitation. But that was all right, as it was where the Royal Marine Commandos did their training. Lots of assault courses and such like, for us schoolboys to test.

Towards the end of that year, so many boys had returned to Shooters Hill School at Woolwich, it was decided that all would return. Although I was pleased to be home with my own family at last, I could never forget all those I had lived with, those I had played with, the places I had seen and the things I had learned during my five long years of evacuation.

74

MARGARET GARDINER

I was born the month after war broke out. Apparently the government was trying to persuade mothers to get gas-proof prams but mothers resisted: 'I'm not putting my baby into one of those things, it looks like a coffin!' My mother, who was a nurse, was asked to demonstrate the prams by putting me in one and showing that 'the baby doesn't mind.' But mothers were not convinced.

My mother was Australian and she decided to take me home to Australia when I was a few months old. She and I stayed there until 1943, but then she decided to come back to England. Apparently Churchill had made reassuring statements to the effect that the real danger was over. We came across the Atlantic on a cargo ship (it was carrying meat) in convoy, thank God. We came right through the Battle of the Atlantic. It was only when I looked at the displays in the Maritime Museum in Greenwich that I realised how slim would have been our chances if we had not been in convoy. It was quite bad enough as it was. We were shot at by U-boats and Focke Wulfs many times during the trip which took twelve weeks instead of the normal six.

We also came through horrific storms. My mother was sea-sick for the whole trip, and I had virtually the run of the ship as long as I wore my life-jacket. The crew adopted me as a sort of mascot, and they used to play all sorts of games with me, for instance rigging up a fishing line over the side of the ship, then surreptitiously tying a kipper on the end of the line and letting me think I had caught it.

Margaret in Sydney in 1943, shortly before sailing back to England.

I remember having a lot of fun. I don't remember feeling any fear, although it must have been terrifying when we were being shot at. I was told the guns were only practising, and they took me down below deck and put cotton wool in my ears. I had my fourth birthday on board ship: the cook made a sumptuous party for me and everyone came. We had all sorts of food I had never seen before like ginger-beer, pop-corn, cakes with wonderful sugar nursery rhyme figures on them. I don't know where on earth he got them from. I never saw any more food like that for years. It was a great shock to come back to war-time Britain after Australia. I remember it as dark (black-out), dirty and freezing cold. We went straight up to the west coast of Scotland because my father's ship was coming and going along the Clyde at that stage. Combined Operators were based at Inverary Castle, and there were intense secret preparations going on for D-day.

Those were very bleak months. Then, just before D-Day, we moved down to Hampshire. I remember my Godmother took me for a walk in the New Forest one day. We turned a corner in the path and came into a clearing which was FULL of soldiers and tanks — all waiting in total silence. It was a very eerie experience!

Wills's Cigarette Cards, A.R.P. Series.

MILLY GARDNER

The continued nightly bombardment of Plymouth gradually faded into the distance when I was finally evacuated to the peaceful greenery of the countryside of Exmouth. Nightly we still heard the planes, and saw the searchlights in the sky, but here, we could rest cosily in our beds, feeling almost certain of a tomorrow.

Friends were made, and school went on apace. 'School' was a hotel, lent for the duration, the owner having returned to America.

There was a market garden adjoining the hotel, which supplied most of the local needs, and with all able-bodied men at the front, was worked short-handed. It being a good summer, the soft fruits were in abundance. There was no time to lose, so the gardener called for volunteers. Six of us applied.

Carefully wending our way along the edge of the magnificent lawn, for we were never allowed to tread upon it, and on through the wooded copse beyond, we came upon the market garden, a miscellany of glasshouses, potting sheds, and numerous netted areas containing soft fruits. We were given baskets, told to fill as many as possible. There was no pay, but we could eat our fill of the plump to bursting gooseberries.

Many such outings later, we had learned not only of growing plants, but of each other as well, and felt great satisfaction in knowing we had helped to put fresh food on the tables of England, doing our small bit, whilst the men did theirs.

DAVE GELLY

My very earliest memory is of being carried, wrapped in a blanket, past a glowing red rectangle. This was the frosted glass window at the top of our stairs, and the red was burning London. It must have been 1940, when I was two.

From that time onwards, for the next five years, I had two homes. One was in the London suburb of Bexleyheath, the other in my grandfather's house at Loughor, a village on the Western edge of the South Wales coalfield, midway between Swansea and Llanelli. Even today, I can't quite sort out exactly when I was in one place or the other.

There must have been thousands of children like me — not evacuated, but taken or sent to live with relatives, usually grandparents. When you come to think of it, we were probably in the majority in the outer ring of London suburbs, the ones built in the 1920s and 30s, because everyone there came from somewhere else. Many, like my father, were immigrants from other parts of the British Isles, which meant that we had a clump of long-distance grandparents, uncles, aunts and cousins 'back home'.

My grandfather's house stood alone, at the end of a muddy lane. It consisted of a two-up, two-down stone cottage and a large number of sheds. One shed was the kitchen, another, made largely from old railway sleepers, was the dining room-cum-everyday room. A stone shed was the pantry. The dog had a shed, the chickens had a shed, the apples had a shed. To get from any one of these to another you had to

go outdoors and in again. My father later explained this state of affairs to me as an example of the Celtic reluctance ever to finish anything.

There was no electricity, no gas, no piped water, no mains drainage. Cooking was done over the fire or in an oil stove. Really big boiling jobs were done in an outdoor brick oven.

The whole place had a kind of grubby, nest-like cosiness, quite different from the rational, electric light and bathroom comfort of a Bexleyheath semi. It had grown, more like a plant than a building, sprouting its sheds and ovens and benches and water butts, over several generations. I think I am alone among all my circle of acquaintance in having spent long stretches of my childhood amid pure Victorian domestic arrangements.

It was at Loughor that I first went to school There was no preparation; one day I was free, unique and treated more or less as a household pet, the next, I was sat at a desk with two others, in a row of desks, in a room containing fifty-odd children and a large old man with a very loud voice named Mr Walters.

I first encountered proper evacuees at Loughor School, and their presence put me in a very complicated position. I was by now, in all visible and audible respects, as Welsh as cawl and leeks, but I could revert in an instant to broadest London. Far from turning me into some kind of valued go-between or interpreter, this facility meant only that I ended up in a minority of one.

I remember when one group of evacuees turned up, because an incident occurred that led to endless gossip and tongue-clicking. It seems that there were enough volunteer families to take all but one of the children in as soon as they arrived, so, as it was getting late, the billeting officer decided to knock on the door of a couple known to be childless and ask them to put the boy up for the night.

Now, any native could have told him that the lady of the house, one Bessie, was notoriously mean and ill-tempered. She came to the door, it was said, 'wiping her hands on a towel' and 'turned the child away'. In those days, everyone in South Wales knew the Bible, and much was made of the Pontius Pilate symbolism of the towel. Eventually, the little boy was taken in, 'just for the night', by a family that already had seven kids, presumably on the grounds that one more wouldn't make much difference. In the morning, neighbours sent presents of eggs and sweets and no-one spoke to Bessie for months.

The little boy, incidentally, settled down quite happily with the big family and stayed with them until the war was over.

It was the other way round with another childless couple, Mr Rees the butcher and his wife. They loved children but couldn't have any, and when the war brought them a tiny, blue-eyed, golden-haired girl, it was as if God had suddenly relented at the last moment.

Never was a child more adored and fussed over. She came from an ordinary working-class London family into a household where nothing was ever in short supply or 'under the counter' — because the butcher owned the counter and more or less controlled the supply. She had a tricycle and a dolls' pram and a little nurse's outfit and went every week to Sunday School in the nicest clothes. What her real parents felt about all this, I don't know, although her mother used to come down and stay from time to time, so perhaps it was all right.

The Reeses were inconsolable when peace came and God took his gift back again.

ALAN GRANT

I was nine years old when I was evacuated and my sister was four years older. I went with my sister's school, Aspen House, an open air school which was situated quite near Brixton Hill. I can remember quite clearly queuing up in the school yard waiting for the transport. I do remember we had the old fashioned paper carrier bag given us, with certain items in it. I presume they were a form of emergency ration to tide the landladies over until ration cards were issued. I remember a big bar of chocolate, and a tin of corned beef, which I have no doubt was put by in the cupboard. My sister seems to remember there was some fruit in the bag, apples and oranges.

We went down to Goring-by-Sea and we were billeted together because it was always done to keep brothers and sisters together if possible. We went to stay with an elderly couple, I think they must have been retired. There was just the husband and wife and my sister and me.

I remember a rather amusing incident with that landlady. She said that we were going to have dumplings for dinner. To my mind, dumplings were those things that broke up in the stew and spoiled it, so I said that I did not want any. But it turned out to be the apple dumplings with custard and so I had to sit quietly while everybody enjoyed theirs. I don't think we were ever served apple dumplings again.

Once, I went into the toilet and I put the light on in the toilet, but the blackout curtains were not drawn. I was told what a wicked boy I was and that I might have had the whole of the Luftwaffe strafing the south coast. But I am happy to say that it did not happen!

Our first school was in a little Scout hut and we were all evacuees. We used to have lessons out in the open, being an 'open air school'. They used to have all the desks out there and it could be quite cold in the winter time. I think the policy was 'Kill or Cure' though most people seemed to survive. The fresh air was supposed to do you good.

I cannot remember how long I stayed there, but I remember at Christmas my school teacher bought every person in the class a little gift. I got a 'Frog' aeroplane which used to be propelled by a propeller and an elastic band, which you wound round. It probably cost about sixpence. And a tin whistle which probably cost about three or fourpence. I don't know how many were in the class at that time but I expect it cost the teacher quite a bit. It was quite a good thought and I expect she was being like a mother to us as well. She was one of the teachers who had come down with us from our school.

I think the education at that time was very, very scanty probably due to the lack of space. What we did do though was, we were quite near the South Downs and we went there to a famous place called Chantonbury Ring, an old Roman site and we used to dig for pottery there. It was only a few years ago that I threw most of it away. I had still been carrying it around with me.

Also, we were quite near the coast and I used to like walking along the coast and looking in the rock pools. I remember at one time I got very frightened. It was always impressed upon us to carry our gas masks everywhere with us, and I left mine on the shore front. There was a sea mist and I was wondering whether or not it was gas but anyway I went back to get my gas mask and that is one of the things that sticks in my mind.

I also liked walking in the fields and we used to see the newts and watch the hawks hovering. I was quite happy there because I was very interested in nature. I also used to like watching the reconnaisance aircraft. Probably all they saw was the evacuees waving up to them. I remember going on an outing on a bus, on the South Down buses. There were about forty or fifty of us. The conductor had a ticket machine and he used to turn a handle and out would come forty or fifty tickets. The children used to say, 'Please Miss can I have the tickets to send home', because they were entirely different from the ones we were used to having on the London buses and the trams. They were different coloured tickets in a wooden rack which the conductor would punch according to the fare and the destination, and these bus tickets were quite a novelty.

My sister says that Mum and Dad came down to visit us by coach but I cannot remember much about it. At Brixton there used to be the Orange Coaches, and I expect they came down on those, but I don't know if the firm are still there.

My sister eventually went on from Goring to Chorleywood in Hertfordshire, because the government thought there was a chance of invasion and so they moved the children further inland. But I was a little bit home-sick and my mother was worried about my stammer, so I did not need much inducement to come back to London. In moments of stress, I still sometimes stammer. I can't quite remember how I developed it when I was away, but I do remember I used to wet the bed as well. I suppose some children did develop it, with nervousness.

I stayed in London for virtually the rest of the war, but towards the end there was very heavy bombing and my mother was worried. She had a sister who was bombed out in East London and had gone to Cornwall and we were sent to stay with her in Wadebridge. I had left school at that point and I was working in a dairy for about twenty one shillings a week. We went back to London before the war ended.

GERVAISE DU BOIS GROUT

*Home Cottage, Wiltshire where Gervaise lived
at the outbreak of war.*

I was fifteen years old when I was evacuated. I was at the City of London School, but I was not evacuated with the school. We went independently. The reason was that my mother had a very old friend, a Miss Jay whom I called Aunt Tilly, although she was not really an aunt. Miss Jay had been a headmistress at a council school at Ealing and she had retired about 1938 and bought a cottage in the country, as they used to in those days, at a place called Lockeridge. This was about three and three quarter miles beyond Marlborough. The City of London School was in fact evacuated to Marlborough and so we went down to stay with her about a fortnight before war broke out.

The village of Lockeridge had a village school, a gospel hall, the church was in a neighbouring village, and a village pub called the 'Who'd A Thought It?' At that time I do not think there was any street lighting, but even if there had been it probably did not matter because there was the blackout. There was no electric lighting or gas heating in the cottage, and so we used oil lamps, but it was a very comfortable cottage with a thatched roof.

I was bought a bike, which I was not able to ride because I had never had one before. The bike was a Rudge Whitworth, whose trade mark was a palm of a hand. It cost I think about five pounds, plus a guinea extra for a Sturmey Archer three speed gear. The intention was that I should ride the three or four miles from Lockridge to Marlborough for lessons. However, as the weather was so severe in the winter of 1939/40,

I was unable to ride. I finished up at Marlborough, billeted like all the other boys, in the houses in and around the town.

That winter was so severe that lots of boys, myself included, got an influenza type illness. The College had a sanatorium and that became so full, because it was catering not only for the Marlborough boys but ourselves as well, that there had to be an overflow of beds in the gymnasium because it was so severe.

We shared the premises of Marlborough College for lessons. As they were also used by the college boys there was a careful dovetailing exercise. As far as I can remember we used to have morning assembly about a quarter past eight, and then one lesson for about three quarters of an hour followed by breakfast. When we had finished breakfast it was probably getting on for ten o'clock. In the mornings from ten o'clock to half past twelve we would have activities such as the Cadet Corps or sport of one kind or another. We would come in at about half past twelve and have one lesson, then we would have lunch. We would go back after lunch, and according to what day of the week it was, we would have four or five lessons to fill up the rest of the afternoon. We would have tea at the college and after that we would go back to our respective billets.

Gervaise, in glasses, in the Cadet Corps.

I belonged to the Cadet Corps. I enjoyed being in the Signals section, and when I went into the full-time Army later on I was also in the Signals section. I liked the Morse codes and that sort of thing. In the Cadet Corps we had drill and weapon training, tactics lectures and map reading. Once a term we used to have what was known as a 'field day' and we used to go out on exercises.

My mother stayed with Miss Jay for the period which was known as the Phoney War, but as there were no bombings, she decided to go back home. I was then, in common with a lot of other boys, just on my own. I did come home for Christmas in 1939, which was in many respects like previous Christmases, and I came home again for the Easter holidays 1940, which was before the Battle of Britain. When the Summer holidays came, however, things had 'hotted up' in London. I came home for a short period but I was soon sent back to Marlborough for my own safety. Christmas 1940 I did not go home at all, but stayed in my billet home.

In the photograph of me, taken in 1941, I am wearing a tie which was awarded for proficiency in certain activities, in my case for chess. The tie has a thin stripe which was coloured white but there was a more prestigious tie, in which the stripe was yellow, that was awarded for prowess in rugger and cricket which I never qualified for. I left school at the end of the first term, 1942, in early April. I had a short period as a Junior Clerk in an insurance company, which was also evacuated not far out, at Beaconsfield. After that I joined the Army on Guy Fawkes' day, Thursday, 5th November, 1942.

Gervaise in his chess award tie. 1941.

POLA HAWARD

I remember I'd felt ecxited that morning, September 2nd. 1939, like any other five year old might feel at the prospect of a trip to the country. The trip had come right out of the blue for me. Mother had had my hair cut in a neat semi-shingle especially for the trip. So our parents weren't coming! That didn't worry me too much although I would rather have had them with me, but Bill was with me, he would always be with me, they had told me so. Bill was my brother and my senior by three and a half years, although at that time he seemed much older to me.

I was totally unaware of the reason behind the trip, but then I didn't give reasons very much thought. We were going to the country for a while, that was all I knew. They had promised faithfully that it would only be for a very short while, and then they would come and fetch us home. I believed them, they never lied to us. And so it was, with a childlike feeling of excitement and innocence, that I walked away from my warm cocoon.

It was early September 1939, a few days before my fifth birthday. We each had a small case and some sandwiches and fruit, and a gas mask in a cardboard box over our shoulders, although, at that time, it was a mystery box to me.

The South East London station was only a few minutes walk from our home, and Grandmother accompanied us there. On that short walk I couldn't help noticing that Bill was particularly quiet. I didn't take too

The Government scheme for the evacuation of people in London and large cities was announced on Thursday, 29th. September, 1938.

'Anyone who cannot make private arrangements to go into the country will have the chance to be taken to billets in private houses some fifty miles from the danger areas. Schoolchildren who cannot go to relatives or friends can be sent away in the care of their teachers.

Children will go to school as usual. They will be taken to the station by teachers or other adults connected with the school. They will be given free tickets, and taken by special trains to stations about thirty to fifty miles from London. Homes will be found in private homes. Householders will be expected to give them board and lodging, and to look after them. The Government will pay the householder 10/6 a week if one child is taken and 8/6 for each additional child.

As far as possible, groups from each school will be found homes near each other, and schoolteachers and others who have volunteered to help in looking after them will be in constant touch.

Parents who wish their children to go should note these instructions:-
1) The children should be sent to school as usual.
2) They should be dressed in their warmest clothes.
3) They should be given an overcoat or mackintosh, hand luggage, a blanket, if possible, food for the journey, and an apple or orange, but no drinks in glass bottles.
4) They should take gas masks.

Ordinary railway arrangements at these stations will be seriously disrupted during these hours, which will be roughly from ten o'clock in the morning to four o'clock in the afternoon.'

much notice though, Bill was quiet and serious most days. I, on the other hand, chatted quite incessantly. I was, so I have been told, a highly strung child, lively and talkative, and Grandmother had her work cut out answering the continual flow of questions thrown at her.

We reached the station and, as we walked down the steps to the platform, I was surprised to see a crowd of children already waiting there. I thought it was just going to be Bill and me. It wasn't at all what I had expected. When we got to the bottom of the steps Grandmother led us along to the end of the platform, and, as she did so, a feeling of uneasiness came over me. It struck me, as I looked around, that all the children had labels pinned to their coats just like Bill and me, and gas masks too, and some were crying. I didn't like it at all.

I remember how Grandmother had talked as if the trip were going to be fun and I had the distinct impression, until now at any rate, that the whole thing was optional. 'I've changed my mind Nanny,' I said clutching her hand more tightly, 'I don't think I want to go after all. Come on, let's go home.' I turned trying to drag her back to the steps, but she gently pulled me toward her, 'You must go dear.' she said, looking as if she were about to burst into tears. I didn't understand, and began to protest, but my voice was lost amidst the hubbub.

I saw a few familiar faces among the crowd of children, ones that I had seen at Lucas Vale, my primary school, and normally I would have been anxious to run over and join them, but just then, I wanted more than anything to cling to Grandmother. 'Can't you come too Nanny?' I asked. 'I'll come later.' she answered.

After what seemed to be a very short nervous wait, the train pulled into the station. 'Now you take care of each other and keep together.' she urged. 'Billy, don't forget to send the postcard and let us know where you're staying, and we'll visit you in a few days.' She kissed and hugged us and ushered us toward the waiting train. It took quite a while for all the children to get settled, but she waited on the platform and waved as the train drew away from the station, on the journey to an unknown destination.

The first of many ports of call was Camber Sands, a quiet seaside resort in Sussex. It was very sandy, near the sea, and I thought how I would

Pola with her father and brother Bill at Hastings.

Pola with her mother.

have enjoyed myself had my parents been with me. The girls and boys were separated and housed in chalets, two or three children together, with an older child in charge of the younger ones. For the very first time I was separated from Bill and felt very bewildered.

One of the first things we had to do after settling into the chalets was to assemble in order to practice putting on our gas masks. The teachers started to explain how we were to put them on, the chin inside first, then over the head so that our faces were firmly covered and protected by the close fitting rubber sides of the mask. A feeling of suffocation always overcame me when I had anything covering my face. Even when Bill jokingly held the blankets over my head, when we played at home, sheer panic used to grip me, and I screamed and struggled in near hysteria.

I lifted the bottom part of the mask over and above my mouth, hoping that the teachers would not look too closely, but they were very careful in looking after their charges and solicitous in inspecting each child properly to see that he or she had got the hang of putting their mask on correctly. When the teacher came to me, she simply adjusted the mask to its proper position, over my mouth, explained that was how I was to do it in future, then walked on. I felt that I would not be able to breathe and was going to suffocate. I was greatly relieved when that drill was over, and lived in dread of the next practice.

After a very short stay at Camber Sands we were moved on to Fairlight Glen, a lovely spot in Sussex, where we were billeted in a school. After a few days we moved on to Hastings. If I was unhappy at Camber and Fairlight, there was worse to come.

In Hastings I was taken in, begrudgingly I feel, by Mrs Pool, a woman not given to smiling and rather grim faced. She had one child, a daughter, Stella, a few years older than me. She was used to being the centre of attention and reigned supreme in the Pool household. Stella saw me as nothing more than an intruder and my very presence seemed to annoy her.

By December 1939 quite a number of my friends had gone back to London and so would be spending Christmas with their families. I thought how lucky they were, and how very fond their parents must be of them. I felt that I had been dumped and forgotten. I'd have done just anything to be with Mum and Dad, but they wouldn't have me home. They were adamant about that. I went to bed on Christmas Eve with no childlike eager anticipation.

A Letter home from Pola.

When I awoke on Christmas morning I looked across at Stella surrounded by all her presents, feverishly scrambling from one gift to the other. I was half afraid to look at the bottom of my bed, but Stella was so absorbed in her presents that I dared to raise myself on one elbow and tentatively peered at the bottom of the bed, and there, to my delight, was a long coloured box. I knew without opening it what it contained. I scrambled to the box, opened the lid, and took out a big china doll. They didn't forget me, I thought. I hugged that doll to me for the rest of the morning as if it were a living link with home. Stella, with all her gifts, couldn't have been more pleased than I was at that time. 'That's all you've got though.' she taunted me, but I didn't care, it was the most beautiful gift in all the world and all I wanted.

Downstairs in the living room Stella inspected and played with all her toys and games. Mrs Pool was busy in the kitchen preparing Christmas dinner. I sat quietly on the other side of the room, hugging my doll, watching Stella but not daring to join in her play uninvited. I couldn't help noticing that Stella had been given a beautiful sewing set with different coloured cottons, and some shiny beads of different shapes and colours. 'Your mum bought these for me,' she purred. I remembered I had asked mother to buy me a sewing set and some beads, but she'd bought them for Stella instead. Perhaps it was because I hadn't shown much enthusiasm on that day when I had pleaded with them to take me home, and so they'd decided not to give them to me.

Just before lunch, Mrs Pool came in. 'Come on Stella, you've played with them long enough, you must be fed with them by now. We had better give them to Pola, after all, they are hers,' she said quietly, obviously not intending me to hear. I sat glued to the chair, as Stella sulkily gathered up the cottons and beads. I couldn't believe what I had heard. Nothing like this had ever happened at home. She handed over the gifts to her mother who unceremoniously plonked them in front of me. 'These are yours, from your parents,' she said curtly, 'I made a mistake, I thought they were for Stella.' I sat looking at the gifts not grasping the situation at all. 'Well play with them now that you've got them,' Stella said irritably.

I touched the cottons and the beads feeling too self-conscious to attempt to play. I was happy that they were mine after all, but somehow a dark cloud had been cast over the joy of receiving them. Not even on Christmas Day could they endeavour to make me feel welcome and at home. I wasn't sorry when Christmas 1939 was over. Stella's deep resentment of me soon began to manifest itself. Mrs Pool went over to the wireless set and turned it on, but there was no sound. She twiddled the knobs, but still there was no sound. 'I saw Pola playing with the wireless this morning Mummy,' said Stella. 'I didn't Stella, that's a fib, I didn't.' I said. 'Yes she did, I watched her break it. She did it on purpose.' 'No, no, I didn't.' I protested. 'Yes you did, I watched you.' 'Now Stella, tell me,' said Mrs Pool, red in the face with anger, 'Did you see her break the wireless?' 'Yes, I did, she was pulling all the knobs out.' 'I wasn't, honest,' I cried, at the same time feeling that my protests were in vain. 'Stella says that you did break it and she doesn't tell lies.' said Mrs. Pool, 'I'm going to write to your mother, and she's going to have to pay for it.' 'But I didn't break it Mrs Pool, I didn't touch it, honest.' But it was useless Mrs Pool was completely blind to Stella's tricks, but ever ready to see mischief in me.

I was terrified of wetting the bed. Fear really took a grip. That night I prayed to God that I would not wake up to a wet bed. Nanny had always told me that God would hear my prayers, and if I prayed hard enough, he would answer them. I remember the prayer she had told me to say, 'God bless Mummy and Daddy, Nanny and Bill and all the family. Thank you for the food we eat. Help me to be a good girl.' And then I would add, 'Oh God please help me not to wet the bed, and may the war be over soon so that we can go home, please, please God. Amen.'

I awoke in the morning to find my fears realised. I turned in the damp bed. God hadn't answered my prayer and I'd prayed so hard. I lay in the bed hoping that it would dry a little before I got up, but I was soon called to my breakfast.

While I ate my bread and milk, Mrs Pool went upstairs. The sound of her bounding down the stairs told me she had discovered the worst. She burst into the room, 'You filthy little bitch, I've had enough of you.' Grabbing hold of my arm, she pulled me out of the chair, dragged me up the stairs and into the bedroom. Then, holding me by the scruff of the neck, she pulled me over to the bed. 'If you are going to behave like a puppy, then I'll treat you like one.' My face suddenly struck the centre of the bed and pressure was applied to the back of my head as it was pushed into the wet sheet.

The Government attempts to stem the flow of returning evacuees.

A certain amount of valuable ground was lost in my emotional development, as a result of being evacuated, affecting my confidence, and limiting my ability to interact normally with others.

Many years after the war, when away from home too long, or in strange surroundings, I was still subject to strange feelings of insecurity and disorientation, as if I were in no man's land, in limbo, feelings to which I had become so accustomed. In fact, a day's outing or even a visit to friends was sometimes enough to spark off these strange feelings of unreality and confusion.

Evacuation had a disastrous effect on our education as a result of overcrowded classrooms, varying age groups being lumped together in one makeshift classroom or hall, and being supervised rather than educated by one, sometimes two very tired teachers. For many there was no continuity, being shunted from one school to another.

> The question of the education of the children is receiving very careful consideration, and when the school plans have been completed it is hoped that it will be possible to make arrangements for their amusement and care out of school hours.

> The billeting committee will be most grateful for any offers of children's clothing, bedding, etc. Such offers should be addressed to— The Reception Officer, Urban District Council Offices, Newport Pagnell.
> Push chairs for the quite young children would be specially welcome.

Bucks Standard, 9th September 1939.

Despite the improvements in education made after the war, most of us were so far behind there was little chance of catching up and reaching a reasonable level, unless one was exceptionally bright. The education of many children had fallen victim to the war and, for the first time since education was made compulsory, standards dropped and were extremely low.

For my brother and me, school became a tremendous struggle and a nightmare, and we were just two out of the many, many thousands of children evacuated from London in September 1939.

My brother and I felt very resentful toward our parents and blamed them for sending us away. We felt we had been abandoned, even more so toward the end of 1939 when the great drift homeward began for a considerable number of evacuees, perhaps because families wanted to spend Christmas together. We felt more desolate than ever at that time, we thought we had been rejected and forgotten.

My brother and I would say how we would have preferred to have taken our chance in London, rather than to be sent to live with people who had no love for us, little sympathy, and in some cases were totally lacking in understanding and tolerance. It was many years before we realised just how very deeply our parents cared for us, and many more years before we contemplated whether, given their situation, we might not have done exactly the same thing.

Pola with her family.

VALERIE HEDGES

When the headmaster asked all the children, who were going away to be evacuated, to stand up, I was amazed how few there were. I couldn't wait. I had really wanted to go to boarding school like Shirley Temple, but my pleas to follow in her footsteps had fallen on deaf ears. This seemed to be the next best thing. So, dressed in my Sunday best clothes, with my brown label tied to my button hole, I was taken to the railway station.

It was a very long journey. After hours of travelling, and very late at night, I arrived at a school hall, and sat on the floor with some other children. They were mostly boys, and older than me, so I was pleased that I was soon called and sent for a ride in a car. As tired as I was, I found this very thrilling as I had always longed to ride in a car, but never dreamed that it would really happen one day. It was wonderful to run my hands over the shiny leather seats.

I was so excited by the car ride that I wasn't at all upset that at the first house we called at, the woman loudly refused to have me. 'I have already taken three tonight,' she said. So I was taken to number ten. A nice lady came to the door and picked me up into her arms. 'Look what I've got,' she said. They were all smiling and seemed very pleased with me. I was not used to so much attention. It was lovely. Someone asked, 'How old are you?' 'Six,' I said. They all laughed. They thought that this was perhaps the only number that I knew. They wouldn't believe me, but somehow found out that I was speaking the truth and that I was just very tiny for my age.

The place I had arrived in was Torquay, and the house I was taken to belonged to Mr and Mrs Lane. Mr Lane was a tailor, and went to work every day in the back of a little shop in Babbacombe, but sometimes he worked at home. He would sit cross-legged in a corner of his bedroom sewing away at large pieces of dark coloured material. Perhaps he was making his own clothes.

Mrs Lane was very clever with a needle too. All the jam pots had their own little lace covers, and she once made me a lovely little dress. It was very dainty material covered in little pink roses. I had never owned anything so beautiful.

Mrs Lane was really very kind to me but was also very strict. I was used to this anyway. Children were to be seen but not heard in those days. Mrs Lane tried to fatten me up, but I was very hard to feed. To encourage me, Mr Lane used to challenge me to an eating race. 'See who can finish first,' he would say. I didn't like to lose any kind of competition, so I soon learned to watch his plate. The moment he came near to finishing, I would eat no more. I thought it rather unfair that they wouldn't understand that I had won.

One day, she saved a piece of gristle that had slipped to the side of my plate. Some things I could force down, but not gristle. I found it a few minutes later in my custard. I played with it for a while, but Mrs Lane was obviously determined that I must eat it, and I was going to have to risk almost certain death and do as I was told. I squeezed my eyes very tightly shut and gulped hard. To my great delight and amazement, I was still alive. Now, I thought, she would be very pleased with me. 'You didn't see that piece of meat in your custard,' she taunted me. 'Yes I did,' I protested in some anguish. How could she be so cruel not to see what a great hurdle I had overcome?

I was not allowed in the front room, and I found this very frustrating because there was a piano in there. Mr Lane used to give piano lessons. We had a piano at home and Mum could play anything by 'ear'. One day, I got home from school and there was no one in. The piano was tugging at me, like a magnet, through the door. I resisted for as long as I could but eventually I opened the door and crept to the piano. What a glorious time I had. I didn't know how to play a tune, and just made a terrible din. In my mind, however, I was playing to a packed house, so I got louder and louder as my enjoyment overcame my caution.

I was completely surprised when Mrs Lane arrived back from her shopping trip. I was suddenly grabbed by the collar, and plucked from the piano stool. I can't remember that she ever raised a hand to me, but the shock of her sudden return was enough to teach me that I should never be so daring again. Grown ups had a terrible way of knowing when you were up to something.

The Lanes were very different people to my family. They were quiet. The wireless was put on for the news, but the moment Tommy Handley and laughter came on from the set, Mrs Lane would rush over and switch it off in disgust.

Torquay is a very fine seaside town, but people who live near the sea don't appreciate how lucky they are, so they don't want to spend time on the beach. It was not until my mum and dad managed to come all the way to visit me that I ever went near to the sea. Of course in those days the beaches were barricaded with barbed wire in case the Germans tried to invade us.

There were lots of soldiers, including Americans, in the town. Children used to say to them, 'Got any gum, chum?' I was not allowed to speak to strangers, and thought the ones who did were very brave. The sweet shop hardly ever had anything to sell. I ate a great many cough sweets, I used to eat a whole packet in one go.

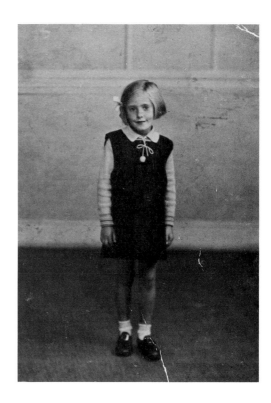

Mum used to save all her's and Dad's rations and send them to me. There would be slabs of toffee, and packets of boiled sweets. The paper was usually glued fast onto everything, and none of it was very nice tasting, but it was all there was, so it was greatly enjoyed. The parcel had to last a long time because you never knew if there would be another.

I was soon settled in a beautiful bungalow styled school. At first, I didn't bother trying to make friends, I just used to wander around the playground, until I found the game I wanted to play, and then asked if I could join in. I often had to stay in at playtime because I couldn't do my sums. This was where I met the little girl who was to become a firm friend. The teacher did not stay in with us, so we spent the time trying to help, but in fact confusing, one another. Later at Mrs Lane's, I was asked how I was getting on, and confessed that I could not get the hang of adding up. With a bit of help, the mystery was solved at last. I had been trying to add up sideways instead of from top to bottom! Then, at school, it was discovered that I knew all about 'Rover the Dog', not because I could read a word that had been written about him, but simply because I had a good memory and could interpret the simple pictures. This resulted in great disgrace, because I was sent back to the beginners group. However, it wasn't long before I was reading as well as the best in the class.

Sometimes, when my classmates were busy with some quiet task, we, the evacuees, would be called to the front to compose a letter to our parents. This was quite outside my experience and defeated me totally. I couldn't think of anything that would remotely interest anyone I had left behind in London. These communications must have been very brief, and mainly of my teacher's invention.

Whenever the siren sounded or when we had an air raid drill, we were shepherded into the shelter, and had to put our gas masks on. Mine had some kind of blockage, and I could only force air into it with the greatest effort. They were only inspected once a year, and I lived very anxiously for months on end. I couldn't convince anyone that it was absolutely useless. The inspector was abrupt and disbelieving, and I was sent away to yet another year of worry. Perhaps there were no replacements, or maybe it was just that evacuees were thought to be untruthful.

YOUR GAS MASK

TAKE CARE OF YOUR GAS MASK AND YOUR GAS MASK WILL TAKE CARE OF YOU. It is possible that in war your life might depend on your gas mask and the condition in which it had been kept.

The official gas mask, or respirator, consists of a metal container filled with material which absorbs the gas, and a rubber facepiece with a non-inflammable transparent window. Some people seem to think that this mask does not look as if it would offer very good protection. Actually, it has been most carefully designed and fully tested, and will give you adequate protection against breathing any of the known war gases. But remember it will not protect you from the ordinary gas that you burn in a gas cooker or gas fire.

HOW TO STORE IT

Your mask should be kept carefully. Never hang it up by the straps which fasten it on over the head. This will pull the rubber facepiece out of shape so that it no longer fits you properly. It should be kept in the special box provided, where this has been issued, but any box which is air tight, or nearly so, will do.

When placed in the box the metal container should lie flat with the rubber facepiece uppermost, the transparent window lying evenly on top at full length. Great care should be taken not to bend or fold the window, or to let it get scratched, cracked or dented.

After two years in Torquay with Mr and Mrs Lane, my mother discovered that my grandparents were fostering children in their house in Surrey, and I was brought back from Devon to go and stay with them.

DOREEN HENRY

It was the second year of the war and the bombing grew heavier. My mum said, 'It's no use, I am afraid we will have to get you evacuated. It's just not safe any longer here in London'. I am sure what made her finally make up her mind was that poor Mrs Watts and her five children were killed the previous night, when a bomb made a direct hit on their house, which was only at the end of our road.

Three weeks later, on the 10th July, my cousins and I found ourselves billeted with Mrs Black and her only daughter at Tonbridge, Kent. It was a frightening experience for a six year old child, to find oneself in strange, unfamiliar and hostile surroundings, away from home and family. Mrs Black obviously did not want to take in evacuees but was forced to do so and had to make the best of the situation.

There were three of us, John, seven and his sister June, who was five, and myself, six. June, being the youngest, was always crying and continually asking to go home, although she was the one who had least to cry about as Mrs Black's daughter pampered and spoilt her. This was understandable, as she was a pretty child, with a mop of fair curly hair and large blue eyes.

Every night, at six o'clock sharp, we mounted the narrow, dark, musty smelling stairs, where we were tucked up for the night in a huge feather bed. It was so enormous, it seemed to fill the whole room. On the mantleshelf was an assortment of objects, vases, photos of numerous relatives, past and present, and one large sea shell that had place of honour. Every night we fought over who was going to listen to the sea in the beautiful pink shell and there was always a skirmish over who was going to sleep in the middle of the bed. June was always being pushed to the outside. It usually took about an hour, and many an annoyed visit from Mrs Black, before we finally settled down for the night.

Each day grew longer and more miserable. At half past eight every morning, come rain or shine, John and I were bundled into our coats and told to go out to play. We were only allowed in at half past twelve for a quick, cold snack, then hustled out again at one o'clock until half past four, which was tea time. Finally, after ten days, we could stand it no longer and John and I decided to run away, back to London. June started wailing, 'I'm coming too', and John shouted, 'Only if you shut up and stop snivelling.'

We knew there was a railway siding at the end of the road, as we used to lie awake at night listening to the hissing of the steam engines and the clanking of the trains – a haunting sound in the dead of night – thinking of home. The next day June insisted on coming out to play as she knew this was the day we had decided to run away. Mrs Black made no objection, so we made our way along to the end of the road to the railway sidings, hoping to get on a train. We assumed all the trains went to London. The huge green gates were closed. Then John saw an opening in the fence a little further along. Being tiny, we all managed to squeeze through the gap and we slowly made our way along the track, which looked very forbidding. Then I said, 'Look, there's a hut. Let's go and wait in there until a train comes'.

It took us several minutes before our eyes focused in the dark. 'What have we got here?' cried the little railwayman, who was sitting in the corner. 'What are you three imps up to?' he bellowed, putting his mug of black tea on the table. It seemed such a loud voice for such a small man. John rambled on about wanting to go home because we were so unhappy in Tonbridge. The man listened with sympathy while wiping June's eyes, who by this time was crying copiously and wishing she had not decided to come on this stupid adventure.

'Do you know your address in London?' he said. Feeling very grown up I told him. 'Fine,' he said, 'Now, if you promise to go back to Mrs Black's, I will write to your mum and explain everything.' By this time we were beginning to feel very tired and hungry. Running away did not seem such a good idea, in fact quite daunting! 'Come on', the kindly railway man said, taking us by the hand, 'We'll go and buy some buns at the bakers, around the corner. You can buy a whole bag full for threepence, if you don't mind stale ones.' We had forgotten what sweets and things looked like, as we had not had any for so long and the prospect of a bag of buns, even stale ones, was tantalizing.

He was as good as his word, because by the end of the week Mum and Auntie Luce had arrived and given Mrs Black a good telling off. She was absolutely stunned and, I am sure, was glad to see us go. I have often wondered what would have happened to us if it had not been for that kindly railway man. I never did know his name.

Doreen aged five.

BILL HERRING

I was thirteen years old and attending the local senior school when war broke out. My younger brother was still in junior school, and it was decided that when we were evacuated I would go with his school.

On the 1st September, we assembled in his school playground with our cases and gas masks ready for the off. The parents who had come to see us off, mostly mothers, were obviously distressed. I already felt out of place as there were very few lads of my age and I was somewhat worried about the responsibility of looking after 'me younger bruvver'.

However, my confidence gradually increased. The whole episode of getting together into our groups, each in the care of a teacher, followed by the walk to the local station, became an adventure into the unknown. I remember nothing of the train journey which (as it ended at Horsham in Sussex, a mere forty miles away) was probably not as long as it seemed.

The clearest memory is of being taken in our groups with a woman who was responsible for finding us lodgings. We were taken along what seemed to be a long residential road, our numbers gradually decreasing as lodgings were found for the other children. The whole process was tiring and our original excitement gradually waned.

Finally, it was my brother's and my turn. The next door was opened by a severe looking, tall, elderly lady dressed in black or some other dark

material. She protested to the billeting officer that she had specified girls, but after some discussion she agreed to take us. Although by this time we were both very apprehensive she made us very welcome, although it was obvious that she had had very little dealings with boys, especially two working class, flat-reared Londoners. I remember a few tears being shed that night as we began to think it was not such a lark after all.

We later learned that our foster mum was a spinster, very religious and what we would call a Gentlewoman. After our initial shock, we settled down in our new home. We looked forward to our letters from home, especially the weekly postal orders.

Schooling was almost non-existent especially for boys of my age, firstly because we were sharing a church hall and secondly because as I was the oldest, there were no suitable classes available. I sometimes ended up looking after groups of younger children.

The countryside was full of adventure. We went for long walks, explored the woods and, it being harvest time, there was plenty of fruit to scrump. A new experience was collecting sweet chestnuts which our foster mum boiled and used as a vegetable. At home we attended Sunday school, no doubt to give our parents a quiet afternoon, but our foster mum expected us to go to Sunday school and church regularly and say grace at meals.

Although we were treated well, we never really felt at home and as the weeks, then months passed without any air raids, it was decided that we should go home. By this time many of the schools in London had re-opened.

One of these was my school, but as some of the teachers and children were still away, we had to share some lessons with the girls' school. One class that has always stood me in good stead was domestic science where we learned to cook, wash and iron.

I particularly remember the evacuation of Dunkirk because we lived alongside the railway along which the returning troop trains passed. My oldest brother was in the forces and last heard of somewhere in France, so we tried to watch every train in the hope of seeing him. The fall of

France made the possibility of air raids almost certain, so a second evacuation was arranged, this time with my school.

Being old hands, the second time was not so traumatic and this time I went with my mates and familiar teachers. Although in some cases this did not necessarily please us, they knew us and we knew them only too well. I again had 'me young bruvver' to look after. During both evacuations the teachers did a marvellous job acting as surrogate fathers sorting out all kinds of problems of so many unruly kids.

This time we had a much longer journey and ended up in Paignton, South Devon. The authorities had learned from their previous experience, and our arrival and distribution to our lodgings was much more organised.

Our evacuee mum ran a small boarding house near the sea-front. Most of the beaches were shut off due to defence work, nevertheless it was great to be at the sea-side. Our previous experience of this had been an occasional day trip to Southend, or perhaps Brighton.

For some reason, which was never explained, soon after we arrived we moved with our foster mum to a much smaller house without a bathroom. We used to bath in a tin bath in the kitchen. Being in my early teens, I was beginning to get self conscious and did not like the lack of privacy. The house was much further away from the sea front, but nearer to the school that we were using.

Our foster mum was a late middle aged country woman. She did her own baking and produced most of the vegetables from a small garden or from an allotment run by the lodger who was the only other member of the household. It occurred to me in later years that he was the tenant of the house and we were in fact living with him.

I clearly remember the beetroot harvest which we had to prepare for the making of beetroot wine, which was later given to us in quite large glasses. Our parents would have been horrified had they known, although I remember them sampling it on a rare visit.

Bill Herring and his younger brother David at Paignton, Devon.

We attended a large, fairly modern secondary school which we shared with the local children. Most of the day seemed to be spent in the grounds tending the vegetables or digging trenches to use in case of air raids. Fortunately, apart from the occasional dog-fight or the stray bomber passing over, there was no cause to use our trenches.

Out of school, we usually spent our time in town going to the pictures when we could afford it, or walking aimlessly along the sea front. Our foster mum would occasionally take us out on trips to nearby towns, or places of interest.

As time went by, we were more and more concerned with the fate of our parents back in London, especially as our eldest brother was seriously wounded. Our parents made a special journey to break the news of this to us. I, particularly, began to feel more cut off and unsettled.

Our foster mum had a very suspicious nature and often built small incidents into major causes of disagreement. This, together with my becoming more self-willed and unsettled, meant that our relationship was not a happy one. I was now well over the school leaving age of 14 years and it was suggested that I found local work but as the prospects of finding suitable work in Paignton were not good, it was decided that I would return home without 'me young bruvver'.

The regular nightly raids on London had ceased. I finally returned home in February 1941 with the object of applying for work as a boy messenger in the GPO, a sought after safe and regular job. After completing the necessary tests and examinations, I started work.

Ironically, some of the heaviest raids of the war came soon after, when I was travelling daily into central London from Brixton, but that's another story.

JOAN HERRING

It's funny how things work out. We didn't have a 'pick your evacuee' session when we arrived in West Worthing on September 1st but were led off in a crocodile down a long road to a modern estate of houses at the end. We turned into the first cul-de-sac and at the first home the billeting officer called out; 'Now, who's going to go in here?' There was total silence and then I heard myself say, 'I will.' That led me to having three billets in the ten months we were there, whereas the girl who went in the next house I believe stayed put for the whole time.

I was nine years old and an only child. Mrs Carns, my first hostess, was living with her parents as her husband was a Chief Petty Officer on HMS Hood. They were very kind and I was well looked after until Mrs Carns went to look after a friend who was expecting a baby and her parents were too elderly to look after me. Her husband was killed later when the Hood was sunk.

I was handed on to the Clintons in St Andrews Road. This was a family with two sons in an older house which was very cold in the bad winter we had that year. They were kind but I think things were quite difficult for them and I got very thin and suffered from horrible broken chilblains on my feet which were in a state with broken blisters and weeping areas under my toes. My mother came down and was shocked at my condition and got me moved again.

1.9.39.

Mrs Carn
37 Lincoln Rd
Canterbury Estate
West Worthing

Dear Mum e Dad,
We went to Worthing after all you said about us going to certain places. I have gone to a very, very, very, nice house. All of our group were seperated, and we don't know where Joyce has gone, but nine of us are in the one road all in different houses. Joan Hyenn lives two doors away. There is a dog named Nell and a bird named Joey in this house. Do you know what you did Mum? you. You did not put a tomb in my case, naughty. I hear war has started in Poland.
Mrs Carn has small apple trees in her garden but you aught

Joan in the back garden, with Mrs Carter's dog, in Worthing.

95

Joan Herring in Worthing.

1

37, Lincoln Rd,
Tarring,
West Worthing.

Dear Mum e Dad, I hope you are
keeping well. You know I said
that the money I had would
last me a month? Well I
have only sixpence left. It
was the pictures that did it
they cost eightpence. I would
like you to bring me the
Worlds Greatest Wonders please
(not the Wonders of the
World). I wrote to Auntie Vic
and she replied yesterday.
I want Mrs Carns Husband
to come home he is a Petty
Officer on the H.M.S. "Hood"
and he has three stripes.

Letters from Joan to her mother.

Is dad working in Victoria Station
? If he is he can come home
to dinner cant he? I am
just munching one of my
chocolates, they are lovely.
The ribbin on the lid is
in peices but I can take
the bow of and put it
on a clip. Please exuse
the writing, I know it is
terrible but you know what
I am for writing.
We are knitting 6" squares to
join to gether and make
into blankets for the refugees. Miss Fanny Fuss Face
Jackson has found us a
ball and we have to
walk a hundred miles to
it It is a terrible long
way to go, Isn't it terrible

about H.M.S. Gouragous going
down. If they can sink that
I hope they don't sink the
"Hood". They say that 681 lives
have been saved and they
say that the men were
swimming about in the
water singing and cracking
Jokes. I shall be ever so
pleased to see you next
week. All for now love and
kisses from Joan xxxxxxxxxxxx
xxxxxxxxxxxxxxx
xxxxxxxxxxxx
X xxxxxxxxxx
xxx xxxxxxx
xxx xxxx
xxx xxxx
xxx

Hitler   Chamberlin

ing, Please, Please, PLEASE, try and come and see me next Sunday even if it is only for half an hour or an hour I wouldn't mind as long as I saw you. There is no one in this house but there is rather a nasty girl next door and I had to go up on the downs with her but she doesn't worry me although I have to play with her. You are silly to worry about my back there is hardly any-thing to worry about.

My Scab.

Last time I looked at my scab it was no bigger than the picture shows. So the is no need to worry I shall love you both for ever and ever now you have sent me an adventure book as well as a school girls story book, you know I like those

I finished this spell of evacuation with Mr and Mrs Carter who also had two sons and they looked after me as if I was their own daughter. With Mrs Carter I learned embroidering, rug making and did a lot of knitting. She used to buy me lots of old copies of 'Girls Crystal' and other books, so I was happy. I stayed there until France fell in June.

The worst thing about this time was that my mother insisted that every Friday night I had to have my dose of syrup of figs — how I hated that stuff! But a good 'clear-out' was obligatory once a week.

School was part time and we spent a lot of time in the recreation ground or the 'Rec'. A garden backing onto the Rec had a big monkey puzzle tree which intrigued us. Knitting seemed to figure largely there too. We put on the musical 'Fat King Melon' again, that we had done in London the previous year.

I was lent a small two wheel bike and proceeded to break one of Mr Carter's prize standard rose bushes in the front garden. I could not get the hang of balancing until I went out on to the road and just did it.

Our parents lost lots of sharing in our experiences. It must have been awful for them to stick to the resolve of keeping us evacuated when all was quiet in London. I remember looking at my children when they were around nine years old and thinking that I could never have parted with them. My mother says she used to go out and walk around because the house wasn't right without me in it. Even at Christmas I was not taken back to London.

The main thing I remember was the scavenger hunt arranged by the hotel for Boxing Day. One of the things on the list was a dead rat which the hotel had 'planted' round by the dustbins. At the checking of the lists, when the man called, 'And who has a dead rat?' My father unrolled a big parcel of newspapers he had under his arm, and held the dead rat up by its tail. There were screams all round! I remember my father laughing, which was something I didn't associate with him. I don't think I'd ever seen him with a crowd of other people before.

Although the 1939 evacuation is what people think of when the subject is raised, it was probably the second evacuation which had the bigger effect on the children's lives because it lasted longer. The first evacuation ended, broadly, at the time of France's surrender. Schools were re-evacuated from their first destination, or parents took their children back to London. My mother's attitude was, 'If we're going to die, we'll all die together!' By the end of August 1940 though, we were receiving the air raids we'd been evacuated to avoid in the first place. My father was in a reserved occupation as a steel erector and was travelling to Leavesden, near Watford, from Bermondsey, daily, and, although he should not have been doing fire watching and fighting, it was difficult to stay in the shelter with everything that happened every night. One day he was sitting on a girder forty feet up and dropped off to sleep, nearly literally dropped off, before his mates shouted and woke him up!

That night he told my mother we would have to either go to shelter in the underground or go away. My mother was against the underground, so on the Saturday morning she put the best bits of china and glass in the boiler and tied its lid on. It was put behind an armchair. We took what we could carry and the dog, and went to lodge in Abbots Langley, near my father's job. That night the house was bombed.

We stayed in Abbots Langley from September 1940 to July 1945, my age being ten to fifteen, quite a time of change and growing up. After the loss of our home, the billeting officer found us something more permanent. It was a large semi-basement room in a farmhouse. There was a double bed for my parents, a large table, a single bed for me, and a wash stand and a wardrobe. My mother had use of the oven in the scullery of the house once a week, and cooked on the small open fire at other times. The fire had to burn summer and winter because of this. The window was in the corner, the window sill being on the level of the ground. Outside there was the sawing horse for the firewood.

Being evacuated with my parents may seem to have been a good thing, but living in that one room for four years with parents who did not get on well and were also under strain because of the way we were living, was not a happy experience. None of us ever had any privacy. My father worked seven days a week and eventually my mother worked in a school canteen.

I first of all joined a London school from St. Johns Wood which was evacuated to the village. I think it was in the Guide hut. It was fascinating on Fridays because a lot of the boys put little caps on their heads and had a special class in a separate room. Most of them had strong accents but I didn't understand the significance then, that they were Jewish boys.

When I passed the eleven-plus, the list of London schools showed that the Aylwin School, which had been at the bottom of our garden in Bermondsey, was at the Royal Masonic School in Rickmansworth. This was a long journey, but I had always said as a small child that that was 'my school'. So in the September I started the daily trek from Abbots Langley to Rickmansworth. I used to leave home at seven in the morning and usually got home at five in the evening or even later.

In November I had a near fatal accident on those buses. The bus from Rickmansworth used to get to the roundabout outside Watford Town Hall as the single-decker I had to catch came up the opposite road and passed in front of my bus. I used to stand at the top of the bus stairs which went straight down to the door, and on the night in question I had a fat book of Dorita Fairley Bruce school stories under one arm and my music case in the other hand. As the bus swung round the roundabout, a Watford schoolboy stuck a compass point in my bottom. I went down the stairs, past my startled friend and out of the door into the road, in the dark, in the rush hour. How I wasn't run over too was amazing.

My mother had the shock of the village bobby coming up the garden path to tell the news. I escaped with severe concussion but did not return to school until January. My father told me never to ride on the top deck again but, of course, I did. And had the satisfaction of seeing the expression on the face of the boy who did the deed! The teachers were very kind and gave me extra work to help me catch up, but I never got to grips with algebra and had years of tears over algebra homework until I was allowed to give it up before taking School Certificate.

In our one room the radio was on all the time in the evenings as it was a most important feature of the war years, but it made it difficult to do homework. My work gradually deteriorated until my Lower Fifth report in 1945 showed F for failure in most subjects. When I returned to London and took school certificate in 1946 I passed with five credits, the difference made by having a room of my own.

School at the Royal Masonic School's lovely buildings was an eye opener. It was a boarding school although of course we were only using a set of classrooms. The girls had a spell of holding their noses as they passed the London girls, but we had little to do with them. The grounds were extensive and our P.E. teacher instituted a daily mile run we had to do every morning. With the tiredness I usually felt with the travelling

1

11.9.39.   37, Lincoln Rd,
                            Tarring,
                            W. Worthing.

Dear Mum & Dad,
            I hope you are both
keeping well. Thank you for the parcel
and for things you sent by Mr. & Mrs.
Steer. The chocolates you sent have
got to last me three years because
that is how long they say the war
will last.
If I have a lovlier time in my life
than I am have-ing now I shall die of
suprise yes I will and with-out you saying that I am silly.
Will you tell me if my writing is get-
ing worse or better Please when you
write again?
I went on the hills yesterday and
had a lovely bath yesterday morn-

Apart from being such important years to a youngster anyway, it seems, looking back, like another world, a dream period that I remember so much of. I can't remember the following five years so clearly. Evacuation gave an intensity to life because we were surviving an unnatural time of our lives through a war, the outcome of which never seemed as sure as the politicians declaimed.

and the anaemia I always struggled with, this was a real torment.

The school holidays were the best things. We were in the country. The Ovaltine Model farm was across the road and in the same lane was a fantastic bluebell wood. There was a ruined manor house nearby with an overgrown walled garden full of huge rose bushes, flowers, figs and other fruit. It was a magic world. My mother and I fled from a herd of curious calves thinking they were bulls. I collected primrose and violet plants and made a garden under a tree in a field behind the house and was furious when the farmer's cows came and trampled it down. Didn't they know how long I'd spent making it?

In the Summer I worked on the harvest. We stooked corn and then I drove a horse and cart to the field, had it loaded with sheaves and then walked the great shire horse back to the farm. It was a wonderful experience. I was astonished when the farmer paid me with the other workers at the end of the harvest.

Other farm work we had to do was not so nice. From school we had days when we had to go potato and pea picking for the war effort. The pea picking meant sitting on sacks, singing songs and stripping the peas from the pile of plants. The potato picking was a nightmare. A full day in the open fields in rain or frost when the spinner came round again and again. There was only the hedge for a lavatory. I was exhausted to tears by it, and still had the long ride home afterwards.

Wherever I lived during evacuation there were boys in the house. During these wartime years the boys were important. Sunday afternoons were spent in the back row of the circle in the Watford Odeon. All very intense but very innocent. I also played goalie for the football team!

So much happened. We watched London burn from the hill top. One of the early rockets dropped near school. The buses ran on gas when the petrol got short. We used to have to walk up one hill near Croxley Green because the gas driven bus wasn't strong enough to get us all up the hill.

When the war ended my mother stayed on with me to finish the school term in July because the Aylwin School building in London had been used as a reception centre and needed repairs.

HEATHER HODGE

In 1939, when war began, I was five and my sister was thirteen and I had two little brothers, one about four and one born in May, 1939. My mother and father had a greengrocer's shop in Brixton. We used to have a shop with shutters. When the war started my father wrote to his brother in St. Thomas, in Canada and asked if he could send all the children out and my uncle agreed that we should go to them. But I think you had to be six to go and so my brothers were too young.

My parents got in touch with the Children's Aid Society about it and though we went with the evacuation scheme, we went privately. You could not tell anybody where you were going so my mum and dad could not tell people that their daughters were going to Canada. If anybody found out that we were going on the boat it could be dangerous. My sister and I continued going to school at Charles Edward Brook School in Camberwell but my mother could not tell the school that we were going away. We went to school as usual on the Friday but on the Monday we did not go in. She just had to say we were ill until we got to Canada and then she could tell them where we were.

Mum took us to Euston Station and waved us goodbye. I did not know where we were going, I thought we were going on a holiday. We got on the train with hundreds of other children and we went to Liverpool. We stayed overnight in some sort of shelter which I think was in a school and I can remember lying down on palliasses all in a row. We were just going off to sleep when there was an air raid and my sister pulled me up

out of bed and piggy backed me across this huge piece of grass into a shelter.

The next morning we queued up to get on to a large boat. I think there were four or five boats in the convoy and the one we were on was called the 'Hilary'. We were all issued with name tags and marched up on to the deck where we had a chat about what to do if we had to put our lifejackets on, how to assemble quickly and quietly on the deck and get into the life boats!

We had been sailing for about two or three days and were asleep in our bunks, fully clothed, we were not allowed to get undressed, when there was an awful ringing of a bell and everbody jumped out of bed. We had to pick up all our stuff and there we were standing on deck with our cases. My sister was quite frightened but trying not to show it because I was only six years old. But I was not frightened at all because I did not realise what was going on. I could see what looked like fireworks in the distance, which was probably bombs coming down and ships on fire, and I said to my sister, 'Isn't this exciting, it's just like firework night!', but she did not think it was exciting at all. Our boat and two other boats got through safely and we landed in Nova Scotia at the end of August and from there we went to Toronto. We were quarantined for a week because one of the children had developed an illness and they did not want to ship us off until everything was clear. By the time we arrived in St. Thomas it was the first week in September and my parents, at home, were worried, they did not know what was happening.

About two or three days after we had left England, my parents read in the newspapers that a ship going out to Canada with evacuee children had been sunk! Because there was no information they did not know whether we had drowned or not. When we got to Canada we were quarantined in Toronto University for about a week.

When our telegram eventually arrived in London, four weeks after we had set out, my father shut the shop up, and he and my mum sat at the table with the telegram between them. My father said to Mum, 'You allowed them to go, so I think you had better open the telegram'. He said that to her because he had insisted that she took us to the station and put us on the train, hoping she would change her mind at the last minute. When she came back without us, he was most upset because he

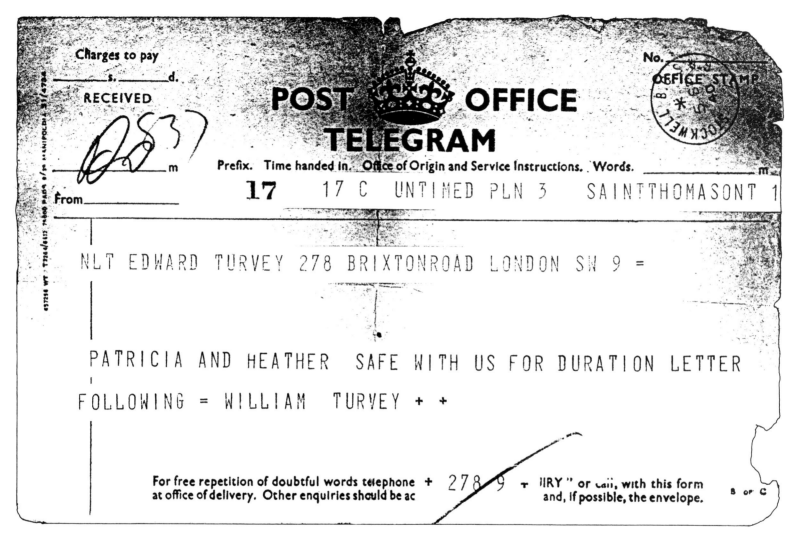

POST OFFICE
TELEGRAM

Charges to pay
_____ s. _____ d.

RECEIVED

_____ m

From _____

Prefix. Time handed in. Office of Origin and Service Instructions. Words. _____ m

17   17 C UNTIMED PLN 3   SAINTTHOMASONT 1

NLT EDWARD TURVEY 278 BRIXTONROAD LONDON SW 9 =

PATRICIA AND HEATHER SAFE WITH US FOR DURATION LETTER

FOLLOWING = WILLIAM TURVEY + +

For free repetition of doubtful words telephone + 278 9 + IIRY " or call, with this form
at office of delivery. Other enquiries should be ac   and, if possible, the envelope.   B or C

had thought she would not let us go. Of course when they did open the telegram there were floods of tears of relief. The worst part was that when people had come into the shop and asked where Heather and Patricia were, they could not tell them the truth. After the telegram arrived, of course, they could tell family, friends and our schools where we had been evacuated.

From then on my sister and I became like two Canadian children, living with my aunt and uncle and my cousin Billy in a bungalow in St. Thomas. My uncle was a Captain in the Fire Service and I have very happy memories of going to the Fire Station and going out on the very long fire engine. If they were just going for a run to see if the engine was all right, my cousin and I used to sit on the back and they allowed us to ring the bell.

CHILDREN FIND WAR HAVEN IN TORONTO

I went to school at Myrtle Street School with my cousin Billy and we joined Brownies and Cubs together and then later on the Guides and Scouts. We went to Church together three times every Sunday, morning, afternoon and evening, and sang in the choir.

In the winter, our school playground became an ice rink and we took our skates to school and at playtime we skated. They had hockey teams, Little Hockey Leagues, and if the ice looked as if it was getting pitted the teachers would get a hose and hose the yard down so that we got a nice surface for a bit longer. I loved the winter in Canada. We lived on the edge of a ravine and when the snow came we would go to the end of our road and ski and toboggan down the ravine.

Christmas was wonderful in Canada because where we lived it seemed always to be snowing at Christmas. St. Thomas was a very small town where, as soon as the snow came down, it went into snow drifts. Cars could not go out and so you went out for sleigh rides. When I was in the Brownies we went out into the country in this open sleigh, about twenty Brownies sitting in the back all singing songs and when we got back to the church hall all the mothers were there with steaming cups of tomato soup and buns. Father Christmas would go through the streets on a sledge and I believed it was the real Father Christmas. The man really looked like him and he would come round before Christmas in the snow and say, 'You be good and I'll come to you,' and I really believed it. It was wonderful.

Heather is ready at Church Parade with Cousin Billy, aged 9. Easter 1943.

They were a very religious community, everybody went to church, and it was the central part of life. My aunt was involved in the 'Parcels for War-torn England' group and she was always collecting for parcels to send to England. People would give toothpaste and soap and all sorts of things. My mother said that in the parcels that she used to get from my aunt, there were packets of something like blancmange, but there were no instructions and so she could not use it.

When we got to Canada, food was rationed, but my aunt, when the war began, had rushed out and bought in as many supplies as she could and filled the basement with sugar, tea, vinegar in barrels, and we used to trip over them. Their rationing was about two to three pounds of sugar, about a quarter of tea and a pound of butter each person a week, and so even though you could not have got through it each week, my aunt dutifully bought all the rations. At home my Mum and Dad were making do with about an ounce of butter and cheese each week. My aunt used to think it was awful having all the restrictions on food but we ate so well. She was a very good cook anyway — she was a Scots lady and we had wonderful food.

When we returned to England I had been brought up on a high protein diet, very good food, but my mother could only give us stodgy food, suet puddings and potatoes which did not help me as a teenager — I swelled up! We were about twelve miles from Lake Eerie and we used to go on holiday on the lake, swimming in it. We had a little cottage there and we would stay there for a couple of weeks. My uncle was a keen fisherman so we used to go out in all weathers while he fished and we would cook the fish on the beach.

We spent a lot of our time going to the cinema because, in Canada, if you went with a grown up you could see any film. I went every Saturday afternoon and I saw them all. I used to know all the film stars' names. We 'refugees' were invited to meet Judy Garland and Mickey Rooney in 1942. I think the film was called 'Babes on Broadway'. Frank Sinatra was just making his name and my sister was a 'Bobbysoxer'. She used to go around with a group of her school pals in an old car to anywhere he would be coming to in Canada. There was a place called London and Brantford that they went to and they would stand and wait for him to appear.

Dear Santa Claus, I hope you are well. Thank you for the things you gave me last year. Well I'd like, a pair of rollar skates, and a reader, a box of crayons, an apron, a pair of slippers, if you have a black doll I will be appreciated.

I will be very pleased if you have them. Love From Heather

Thank You.

Heather's letter to Santa.

In my school there were another two evacuees who were sisters, but in the whole area there were only about six of us, so we were rather special. My sister and I were always being interviewed by newspapers. If anything was going on at school and they wanted somebody who sounded different they would ask me to speak. That was because I had an English accent, although I thought I had a Canadian accent.

The lessons were a little different from those in England. I had been sent to a private school at home from the age of three and when I went to Canada I could already read, write and count. The children in Canada did not go to school until they were six and so when my aunt took me to school, they very quickly realised I was more advanced. I was put into a class two grades up and for the whole of my school life in Canada I was always in a class with children two or three years older than me. When I left I was in the eighth grade, which is the grade before you go on to the senior school, they call it the Junior College, and there were boys in my class of seventeen and I was eleven. If they did not pass they just had to keep taking the exams every year. You did not automatically go to the bigger school; you had to pass the exams before you could go there.

They were very fussy about handwriting and in Canada they all seem to write the same. The letter formation had to be written in the same manner. And so much writing had to be done every day. I have a letter that I wrote to Father Christmas when I was six and it is in proper writing. My grandchildren at six cannot write like that. Instead of reading primers like 'Janet & John' I was already reading books like 'Heidi' and so on. I was encouraged in school to read a lot and I was put in charge of a little library in our class because nobody else liked organising things. I loved school in Canada and I got on extremely well there. I think if I had stayed there, as my aunt and uncle wished, I would have gone on to University.

Coming back to England, when the war ended, all the schools were full, so my mother and father had the choice of either sending me to the local elementary school or arranging for me to go to a Catholic convent, which they did. I absolutely hated it because I was not a Catholic and my religious background was very strong. I had only been back in England for two years when my father died and I persuaded my mother to let me transfer to St. Martins in the Fields. Some lessons were a little difficult

Heather, aged 10, sledging with Billy, in winter 1944 in Canada.

106

to cope with here, like money sums. Of course I knew nothing about pounds, shillings and pence, and weight was different too.

We came back to England in 1945 but we did not want to come back. Although we wanted to see our parents and our brothers, we did not want to leave Canada. My uncle and aunt wanted to adopt us. They were like parents to us and my cousin, who was just a year younger than me, was like a brother and we had done everything together. Our parents would not agree to adoption. We filled our trunks with things like green bananas, oranges, huge bars of chocolate and all the things we knew they could not get in England.

We came home in June, leaving the most glorious hot weather and when we reached Euston station, it was pouring with rain. I remember my mother and father were standing on the platform, and my sister was so eager to attract their attention she banged her hand on the glass of the window and broke the glass. We all got in this old taxi and we both felt so strange. There were these four people who were like strangers to us. We had recognised them because we had had photographs and we knew who they were but we did not know what to talk about.

When we got to our house in Brixton we looked up the road and saw all these houses joined up together. We wanted to know where all the gardens were. We had been living in a bungalow with lots of space around and big gardens. Some of the houses had been bombed and there were big gaps. We could not believe it. We went into this tiny terrace house and it seemed so strange. We sat down, and when we unpacked the bananas, my two brothers did not know what they were. My sister said, 'Would you like a banana?', and they said, 'What's a banana?'

My mother and father were most upset because my sister had grown into a young woman and I was quite big and very self assured for my age. I did not want a fuss made and yet in a way I did. I felt I was too old for anybody to cuddle me and make a fuss of me but I needed something. My mother said, many years later, that if such a situation had ever occured again she would not have let us go away. Five years out of your children's lives was too much and at one point she began to think that she would never see us again.

Heather, aged 7, ready for a drive in Uncle's Chevrolet. Summer 1941.

My father was very pleased that his two daughters had come back. Dads always love their daughters don't they, and he made such a fuss of us. But my brothers did not seem to like us at all. I think they were very wary of these two strange people who had come into their home. I can remember feeling very sorry for my brothers; they seemed to stand in the background wondering whatever was going on. One was ten and the other about six years old. They had little school caps on and long grey shorts and they looked so funny to us because nobody dressed like that in Canada, they dressed very casually.

My sister was nearly twenty when we came home. She had met a young Canadian airman before she left Canada, and she had started going out with him. He wanted to marry her, but we had to come home to see our family. My sister settled into a job in London, but in 1952 she went back to Canada. She had never corresponded with the boy that she had left behind, but she bumped into him at a party and within six months they had got married. They are still very happily married and living in Toronto now with their two sons. She did not come back to England until 1976 when she brought her family to spend Christmas with us. We had our four children too and we had a really lovely time. We went to Canada for their son's wedding and stayed for three weeks in 1983. I met many of my old friends and spoke to some of those who had moved away. I would love to go and see them all again but I would not like to stay. It is a lovely place for a holiday but I think I will stay living where I am. It's not a bad old place, England.

These English Girls Have Enjoyed Their Stay Here

PATRICIA AND HEATHER TURVEY

If you happen to see two nice looking English lassies somewhere on the streets of St. Thomas in the next few days looking rather wistful, it is more than likely they are the Turvey sisters —Patricia, 19, and Heather, 11, who received marching orders over the past week-end to return to their home in Brixton, a section of old London. They report at Toronto on Sunday.

The two girls, daughters of Mr. and Mrs. Edward Turvey, have been war guests of their aunt and uncle, Mr. and Mrs. William Turvey, 79 Chestnut street, for almost five years, and since their arrival one August day in 1940, they have lost little time in getting the most out of the Canadian way of life.

Although they have been far removed from their parents in point of distance, the girls have been in constant touch by letter and cable but they missed hearing their mother on one of the special broadcasts for Canadian war guests that were featured a few years ago. That was a heartbreak, but there have been many compensations. There have been trips in the country, and a stay at a cottage last summer at Port Stanley. Special mention was made, too, by Patricia, to the ice skating and snow, which she said she enjoyed very much.

To commemorate their visit to Canada, a Mackintosh Red apple tree was planted in 1941 in the Turvey back garden, and it has attained quite a size already.

Canadian newspaper photo and headline 1945.
Heather and her sister are celebrities in Canada.

DORIS HOLLANDS

When the war broke out, my three sisters were evacuated but being the eldest, I went to work in a factory making relays and morse code boxes.

One day we were asked by our foreman at the factory if we would like a working holiday helping the farmers to pick their vegetables such as potatoes, peas and beetroots. My friend and I picked peas. We sat on upturned buckets, which was not very comfortable, and filled a large sack for a few pence.

We slept under canvas on palliases. They were mattresses made of straw. At night we tied scarves around our heads to keep creepy crawlies away.

There was a white line in the middle of the camp — boys on one side, girls on the other. If you ventured over it at any time, 'the Major', as he was called, that is the gentleman who watched over us and ruled with a rod of iron, would give you a severe reprimand or send you home.

At home the 'flying bombs' were dropping, they were known as 'doodle bugs' and 'V2's'. The first rockets that came over were very noisy but when the engine cut out you ran for cover. The second rockets that came were silent. They were dreadful. They just dropped anywhere and exploded, so now you can understand why a fortnight away from all of this was so wonderful.

Families separated by evacuation.

JIM HUGHES

I was ten years and nine months old when I was evacuated with my sister Barbara. We lived in Bow, in East London and we went to St. Paul's Way Junior and Mixed Infant School. On lst September we went to Paddington and caught the train which took us to a little railway station called Andover Spaul which is near Cheltenham, although we did not know then where it was, and we went from there in a bus to a little village in the Cotswolds called Colne Rogers, about seven miles from Cirencester. We were billeted with a lady called Mrs Guest. She was a widow and she had two grown-up children.

We quickly adapted to the country way of life. We used to go out in the fields and streams and get wet, and when there was snow or ice we used to go out to enjoy ourselves. Very often we would fall through the ice up to our knees in water.

Mrs Guest was a rather old-fashioned sort of woman. She was different from my experience of women. They used to run an agricultural machinery business for threshing and harvesting. She and her son ran it together as a business when her husband died. She was definitely not working class. She used to discourage us from playing with the local children and the other evacuees. She was kindly but she was old-fashioned in her ideas. She used to want us to stay in during the evenings and read books and so on and we wanted to get out.

Jim Hughes with his mother and sister.

To some extent when we went to school we were free, and so we used to climb trees and go in streams and over fields. But when we got home, muddy and wet, she disapproved of what we had been doing. She treated us pretty well though. She was not unkind, she was just different, rather straight-laced. She was also Church Warden of the local church and she encouraged us to go to church. I don't think it did me any harm because I was a bit of a harum scarum before. Apart from getting wet or muddy I don't think we did anything shocking.

One of the things we used to take delight in was building 'dens' and 'camps' and we used to go in the waste ground and get branches and weave them and get rubbish from the local rubbish dump, which we found fascinating. You can understand that she was concerned about us not getting injured from glass and rusty tins and things like that, but that was a world we delighted in. We used to catch frogs and try to keep them in tins or old troughs. I am very much interested in wild life and I think that was the start of it. I remember the local children trying to catch rabbits. They had ferrets and they used to catch rabbits and rats.

Jim helping out on the farm.

I also remember a swan flying into and hitting the telegraph wires and falling. It was not killed, but got up and walked back through the village to the river. One day, going to school on the bus with the other children, I saw a fox for the very first time. We experienced many new things like that.

We were totally unused to snow drifts that you could not get cars through. We had arrived with ordinary town shoes and no Wellingtons or boots of any kind, so we were unprepared for that winter, which was a hard one. But I look back on that time as being a highlight in my life.

Strangely enough, I was later on stationed in that area as a National Serviceman and went back to see Mrs Guest. We also visited her again later on when we were on a cycling touring holiday. There were more cars about, but I don't think the village had altered. Some of the old people that we knew had died and there were fewer children around, but basically it was the same. I think my sister enjoyed being evacuated and so did I. I cannot ever remember being upset or crying. With the other evacuees we enjoyed the Christmas parties and other school activities.

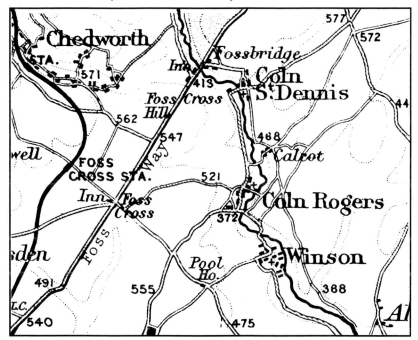

Jim's cycling country.

IRIS HUMPHREYS

I was eight when the war broke out. I lived at Sayes Court Street, Deptford, with my mother and father and elder sister. I was evacuated from Clyde Street School, Deptford, to Tunbridge Wells a few days before the war started. I can remember walking up Amersham Vale to New Cross Station but I can't remember the journey to Tunbridge Wells.

I was billeted with a Mr and Mrs Tapp. He was a plumber and they had a daughter also called Iris. They were very kind to me and the other evacuee, a girl called Winnie, who was from Clyde Street School too. I was terribly home-sick and in fact only stayed in Tunbridge Wells for five weeks before going home to my family.

Wills's Cigarette Cards, A.R.P. Series.

Iris just before the war.

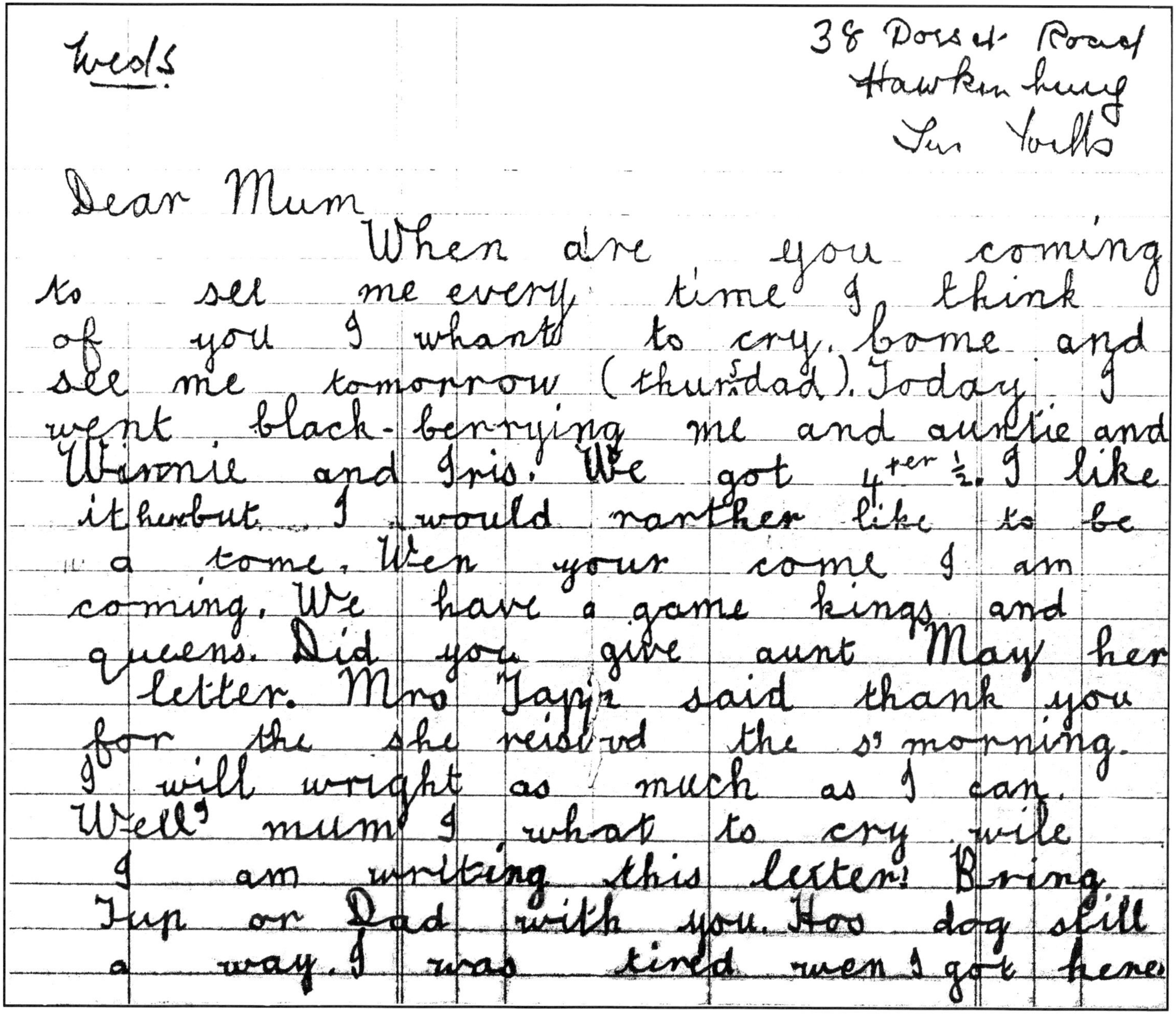

Weds

38 Dorset Road
Hawkenhuny
Sus Yorks

Dear Mum
          When are you coming
to see me every time I think
of you I whant to cry. bome and
see me tomorrow (thursdad). Today I
went black-berrying me and auntie and
Winnie and Iris. We got 4 ter ½. I like
it herbut. I would narther like to be
a tome. Wen your come I am
coming. We have a game kings and
queens. Did you give aunt May her
letter. Mrs Tapp said thank you
for the she reisbved the s morning.
I will wright as much as I can.
Well mum I what to cry wile
I am writing this letter. Bring
Tup or Dad with you. Hoo dog still
a way. I was tired wen I got here.

Iris writes home.

14th June 1940, waiting for a train along with 20,000 others, bound for the West Country.

JOAN JACKAMAN

I was about ten years old when the war started. I did not go away with the school. I don't know how long it was after the outbreak of the war, but my mother decided to go away to West Malling in Kent with the five of us, six with my mum. She lived in one house with my sister Eva, brothers Albert and Lennie, and herself. Margie and I lived next door with another family. After two weeks my mother and the others came home. She never had enough bus fare for us all, so she left me and Margie behind and she said that she would send for us.

They seemed a nice young couple that we stayed with. He used to ride around on a motor bike. I don't know if he was a dispatch rider or something, a messenger. We started school down there. About a week or so after my mum came home the young couple started to take a lot more notice of Margie than me. Because I was two years older than her, if anything went wrong it was always my fault! It was just because they had taken a dislike to me, but I don't know why. They used to send us out to play in the meadow, that was just up the road, and if Margie got mud on her shoes, when we went back, it was my fault!

We were told not to go into the house next door but one. Well, about three weeks after my mum went back to London, the lady that lived there, called us in and gave us a banana. I don't know where she got it from. Whilst we were in there eating it, she was talking to us and Margie was telling her about some knitting that we were doing. I think her name was Alyon and she was quite a bit older than the young couple we lived

Three girls arriving at Redbourne Common, Herts, on 1st September 1939.

with. Anyhow I told Margie to go and get the knitting but she did not come back so I went to see where she was and I got sent to bed.

So having been sent to bed I was not very 'polite' and I swore. Now I could swear, but I used to know how to behave myself and up to that point I had never sworn at them, but now I called out all the names that I could think of. Anyway they put me up to bed and after about a half an hour, the man came upstairs and said I could get up. But being obstinate, I decided I did not want to get up ever again and I stayed there. Well Margie started playing up and crying 'Get up, please get up', and so I got up.

Then my uncle came down to see us on the Sunday and we'd been sent to Church. ' Well' he said 'I hear that you swore at Mr. Russell.' So I swore at my uncle, and said that if they did not come down and get us the next week I was going to walk home. The very next day, while we were at school, my Dad came to fetch us back to Woolwich. When we got to the house to get our things, the people wanted to keep Margie and send me home. So that was my first evacuation at West Malling which seemed then miles and miles away, but I realise now I could have walked home, couldn't I?

I think we stayed in Woolwich for a couple of years and went through all the Blitz. We used to live in the old Warwick Street and a bomb fell at the end of the road. It blew the slates and things off the roof of our house. So then it was 'Oh, we'll go away again'. I don't know who it was you went to, to arrange things like this, but three families went from Warwick Street. Maudie King and her four children, Mrs Alice Ansell, with her two girls, Jessie and Ruth, went with us to Yorkshire, to Wakefield and we stayed in an empty hospital for three nights. Then along came some coaches and they took us all in different directions. We did not know where we were going.

We landed up at a place called Whitley Bridge. It wasn't a town, it wasn't even a village. There were just a few houses scattered about. It had one little shop. The house that we were in was very, very old. I don't know if it had been a farm house at one time, but it stood in its own grounds. When we walked in, there was a man and a woman. I think they must have been fifty to fifty-five, because they had a son

An ARP warden helping homeless mothers and babies to move to places of greater safety in East London.

about thirty. I don't think you realise ages when you are a child. The old boy was mending shoes and spitting in the fireplace. He said 'We Yorkshire people welcome you Londoners and there's a Post Office up the road if you want to go and buy some stamps.' I cried to go and buy some stamps, I do remember that. I didn't want to stay there.

The house had two entrances, one going up the side and stairs leading up to two bedrooms. One was quite a fair size and the other one was very small, so that we were really separated from the family. My brother, Len asked to go to the toilet, and the toilet was a hut thing with a wall built round it and the hut had a hole in the side. Inside was a big wooden toilet seat with excrement all over it, because it was so full that it was coming up over the top. The idea was that you had to get a long rake and put it over the 'lavvy wall' and rake it all out. That was not for the family's use that was for our use. But we used to use a chamber pot and empty it out over the wall.

We had one saucepan and one frying pan to cook for six people, so that if you cooked cabbage you had to cook it first and then put it on to a plate in front of the fire to keep warm while you cooked something else. All the cooking had to be done on the fire of course. The butcher used to come round on Wednesdays, because we were stuck out in the middle of nowhere, and although it was cold you could not keep meat from Wednesday until Sunday, so we used to eat the meat then. Come Sunday, my mum used to open a tin of pilchards and cook some potatoes with it. She used to sit and cry over that, about what she had to give us for Sunday dinner.

There was one single bed and a double bed, and on the beds was a sheet, and a cotton counterpane on each bed. So what we planned to do was to have two in the single bed and four in the double bed top to toe, but it was so cold and there were no blankets that all six of us ended up in the double bed with coats on. The houses did not have any running water. The water had to be fetched from the side of the shop that was across the road where there was a well, and if you did not bang and make a lot of noise when you were over there you used to get a bucket of frogs! It was really primitive. Washing up was done in a bowl and the dirty water went over the 'lavvy wall'. There was one big table spoon and one day that went over the wall with the washing up water and we made Margie go in and get it.

If we were not in bed by nine o'clock, Mum and all, the people in the house used to turn off the electricity at the mains, so you could not stay up even if you wanted to. We decided, after we had been there for about a week, that we would go for a walk. We went about two miles and we came to a pub. My mum went into get a drink and we all used the pub's toilet so that we would not have to use the pot and empty it over the wall. After that, we made that our daily walk.

WHY EVACUATION?

There are still a number of people who ask " What is the need for all this business about evacuation ? Surely if war comes it would be better for families to stick together and not go breaking up their homes ? "

It is quite easy to understand this feeling, because it is difficult for us in this country to realise what war in these days might mean. If we were involved in war, our big cities might be subjected to determined attacks from the air—at any rate in the early stages— and although our defences are strong and are rapidly growing stronger, some bombers would undoubtedly get through.

We must see to it then that the enemy does not secure his chief objects—the creation of anything like panic, or the crippling dislocation of our civil life.

One of the first measures we can take to prevent this is the removal of the children from the more dangerous areas.

THE GOVERNMENT EVACUATION SCHEME

The Government have accordingly made plans for the removal from what are called " evacuable " areas (see list at the back of this leaflet) to safer places called " reception " areas, of school children, children below school age if accompanied by their mothers or other responsible persons, and expectant mothers and blind persons.

The scheme is entirely a voluntary one, but clearly the children will be much safer and happier away from the big cities where the dangers will be greatest.

There is room in the safer areas for these children ; householders have volunteered to provide it. They have offered homes where the children will be made welcome. The children will have their schoolteachers and other helpers with them and their schooling will be continued.

WHAT YOU HAVE TO DO
Schoolchildren

Schoolchildren would assemble at their schools when told to do so and would travel together with their teachers by train. The transport of some 3,000,000 in all is an enormous undertaking. *It would not be possible to let all parents know in advance the place to which each child is to be sent but they would be notified as soon as the movement is over.*

One day when we were on our walk, who should we meet coming from the opposite direction but Maudie and Alice, our friends from Woolwich. So there were tears when we all met. Maudie and Alice had stayed together in a house, but the owner was not there. They also had a shed in the garden for a toilet, but at least the Council used to come and empty theirs so it wasn't so bad.

The School Inspector came for us to go to school but Mum said, 'Oh, we're going home tomorrow.' After two or three days, the School Inspector came again and he was told that we were going home the next day. We were always 'going home'. We used to go on quite long walks and one of them was to a sand quarry. Looking back on it now, it really was very dangerous, because there was a small truck on rails and we used to push it up the quarry and ride down on it.

One day when we were coming back from one of our walks we saw a great big field full of what looked like swedes. Mum said, 'Ooh, lovely swedes.' 'I'll go and get you one', said Margie, and she went in the field and got a swede. When we got back to the house, Mum said to the woman, 'I've got a lovely big swede here. Would you like half?' But when Mum cut it in half for her she said, 'That's not a swede. That's a Mangelwurzel!' Apparently they grew them for feeding to the cows.

One day Margie went into a field to fetch a cabbage and a bloke caught her. Margie was always in trouble. I remember once, a tree was blown down and we all had to go and help to collect pieces from the tree. I would not go but Margie and Lennie went, Albert was too little to go. They dragged back loads and loads of wood and it was locked in a shed. The people used it but we were not allowed to use any of it. We had paid for coal but one day the family went out and locked up the coal shed and we could not get any coal.

There was an Army camp nearby and Eva got a boy friend. Margie was going out of the door one evening to empty the pot when he was just about to knock at the door and that embarrassed Eva so much that she would not go out with him any more.

The ice cream man used to come round and Mum would buy us all an ice cream. But all the time she was trying to save up enough money to pay our fares back to London because it was quite expensive for all of us to come home from Yorkshire. We must have been there about ten weeks altogether. I don't know how far from Doncaster we were, but that was the nearest station and we started to walk to Doncaster. We did not seem to have much luggage to carry but along came a lorry and gave us a lift. So that was how we came back.

We were at home for most of the war. I did not like being in the country. I think I hated it from the minute I got there. Mum used to wait for the postman to come to get letters from home.

Government Evacuation Scheme.

EASTER HOLIDAYS.

Dangers of air attack are in no way less.

You are earnestly advised not to bring your children back to the evacuation areas.

March, 1940.

MINISTRY OF HEALTH,
LONDON, S.W.1.

[77458] 50854 3/40 **706**

Returning evacuees, Stepney. June 1945.

JOYCE KERR

I lived in Portsmouth. My father was in the navy and there was my mother and my sister, and me. I was thirteen and my sister Barbara, was ten. Not many of our set got evacuated, and when we left Portsmouth Town station on 1st September, it was before the war had actually started. What impressed me was that we did not use the ordinary platform but the goods platform. We had this huge train, but there were more people to see us off than were going into the train. We had our little packs on our backs. We had had to get haversacks to put our goods in and everything had to be labelled. My sister and I went along with my mother, my aunt and cousin, from up the road, and my grandparents from Battersea, who were staying with us for their summer holidays. They all came to see us off and they were weeping to see us go, and then off we went. It was rather ludicrous because we were being evacuated from Portsmouth and we were taken to a place seven miles from Southampton, although we did not know that at the time.

We were told to bring some barley sugar to eat on the way. As we went over a big bridge, going into Southampton, one of the teachers told us we could eat our barley sugars. When we got up to get our luggage down, somebody must have inadvertently grabbed hold of the communication cord because the train came to a standstill on the bridge. There was a lot of excitement. Everyone thought that somebody must have fallen off the train, over the bridge and into the water. Anyway, it was soon sorted out and off we went again.

We got to a place called Bartley, in the New Forest. It had been a long day and I think a gaggle of us were put on to a platform to wait. Everybody else seemed to be going off somewhere and we fifteen were left sitting there. The fifteen girls ranged from about five years old to fourteen and we were all children from the same school. We were then told we were going off together to a place called Paultons Park, which was a big country house and that is where we landed up. It was about three miles south of Broadlands, at Romsey. The next morning when we woke up we were amazed to see the house.

Paultons Park.

The people who owned the estate were a Major Sloane-Stanley and his wife, Countess Cairns, and they were really delightful people. They could not do enough for us. When we first arrived we were bought a jersey each and given other clothes, and a present. I think, in the beginning, they had wanted boys because Scouts used to go there for their Jamborees and they were used to having boys, but they were really very good to us girls. They had bought us a set of books which were obviously boys' books, like Conan Doyle's and "The Exploits of Brigadier Gerrard" and things like that, but we read them.

We lived in the servants' quarters of this large house. We had our separate bedrooms and we used to have a 'common room'. This was a huge room where we spent most of our time when we were not in bed or at school. Around the walls there were two big stuffed pikes and a big stag's head, over a huge fireplace. There were great big logs that went into the fireplace. There was a piano too. We were looked after by one of the mistresses, who had come with us, and her sister and mother who had come as helpers.

Our bedrooms looked out over the lake and on that floor was our bathroom. Above the bathroom was a tower and in the tower there was a bell with the rope hanging down. In wartime, if you saw an enemy parachutist coming down or any other mysterious happening, you had to pull the rope to ring the bell. Many a time I sat in the loo, visualising myself as a heroine, looking out of the window, seeing a parachutist descending, and pulling the rope to alert the neighbourhood we were being invaded!

The girls at Paultons with Shinty sticks.

Major Sloane-Stanley and his wife had two daughters. The eldest, who had three small children, when staying at the house often joined in our games of hockey. We used to go to school in what was the cricket pavilion and it was a bit of a mixed kind of schooling because of the range in ages. It must have been quite difficult really. Most of the other children had gone to Bartley School and some of the mistresses that had gone with them came up to our pavilion school, sometimes, to take our lessons. We used to play games on the cricket pitch, outside the pavilion. The Major bought us Shinty sticks, which are like walking sticks turned upside down, and then later on he bought us proper hockey sticks.

At the beginning of the war the weather was lovely and we were able to wander around the estate, exploring. Every morning we were given an apple from the estate. The house was very self sufficient. I remember having rabbit pie which obviously had come from rabbits in the park. We also had pigeon pie and quails on one occasion. We did very well for food and most of the children put on weight.

There was a lake, surrounding the house, that had a lot of fish and ducks on it. It was suggested that we had a nature study lesson there. We needed nets on sticks to go pond dipping and the Chef was asked for some muslin that they used to wrap the meat in. Major Sloane-Stanley

Resting in the grounds of Paultons.

got to hear of this and he thought instead of having fishing nets why not have fishing rods and so he bought us a set of fishing rods. On the lake there was a boat house with small punts. We had spent the morning looking for worms, unsuccessfully, and so the Chef gave us some bread to make our own bait. We got to the boat house and set out the rods and our first catch was one of the ducks! That did upset us. I don't think we did much fishing after that.

The first winter was terribly bad. I don't know how my mother managed to come and visit me. All the signs were taken down on the stations. During that winter, the lake that surrounded the house and wandered through the park froze over. We had great fun and games sliding on the frozen lake. Major Sloane-Stanley saw us there and the next day the attics and cupboards were investigated to find ice skates and boots that we could use. There were not enough for all of us and they were all different sizes so we had to take turns. When we were not skating we slid around on the ice on the wicker chairs from the cricket pavilion, which was near the lake.

On the ice in the cricket pavilion chairs.

At Christmas we had a lovely party in the main part of the house. It was in a beautiful room and we sat at a big table, on chairs that were so wide that I think they must have been from the time when ladies wore crinoline dresses. I had my first long dress for that party. My aunt had made it for me. We had lovely presents too. I had a leather writing case from Harrods and I still have it now. I did not know what Harrods was in those days. They were very generous to us. We did a Mummers' play with St. George and the Dragon and we went round to the different cottages in the village doing our show.

The Mummers Play at Paultons with Major Sloane-Stanley.

The servants were very good to us as well. One of them used to play the piano so that we could have sing-songs. It was very nice. We had a trip to the seaside and once we went to a large house where we were told Marconi had done some of his experiments. My mother used to come and visit us and sometimes my father and other relations. Occasionally we went home for a short holiday particularly at Easter. Some of the children who were left at the house went over to Broadlands for an Easter Egg hunt.

When Southampton was being bombed, we used to go down into the cellars to shelter. But although we used to go down there when there was an air raid alert, we were not really bombed. We did see Southampton Docks on fire though. There was also a land mine that landed near the entrance to the park, later on in the war, and an enemy plane crashed down in the park too. Every time we were playing in the fields and an enemy plane flew over, our mistress used to blow a whistle and we then used to hide under a huge cedar tree.

We were going to present 'A Midsummer Night's Dream' beneath this big tree. There were only ten of us in it and so we had to double up on some of the parts. I rather feel that that was what made me ask my mother to take me home, because I was not too keen on going on the stage at that tender age. Also, to be honest, I was homesick.

In August of 1940 we returned home to Portsmouth. My mother was on her own and my father was away in the Navy. So although we were away for the first year of the war we were back in Portsmouth for the Blitz. We have recently had a reunion of some of the people who were evacuated to Paulton's and we plan to have another next year. We went back to Paulton's Park which is now a Leisure Park. The house is no longer there, just the remains of the cellars. It got burnt down one Guy Fawkes' night and because it was so far away from the road and village, the fire engines did not get there in time. We spent a very nostalgic day talking about those times.

We all got on well together in those far off days, having our friends and enemies within the group as children will. We used to mix with the village school when we had hockey matches, but by and large we were a little community on our own and when I read about other evacuees' experiences I realise how lucky we really were.

Children at Paultons wearing blouses they made with smocking.

MARGARET KIPPIN

I remember the long discussion between my parents and me as to whether we should let my youngest brother be evacuated. He was eleven years old at the time, and, being the baby of the family, rather made much of. Eventually, it was decided that it would be sensible to let him go. At the time, we all expected that as soon as war was declared, we would be subjected to air attacks. He was quite happy about it, looking upon it as a sort of adventure, and we fostered this idea.

It was arranged that, in the evening following the evacuation, parents would be able to call for information at the school from which the boys had gone. My mother and I accordingly went along, but apart from saying it was in Sussex, we had no definite address. However, the children were all given post-cards to send home, and within a day or two, we had his address.

The following week, my mother decided she wanted to go down and check that all was well, and having decided on this, it was all stations go! I happened to be on holiday at the time, and had a friend staying with me, so off we went.

We eventually located the place, and he was with two other boys housed with the Billeting Officer, who occupied a large house by a windmill. She was not at all pleased to see us, doubtless she thought it was too soon and would unsettle him. She was rather a snooty person. We were not invited into the house. The housekeeper, who occupied a nearby cottage, brought us a tray of tea into the field by the windmill! With hindsight, I suppose it was a bit of an imposition just arriving out of the blue, but that was what my mother was like — act first, and think about it afterwards. Anyway, my brother appeared to be quite happy.

We wrote to him very regularly. He had at least three or four letters a week from us. He recently told me how he regretted not keeping these letters as he recalls that they were very special.

However, Miss White (for that was her name) did invite all parents to lunch on the following Boxing Day. My parents could not go, so one of my brothers and I went. There was not a very warm family feeling in the house. The school, which had taken over the local school premises, put on a show in the afternoon and provided tea, which gave me an opportunity to chat with the masters. They felt he was settling in well.

As my brother and I left to catch the coach home, my young brother stood in the middle of the road, waving to us until we were out of sight. I remember the temptation to run back and give him another hug, but felt it was unwise. It might just have upset the balance, but I did have a lump in my throat. We were a united family, and I realised that whilst we were returning to the family home and our parents for back-up and support, he was alone, and because he was the baby of the family, the rest of us always felt protective towards him.

Two or three weeks later, my mother visited him — this time by arrangement! When she returned home, she burst into tears, said she had found it hard to leave him, and that he was very unhappy. So, we decided to bring him home. At that point, we had not suffered any air raids. He has since told me that he felt it was a mistake to give in to what was a temporary show of tears, and that he should have remained there, particularly as it interrupted his schooling.

As time progressed, we were to experience a spate of 'nuisance' raids, and then, early in September, the blitz got under way. We did not have an air raid shelter, as we had moved into the house after they had been distributed and so missed out. However, my father made our dining room as safe from bomb blast as possible. He used our large mahogany table as a screen by fixing it against the French windows, and moved all the beds downstairs. My mother did not feel safe even then, so she used

STAY WHERE YOU ARE

IF this island is invaded by sea or air everyone who is not under orders must stay where he or she is. This is not simply advice : it is an order from the Government, and you must obey it just as soldiers obey their orders. Your order is " Stay Put ", but remember that this does not apply until invasion comes.

Why must I stay put?

Because in France, Holland and Belgium, the Germans were helped by the people who took flight before them. Great crowds of refugees blocked all roads. The soldiers who could have defended them could not get at the enemy. The enemy used the refugees as a human shield. These refugees were got out on to the roads by rumour and false orders. Do not be caught out in this way. Do not take any notice of any story telling what the enemy has done or where he is. Do not take orders except from the Military, the Police, the Home Guard (L.D.V.) and the A.R.P. authorities or wardens.

What will happen to me if I don't stay put?

If you do not stay put you will stand a very good chance of being killed. The enemy may machine-gun you from the air in order to increase panic, or you may run into enemy forces which have landed behind you. An official German message was captured in Belgium which ran :

"Watch for civilian refugees on the roads. Harass them as much as possible."

Our soldiers will be hurrying to drive back the invader and will not be able to stop and help you. On the contrary, they will

---

to spend the nights with the next door neighbour who had a Morrison shelter. My father, brothers and myself would play games. 'Battleships and Cruisers' was the favourite, and every time we heard a stick of bombs on the way, we would call out 'Duck!' and crawl underneath the beds. On one occasion, one of my brothers got stuck, and we had to move the bed to retrieve him.

After a week or so, and after a particularly noisy night, my mother said she had had enough, and she was taking my youngest brother to find a safe area. She assumed that I would go too. I was quite adamant that I would not go — I would stay at home to look after my father and the boys. What was more, I had a job of work to go to. There were tears and arguments, and finally she said we should phone my father and see what he had to say. It was very emotional. I spoke to him, and in the end we were both in tears. He begged me to go, saying it would be one less for him to worry about. I remember vividly going up to my bedroom, getting out a suitcase, and wondering what to take and what to leave. By now, I was beginning to be infected by my mother's panic.

We boarded a train into Kent which was crowded with people with the same idea. We shared a carriage with families from Silvertown, who had experienced a dreadful ordeal the night before, mainly with fires. Their language was choice, and what they would have liked to do to Hitler is unrepeatable... Most of them had decided to go to Paddock Wood, the scene of their hop-picking days. They felt that as they knew the local farmer, they would get help in finding accommodation.

My mother decided that we should make for Tunbridge Wells, and upon arrival, she telephoned the house-keeper where my brother had been billeted to ask what the chances were of finding rooms. We were very lucky, for her niece had recently gone up to join her husband, and her bungalow was available for rent. So, we boarded a coach for Rotherfield, arriving feeling quite exhausted and disorientated.

I remember that first night, my brother and I cuddled together in this strange bedroom, but we did not feel relieved to be out of the bombing. We could hear the planes going over to bomb London, and worried about the rest of the family still facing the danger.

Margaret at Tunbridge Wells in 1941.

On another occasion, I saw a bomber from the train which had been brought down in a field, and beside it, covered in tarpaulin with just their jackboots showing, were the bodies of the crew. Despite everything, I felt sad. They were only doing their jobs and were someone's sons, husbands or brothers. Three years later, when my own brother was shot down and killed over Germany, this scene re-appeared in my mind.

My mother was shopping in the village one very cold day and she saw a small evacuee boy with no coat on and the seat out of his trousers. She was so incensed, she brought him home, kitted him out, then created such a stink that he was found another foster mother.

Soon, I returned home to London, and was able not only to look after my brothers, but restore the house to some sort of order. Very little washing up or cleaning had been done, but they could not altogether be blamed, because as soon as they got home from work, they would have a scratch meal and then go down to the air raid shelter — it was no longer safe to rely on the arrangements made earlier in the house. My father by now was having to remain up in Westminster, travelling being so difficult, although he did manage to pop home some mornings to make sure we were all well.

This situation lasted for about three weeks. My brothers and I would travel down to Rotherfield at the week-ends after visiting the butchers to purchase the week-end joint for my mother, who had not yet re-registered. It was all rather grim. I was having to travel to Beckenham where the company were now installed and this often meant walking all or most of the way as transport was disrupted due to the damage caused by the raids. On one occasion on my long journey home from work, a kind policeman took pity on some of us and I was brought home in a Black Maria! Then it was a quick meal followed by preparations for the night in the shelter.

The decision to leave London once again was then forced upon me. One of my brothers was to move to Surbiton with his firm, and my other brother had received his call-up papers and was due to go off for RAF training. It was decided that I could not remain in the house alone and since my resistance was now at a low ebb, I gave in.

One day, we were watching a 'Dog Fight' taking place overhead when a plane went hurtling to the ground on fire. We could not tell whether it was one of theirs or ours. We then saw a parachute descending, which landed in the field opposite our bungalow. In no time at all, about half a dozen evacuated Londoners, who had been helping out the local farmer, appeared with pitchforks and various other weapons. It transpired that the pilot was in fact a Canadian — had he been a German, I dread to think what might have happened.

I have since felt so guilty, because he stood by the side of the road outside our house, waiting for the police to pick him up. That was the procedure, and he was not allowed to talk to anybody. He was burnt in the face and limped, and we just stood around and stared. Why, oh why, did I not pop indoors and make him a quick cup of tea, or even a cold drink, or offer him a cigarette? I have always felt bad about it.

I was offered a position in the Telephone Manager's office, and my aunt and uncle felt I would be better off going to live with them in Tunbridge Wells to avoid the long journey to work each day. So, despite all my efforts, I was now an evacuee.

What was it like to be one of these? One was grateful for the hospitality and care, but the feeling of being there under sufferance was always present together with the worry and anxiety for those in London, especially as the nightly sound of the bombers on their way reminded one. Looking back, I sometimes think that it was more difficult to have a break from London, because one had to get one's nerve back when returning. I remained in Tunbridge Wells for just over a year. My parents had moved to Surbiton in the late summer, where I later joined them.

I was to be an evacuee on two more occasions before the war was over, firstly for the birth of my daughter, when I was in Surrey for seven weeks, and then, when the doodlebugs were at their height, I was persuaded to take my one year-old daughter to my aunt and uncle in Bedford, where we stayed for about three months.

Margaret (standing end left) with friends
from work in Tunbridge Wells, 1941.

DOREEN KNIGHTS

I was twelve years old when the war started, and therefore old enough to understand what was happening. The thought of leaving parents, brother and sisters seemed unimportant compared with the adventure that lay ahead as we set off for school on the 2nd. September 1939. After roll call, we assembled in the playground, each wearing a luggage label tied to our button hole, bearing our name and the name of the school, but no address. We then walked the mile or so to our local railway station.

We crammed on to the platform, and saw our relatives waiting outside the fence. They had no idea where we were going, nor how long it would be before they saw us again. My brother was also there with his firm's camera. He had recently started work for a local photographer, and took snaps of us all waiting for the train.

<table>
<tr><td colspan="2">

4.—The " School " Party.

Each school, including all departments on its site, will form a unit for evacuation and will be known as " the school party." Each department of the school will be kept together within the party with modifications as follows:—

(1) Children will march in squads of 50 Children of a family, from whichever department of the school, will be in the same squad. If a school party has to be divided because the whole party cannot be taken in the same train, it will be arranged that complete squads will be entrained.

(2) Heads of departments will arrange for each squad to be in the charge of a teacher, assisted by a suitable number of other teachers or helpers.

5.—The School Number.

The school number is of the greatest importance. It is to be used on armlets, labels, etc., and should be quoted in correspondence from the Reception Area. The number of your school is on the front page of this letter.

</td></tr>
</table>

Doreen Knights (nee Spicer) looking out of train window at Eltham Station.

The moment the train left, we devoured the sandwiches, which were supposed to be for lunch, and then felt very hungry for the rest of the journey. We were only allowed into the corridor, in the company of a teacher, when we needed the toilet. Those poor teachers must have walked miles by the time we reached our destination, as we kept wanting to go because it broke the boredom of the journey, which seemed endless although it was only about sixty miles.

We tumbled out of the train when it finally stopped at the small seaside town of Deal. We were then marched into a big hall, and told to stand at one end. Each child was handed a tin of corned beef and a bar of chocolate. Lots of adults who had been waiting, suddenly surged forward and began choosing the children they wanted, or rather had been requested to accept.

The children went off in twos or threes, until just one child was left....me! Luckily one foster parent was persuaded to take a third child, and that was that. The poor woman had no children of her own, but there she was, landed with three growing girls of very different temperaments. However, being a Scot, she managed to cope extremely well, being firm but kind. Once we had carried out our respective tasks for the day, we were free to do as we pleased within accepted limits.

Next morning, we met our friends on the beach at half past ten, all talking excitedly about our billets. Suddenly the air raid siren wailed out over the town, and we all ran for the safety of our new homes. The war had started.

After initial skirmishes with the local children, who had been compelled to give up part of their school to us, most of us settled into the life of the community. We had occasional weekends at home, and it was on one of these that we were all summoned back to Deal.

Since the evacuation of our troops from Dunkirk, the town was no longer considered a safe place to be. Invasion was a serious threat, and we were to be re-evacuated to somewhere safer. Once again, we packed up and bade fond farewells to our 'foster parents', before embarking for the unknown.

There wasn't the same excitement this time. We all began to understand the seriousness of the situation, and felt apprehensive about our families in London as well as our new found adopted ones in Deal.

After an interminable train journey across the southern part of the country, we went through the Severn Tunnel. I thought that meant it was seven miles long! We finally found ourselves at Newport station in Monmouthshire. Then buses took us to Rhiwderin, a mining village that consisted of virtually one street. Again, we were shepherded into a hall to be chosen by the local residents, and taken home by them.

I was lucky, a childless couple took me in, and looked after me as their own. My closest friend, Margy, was taken, along with another girl, to the village shop people. I thought she had it made! The shop had lots of sweets and plenty of food. Later, she told me she never had a cooked meal, except for Sundays, although the rest of the family ate well. They also had to spend any spare time serving in the shop, or keeping their living quarters clean.

My billet was idyllic. I was well fed and well cared for, and free to take the dog for walks, or visit friends once homework was done. The only condition was that I attended church three times each Sunday, and helped at table when the vicar came for high tea.

The house had wooden slats for doors, with latches that rattled in a high wind. They always had a blazing fire all day, which was only dampened down overnight. It was snug and warm. The toilet was outside, but under a covered passage-way. The trip was made eventful by having to take a hurricane lamp for light, and by the fact that for some obscure reason, they always had nursery rhyme toilet paper!

They were kind people, I was given good food, fresh eggs, and even homemade jam. I also had my heart's desire, a dog to take out and care for. It all added up to making me a very happy and contented evacuee.

At school in Rhiwderin. Doreen is on the second row right of the Master.

PAMELA LYNE

1940 is a long time ago, so for someone with a bad memory anyway, I've had to think very hard, but I do recall easily the exciting journey to the country on a train with the other children, arriving at Chard Junction and going into a huge shed place that smelled of milk and then being segregated from my friends because I had a big red cross on my label which was tied to my coat, due to the fact that I had been in contact with chicken pox.

After a few days spent in a big house (which must have been a sort of army hospital because the patients wore blue uniforms), I was taken to Chard and billeted on a very old lady, Miss Hawker, in a tiny house (two up, two down) in Duck Lane. There was no gas or electricity, so we used candles and Miss Hawker cooked on a big black stove thing. My bedroom was very tiny and as a small eight-year-old, I couldn't see out of the window as it was too high for me. The lavatory was at the end of a long path in the back garden — one in a row of others — which had a horrible smell hanging over it, so I had to hold my nose!

I must have told someone that I was unhappy because I was collected from Duck Lane and walked to a few streets away to Church Street where Mr and Mrs Miller (soon to be known as Uncle Stan and Aunty Linda) seemed very pleased to see me, and very soon afterwards, I was joined by my younger sister, Jessica, now recovered from her chicken pox. She was only six, and can't remember this, but like me she can recall only being allowed jam on one piece of bread at tea-time, and being taken on some Sundays to the seaside (Charmouth or Seaton) in Uncle Stan's Austin 7, when there was petrol to be had. I did have a secret fear that I might forget what my mother looked like.

The Millers never had children of their own except us, and we have kept in touch. Both Jessica and I have taken our respective families to Chard when we have visited the West Country. Aunty Linda died just a few years ago, but we often speak to 'Uncle' on the telephone, and he has a very special place in our affections.

Please read Stanley Miller's story with this.

Stanley Miller, Mrs Elgood (Pamela's mother), Mrs. Miller, Jessica and Pamela (chin on hand).

JOAN MARRIOTT

In September 1939, I was one of the thousands of evacuees who set off from Surrey Docks Station for the country. At the time, I was attending Rotherhithe New Road School and, having just passed the Junior County Scholarship, I was due to start at Lewisham Prendergast when war was imminent. I therefore went away with my school in Rotherhithe (nick-named R.N.R. Red Nose Robbers!).

After what seemed an eternity, I remember arriving at Polegate Station in Sussex. We alighted there and all had to board many buses, arriving at the Village Hall in Hailsham.

After being housed twice and not being able to settle, I finished up in the house of Edna and Charlie Hayler in Hailsham. They were wonderful to me. It was a difficult time for me as my father had died in 1938 and my mother was working in London. I had no brothers and sisters and it was a very lonely time for me.

I must now say that, despite the loss of life, the war was instrumental in making life-long friends.

I stayed with Edna and Charlie from September 1939 until June 1940, travelling each day to Bexhill and attending the Roan School. The Christmas of 1939, I came back to London just for the holiday and I remember Edna travelling up to Victoria on the coach with me before handing me over to my Grandmother.

Joan and her mother in 1940.

After Christmas I returned to Hailsham and oh! what fun — the Common Pond opposite where I was staying was frozen and we evacuees had a wonderful time with our old shoes on and making the most fantastic slides on the Pond. There was even some ice skating which I had never seen before.

June 1940 was upon us and, with the fall of France, we were again on the move, this time to Peniel, a little village four miles outside Carmarthen. Another new school for me, this time, Carmarthen County Girls School.

I spent two years in South Wales on a farm in Peniel with a Mr and Mrs Evans. Gradually, by 1942, the evacuees were finding their way back to London and I too returned home. I am sorry to say I never kept in touch with Mr and Mrs Evans.

But Edna and Charlie in Hailsham, yes. They came up to London for my wedding in 1951. We have spent holidays with them over the years. They welcomed my children — John and Ann — and John has spent many a happy time with them fishing on the marshes between Hailsham and Pevensey.

The Haylers attended the weddings of John and Ann in 1979 and now my grandchildren are popping in. My husband and I became very attached to Edna and Charlie who provided a home for me in 1939. In 1985 we bought a caravan at Norman's Bay, about six miles from Hailsham, and so my husband and I are now able to call in more regularly. They say it is the best day's work we ever did.

They still live in the same little house that I remember so well as a child. Edna is still a wonderful cook at the age of 83 and Charlie still keeps in touch with his friends and is forever helping out. Truly, they are a wonderful couple. My husband and I think the world of them. We collect them sometimes and bring them down to the caravan. We spent their Golden Wedding with them a few years ago.

This is just to say thank you to Edna and Charlie Hayler whom, but for the war, we would never have met. They have proved life-long friends to me and all my family. Some good did come out of that dreadful war — and the friendship formed between them and their 'little evacuee' will surely last forever. We shall be seeing them again shortly as soon as we open up the caravan again.

The village of Hailsham where Joan stayed.

Boys from St. Georges C. of E. School, Battersea, stooking barley in Pembrokeshire.

OLIVE MARTIN

My daughter was only fifteen months old when evacuation time came. We were all told to go to Hornsey station but we did not know where we were going. A lot of our mothers and relatives came to see us off, but it must have been terrible for them because they did not know where we were going either. I had a big haversack on my back. I did not know quite what to take with me of course because I did not know how long we were going to be away.

We were on this crowded train and my little daughter was very heavy. She was just beginning to be able to walk, but I had her on reins most of the time. A very kind lady gave Lorna some chocolate in the train. Eventually we came to a little station in Sandy in Bedfordshire. We got out and we were all taken into what I think was the coal yard, it was all cobbles. I could not hold Lorna for very long and she sat down in the coal with chocolate on her face and all down her coat.

There were a lot of organisers waiting for us with lists of people who said that they would take the children and their mothers. My name was not called out, so I stood there in this courtyard and the cars drove away with a lot of the other people. Then there were just a few of us left. A man, whom I knew afterwards as Mr. Portman, one of the chief organisers, said 'We are going to take you to the Church hall. We can try to find accommodation for you from there.'

We did have a cup of tea when we got to the Church hall which was more than welcome after the train journey. Lorna and most of the babies were getting fretty by then, out of their normal routine. However, it seemed that they had not got an address for me. Mr.Portman told me afterwards that he looked at me and I looked so tired. Lorna was crying by then and so, in spite of the fact that he had an eight year old daughter of his own and two neices about the same age staying with them, he thought his wife would not be able to say 'No' if he took me home to his house.

They were so kind to us. However, I think Mrs Portman was a little bit dismayed when she first saw this mother and baby. The girls, of course, were thrilled to bits with the baby to look after. They had a big doll's pram which they thought Lorna would fit into. When my mother knew where we were she did eventually come down with my own pram.

Baby Lorna Martin at Sandy in Bedfordshire.

I stayed with them for some time. They were very busy people. They had a couple of fish and chip shops. Apart from the ordinary chores which I did anyway, I went to help them a couple of evenings a week in one of the fish and chip shops, just serving people at the counter. I do remember that my coat for ever after seemed to smell of fish and chips.

After about six to eight weeks, when there had not been any raids in London, I went home again. I stayed home until I had my son. He was born on top of a Morrison table shelter! My husband had been in a reserved occupation at first but then he was called up and he had to go.

He went to North Africa. My little son was only three months old then, and he did not see his father until he was nearly five when my husband eventually came home. He did not really get to know his father because my husband was only home for two years when he died.

Olive with her children Lorna and Christopher in 1943.
Photo was taken to send to her husband in the army in Africa.

One day they bombed Hornsey station which was very close to my parents' house where we were staying. My father came home in the lunch time because he had heard that they had bombed the station and he said, 'I can't stand it any longer; you must go away.'

My brother lived in Derbyshire then and so we went privately and stayed with him and his wife. While I was there my sister−in−law went into hospital to have her second baby. There was only two months between their daughter Jacqueline and my son Christopher; they were more like twins and I used to take them about in the pram, one at one end and one in the other.

I had been there some time and the neighbours must have seen me coming and going and knew that I was an evacuee mother. Now some evacuee mothers did not have a very good reputation. There was a sweet shop near my brother's house where I used to go and buy sweets for the children. One day, soon after her baby was born, I was in the shop and the lady in the shop asked me how Mrs Smith was. I said, 'My brother came home with the news last night that he has another daughter'. 'Oh,' she said 'he's your brother!' Goodness knows what kind of stories were going around about me! They must have thought, that poor woman, Mrs Smith, is in hospital having a baby and that evacuee woman is there 'looking after' her husband.

SMALL CHILDREN'S RESPIRATOR

INSTRUCTIONS FOR PUTTING ON

To put the respirator on to a child:—

1. Stand the child in front of you with its back towards you so that its head rests against your body.

2. See that the hook and eye on the head harness straps are undone.

Put your left thumb under the bottom and middle straps on the left side of the head harness, and your right thumb under the bottom and middle straps on the right side, and hang the respirator from your two thumbs.

3. Catch the chin of the respirator under the child's chin and then stretch the head harness over the head.

4. See that the respirator is straight on the child's face and that the chin is properly in position. Then join the hook and eye on the two bottom straps to secure the respirator in place.

NOTE.—Most children quickly learn to put on the respirator themselves. They should be taught to do it in the way described above.

MARIANNE MASON

I was evacuated to Ascot in Berkshire for part of the war and we lived in a gardener's cottage. This was situated in large grounds belonging to 'the big house', and was right next to the Royal Ascot Hotel. My father's firm evacuated the London office staff to work from the big house and my mother, grandmother, brother and I were allowed to live in the gardener's cottage. It was quite big and had stables attached on the side. There were no horses in the stables, but we were allowed to play there if it was raining.

I went to the village infants school, which was quite a long way to go down a country lane, and I was taken every day by Jean, who lived nearby and was about three years older than me. I remember there were a lot of soldiers stationed near the Ascot Race Course. They used to wave to us as we went to school, and I was very frightened of so many soldiers and their huge tanks.

I used to go to the big house to play with Jean. She also lived in a gardener's cottage, which was in even bigger grounds. Her father was the gardener and she was a country child. She had lived in Ascot all her life. Once we paddled in the duck pond and got told off!

While we were there, my brother Brian was taken ill and the doctor laid him on the table to examine him. I was frightened of the doctor and of not knowing what was wrong with my brother. When Brian got better I can remember him smashing my dolls. I was screaming my head off and

my mum really told Brian off. Once, when Mum was ironing, the iron fused and she burnt her arm. She rushed out into the garden and plunged her arm into the cold water butt. I was very frightened again.

We came back to London and we stayed at my grandmother's house in Blake Avenue, Barking because our own house was let. One night, Nan was unable to find her way to the shelter and Mum was trying to find her in the dark. The air raid siren had gone and Mum rushed Brian and me

Marianne (back row right) with her cousins.

136

into the air raid shelter. Nan was making her own way down the garden and in the dark she missed the shelter entrance. She found her way instead to the garden shed. Brian and I came out of the shelter to see what was happening and Mum was frantically trying to help Nan to find her way and also ushering us back into the shelter at the same time.

I was aware of missing my schooling and feeling inadequate beside the other children. I had to wear secondhand shoes and I hated them. I said that they were not comfortable so then I got a new pair. I can remember having only one present for Christmas for two years running.

We were re—evacuated to a farm in Bury St. Edmunds, Suffolk. I went with my mother, my brother, grandmother and two cousins. We lived with Aunt Florrie and Uncle George and old Gran. Old Gran was my great grandmother and a real old Tartar! She was about ninety years old and always dressed entirely in black.

We had to collect our water from the well, and I was fascinated by how far down we had to send the bucket. I had skin spots like huge mosquito bites and I had to go to see a skin specialist. The trouble was caused by drinking well water. From then on, I was only allowed to drink boiled water, and I hated it. The toilet was down the bottom of the garden and there was an awful cesspool right next to it!

We had fun playing on the farm. We used to play in the hay stacks and I always used to go home with no bottom in my knickers. I liked riding on the horse and cart too, when the farm workers were gathering in the harvest. I loved to see the pigs but I hated their smell! I traced a picture of a pig in a tracing book at school. Brian always had to be chased to school and my mother always waved an umbrella at him. I liked playing in the playground and watching the dragonflies, and the bats fly in the church tower. I can remember making a tiny doll's crib from dock leaves, folded up and sewn together, and also using old stockings, plaited, to make dolls' hair.

In conclusion, I seem to have spent a lot of my time during the war years feeling frightened, but I was not really old enough to know why.

Marianne with her little brother Brian.

RUBY MAW

During the height of the war, approaching Christmas time, when I attended a village school, I overheard my elderly form mistress, a delightfully kind and motherly soul, say to the mistress from an adjoining classroom, "Poor little things, we must do what we can for them. It's probably the last Christmas they will ever see." I can't quite remember what they did to make the approach to Christmas special, but I do recall that we were all given a chocolate coated digestive biscuit — a very rare treat in those days!

JOYCE MILAN

1945 began with heavy falls of snow, and as we saw the start of the year, we also saw the first signs of peace after six years of war. For me it was also a sign of new life as my first child was about to enter the world. Flying bombs were still a hazard and, without any warning, there would be a sudden explosion and more poor souls would lose their homes, their loved ones or even their life. Our forces were now on French soil and pushing the enemy back, but pockets of resistance remained and therefore we were still under threat.

On my routine visit to The British Hospital for Mothers and Babies in Samuel Street, Woolwich, it was confirmed that my baby would soon be due, and because of the danger from 'doodle-bugs', it was suggested that I, along with others, should depart on 4th. January for 'Moatlands' in Paddock Wood, to rest and await the birth.

Four of us were taken by car, a rare event as no one had cars in those days, along snow-covered country lanes, through the hop fields. Miles from any town, we eventually pulled up at a large country mansion, and entered into a palatial hallway. It was beautifully oak panelled, and ahead was a polished oak staircase, guarded at the bottom by two splendid suits of armour. The walls to the top floor were covered with paintings of past generations of the owners of the house, the Podmores. The house was loaned to The British Hospital, to house expectant mothers, by the family, who had gone abroad away from the war.

A Sister sat at her desk behind a screen in the hallway, and we registered our names. We were taken up the oak staircase, past the 'labour room' and doctors' room, to the 'waiters room', where we were to sleep while we waited to give birth. It was a bare room with six beds and a table and chair. The outlook was wonderful, with fields and trees for miles around and not a house or human being in sight. I once saw a horse, and spread the news to all the others. It was a sensation.

We were not allowed to wear our own nightclothes and were issued with well worn coarse linen Victorian nightdresses with lace edged collars and cuffs. The beds were the most uncomfortable I have ever known, they sank in the middle from months of supporting the weight of large expectant mums, and groaned at each turn.

We were told the large bottle of liquid paraffin in the corner was for us, and that we should take a tablespoonful every morning. We took turns to collect the early morning cocoa. This meant going down the back spiral staircase, which had been the servants' stairs, to the kitchen. It was only available at five o'clock in the morning. I remember going down those stairs on bitter cold mornings, in the dark and half asleep, only to be rewarded with a jug of luke warm cocoa. It was horrid. Tea was not supplied as it was rationed. Breakfast consisted of 'gruel', a kind of porridge and one slice of toast with a scrape of margarine on it.

The rest of the day we had nothing to do. Word was passed around that we could go for a walk outside the home to collect sticks to light our fire, so we began to do this. We gathered as much as we could, but the sticks hadn't time to dry out and were green and wet. So, necessity being the mother of invention, we found the liquid paraffin a boon as, when we poured it on the sticks, they burned and we had a bit of heat. One nurse remarked what good girls we were to take our paraffin so regularly.

We were certainly not living in paradise at 'Moatlands', and yet we had such fun. One of the focal points of hilarity was the bathroom. There was a ceramic toilet bowl decorated in blue and white, a washbasin with an enormous hole in it that did not hold water, and an antiquated bath with no enamel on the base. It was a common occurrence to go to the bathroom and find one girl trying to get hot water for a bath, another washing her hair in a bowl in the hand basin, and some poor girl stuck on the toilet, having been dosed up with castor oil, feeling humiliated.

To pass the time, I attended chapel twice a day. This was taken by a little Sister who we called 'Snow White' because she had short white hair. The entire staff of 'Moatlands' were women, and the doctor, Dr. Groves, was a lovely lady. They did everything necessary to run the home including the manual work.

A new arrival of expectant mums came in four days after me, and I recognised one of them as a girl I had seen each day, and sometimes walked home with, when we worked for the Ministry of Defence. Her name was Mary O'Shea, and we became very close friends. Almost all our husbands were in the services. Vic, my husband got leave as much as possible, and travelled to 'Moatlands' to visit me. The weather was atrocious with thick heavy snow. We were cut off for days on end, so Vic found a farm in Brenchley to stay overnight. He obtained eggs for Mary and me at the farm, a real treat, and walked the rest of the way in snow up to his knees. The Sister said to me, 'I don't know how your husband does it in this weather.' He used to arrive, looking like a snowman, but very handsome in his Chief Petty Officer's Naval uniform.

When Vic couldn't visit me, he used to telephone me. Our phone was in the bottom hallway, so, knowing he was in a call box, I would rush to it. The Sisters feared that I would slip on the stairs and collide with the suits of armour. I reckoned there were ancient corpses of Podmores inside that armour and some of the girls were scared to get up in the night for fear of this.

I was 'waiting' for three weeks, longer than most. The doctors attempted to induce the baby, which meant a morning of hot castor oil, enemas, and hot baths. I was disappointed to have to wait another week when the same procedure took place, this time with success. It was snowing hard when Joy was born but the 'theatre', as they called it, was warm, brightly lit, and cheerful. As soon as I had been attended to and given a beautiful cup of sweet tea, little 'Snow White' asked me if I would like to pray. She knelt at the side of the bed. I can still see her, her straight white hair under the flowing white traditional nurse's head-dress, kneeling to give thanks.

We were kept in bed for two weeks after the baby was born, bound very tightly around the stomach, and we had to sleep on our stomachs. A bed

Joyce and her baby girl Joy, born in the evacuated British Hospital for Mothers and Babies in Kent.

was kept for me downstairs next to Mary, who had just given birth to Meira, and we had plenty of laughs together. Her husband, Mike, sent her parcels, and one day the Sister said, 'I hope that doesn't contain food.' It was a rule that we were all treated equally with no extras for anyone regardless of financial status. Well, it certainly did contain food. There were pigs' trotters, dry biscuits and fruit!

One of my problems was the inability to pass water, so they lifted me out of bed each day to sit in a pot, a large blue decorated bowl on a three legged stand about three feet high. Whilst behind a screen one day, attempting to perform, the pipes in the lavatory, at the end of the ward, burst due to a thaw in the weather, and water gushed into the ward. They all said they thought it was me managing to pass water!

We had a few sad moments. One of our girls had been notified that her R.A.F. husband was missing, presumed dead. When she had a lovely son she cried bitterly for two days. When our babies were born, we all sent telegrams of joy to our husbands, but she no longer had a husband to tell. We all felt for her and shared her grief. She was quite wealthy and found our 'roughing it' routine hard to accept, but she took it like the lady she was. We all liked her a lot.

The British Hospital for Mothers and Babies had a worldwide reputation as the finest training establishment. Any nurse, lucky enough to train there, was well set up for future positions. We had the greatest admiration for the staff, and were unanimous in saying we were cared for devotedly. I felt completely secure in their care, they had never lost a mother, and while I was there, never a baby. Our very basic conditions were not due to lack of care by the hospital but, as we always said, 'C'est la guerre!'

When I left 'Moatlands' for home, I had been there five weeks. The following July, and the war over, I had my son, Peter, at the same hospital but back in their original building in Samuel Street, Woolwich. I still received the same loving care as at 'Moatlands' but not in such primitive conditions.

STANLEY MILLER

Imagine the time and place. A little market town in the south west corner of Somerset. The population was then about five thousand. At the beginning of the war, we were a young couple rising thirty years of age, childless, living in a small cottage and with very little money. Not that that mattered a lot because, what with rationing and general shortages, there was very little to buy anyway. About this time, evacuees were arriving in droves.

A Welfare Officer called on everyone in the village to see if they would be prepared to offer a home. It was more a question of, 'We want volunteers, you, you and you!' We agreed to take two little girls and we waited with interest and not a little aprehension.

The first to arrive was a little girl of seven or eight answering, rather timidly to the name of Pamela Elwood. We later learned she had already been evacuated to Chard but was being transferred to us from the other home where she was apparently rather unhappy. There followed in a day or so her sister called Jessica, who when asked, volunteered the information, 'I thall thoon be thix!'.

We felt very sorry for these poor little mites and resolved to make them feel loved. This was not as simple as it may sound, because although we thought them little angels, they were not always angelic! We had to learn all about the capricious ways of children and even sometimes, their cunning little tricks. Of course, all kinds of children were evacuated. Some were good and some were little horrors. My Mother was very unfortunate with her evacuees, whose escapades worried the life out of her.

After nearly half a century, most of my memories are becoming a little hazy, but a few incidents come readily to mind. For instance, Jessie fell down and shed a front tooth, temporarily increasing her slight lisp. Another day both girls came home after mixing with an unfortunate little friend and this resulted in a minor invasion of visitors in their hair. This caused 'Auntie Linda', my wife, major concern and prompted immediate drastic action.

Pam sometimes became a problem and needed a firm hand. She went through a phase whereby she refused to eat one thing after another, much to Auntie's concern. I said 'O.K. Pam, compile a list of all the things you dislike, because I would hate to force you to eat something you dislike. We will not offer it to you again.' This rule was rigidly adhered to for a couple of days and soon it was 'Perhaps I'll try a little of that, Uncle' which meant that her appetite improved enormously. Thinking back on it, I realise how difficult it was for Auntie Linda to provide meals with the limited rations, dried egg powder and substitute foods, but we seemed to survive.

Jessica was a more happy-go-lucky child and quite imperturbable. We often used to laugh about an incident when she was banished from the dining table for some forgotten misdemeanour, and was made to sit at a side table. A couple of minutes silence ensued shattered by a little voice shouting 'This is the one o'clock news and this is Alvar Liddell reading it'. Actually she pronounced it 'Aba Diddel'. The curious thing was that although I was the one that did all the reprimanding, it was my knee that they wished to sit on.

Life was not all reprimands, but when little things went wrong we felt responsible for moulding their characters. So that when they left us they would be at least as good as when they came to us. We could, of course, never guarantee their safety but felt they were much safer with us than in London. I remember one night when there was the tail end of a raid over the town. I grabbed the girls from their beds and carried them down and put them under the dining table. This had enormously strong legs and a very thick top. I thought it would at least protect them from falling masonry.

I suppose it could be said that whilst we were trying to teach the girls the right way to live, we were, ourselves, learning about life. I do know that when the girls eventually returned home, a great void was left in our hearts. Throughout the years we have kept in touch and I thank God for the privelege of knowing Pam and Jessica.

Please read Pamela Lyne's story with this.

Pamela, aged eight, and Jessica, aged six-and-a-half, at Chard in Somerset, February 1941.

JOSIE MOIR

I was evacuated to Sevenoaks with my school from Camberwell. I was twelve years old, going on thirteen. We arrived at the railway station at Sevenoaks, and were sorted into different catagories. We were put in cattle pens! The teachers were standing there, looking horrified. It wasn't so bad for us twelve or thirteen year olds, but there were little five year old toddlers put in the cattle pens. Then we were all taken into the church hall, where everyone was given a carrier bag with half a pound of chocolate, a tin of evaporated milk, a packet of cornflakes, and a tin of corned beef. Then the people came in to choose who they wanted.

My friend, Olive, and I were the first to be chosen. We were taken by the vicar's wife. She took us to the vicarage, and showed us into the kitchen. She said, 'We can't afford servants, so I hope you'll help us with the housework.' We were left with the cook, and given a meal of corned beef, from our carrier bag supplies, and mashed potato.

The next morning all the silver and brass was put on the kitchen table on newspaper, and Olive and I had to sit there cleaning it. The other children had got together, and were all standing round the gate calling for us. The vicar's wife said, 'I'm sorry but they've got a few jobs to do, but they'll be out later.' There were two baths we had to clean, and a sink, and we had to help with the washing up which was left from their dinner the night before. We weren't allowed out at all!

There was a helper called Mrs Smith who had been evacuated with us, billeted in the house opposite with Mr and Mrs Ascot who were retired schoolteachers. The other children told her that we were not allowed out, and had to do all the chores, and on the Monday we were taken away,' and billeted with Mr and Mrs Ascot. Mr Ascot said, 'There's more Christianity in my front garden than there is in that vicarage.'

Mrs Smith then slept on a camp bed, and Olive and I had the double bed that she'd been sleeping in. Then we got scabies, and that was awful. Mrs smith eventually went back home because her husband missed her so much. Mr and Mrs Ascot were really too old to look after us by themselves, and she was an invalid, so we went to live with Mrs Walton. Then we got scabies again, and everything had to be fumigated. She

didn't like this, she was quite upper class, so, in the end, the billeting officer took us in, and we lived in her house.

She had a cook, who we stayed with all the time. As we were further away from school, we were too far to come home for dinner, so she used to do us sandwiches. They were broad beans in bread with a sprinkling of gravy, and by the time we ate them they were cold and wet! From that day to this, I don't like broad beans at all.

There were only two classes at school which was held in the church hall. Our own teachers had been evacuated with us of course, but we didn't have proper schooling, we just sat around talking most of the time. They did teach us how to write letters home.

Sometime in August, Olive and I were sitting on a fence and suddenly there were Spitfires and German fighter planes overhead, and they seemed to be machine gunning us. This was the first thing we'd ever seen of the war. We ran towards a great big house with a hedge in front of it, and ran into the lodge. We put the settee up against the wall, and got behind it. I don't know what we thought would happen. It was rather exciting at the time, and eventually I wrote home and told mum about it.

The next thing I knew, my brother-in-law hired a car, and came down to fetch us. Of course not many people had cars in those days, and not many people knew how to drive, but his job was to drive a fire engine. He took us home. My mother had been in touch with Olive's parents, and they said that she'd better come home as well.

It was September and the bombing had started in London. Mother and I used to stay in the shelter all day long with blankets and her bag of treasures which contained insurance policies and photographs. The bombing got worse, so we went to stay with a friend of my mother's who lived in Somerset.

When I was fifteen, I came home and worked in Dorothy Perkins as a cashier. In effect, I left school when I was twelve because I got very little schooling in Sevenoaks, and none in London or Somerset. I don't look back on my evacuation with great pleasure. Some people found their feet, but we were Londoners and looked down on. I really didn't make any friends at all.

Boys from Creek Road LCC School Greenwich, evacuated to Llandissilio in Pembrokeshire, bringing in farm horses and helping

ALAN MORGAN

I was six years old when I was evacuated and I think we were taken down by car. I was not evacuated with the school, but to relations in Newport Pagnall. It was quite a small place but there were a lot of us staying there. There was me and my sister, and four cousins and their mothers; their fathers were in the Army. My father and mother stayed at home, and they came down at weekends. Being the only boy living with all those girls must have produced something in me that has made me very quiet and wanting to keep myself to myself.

We went to the local school and it was girls and boys separate. I think I enjoyed school. I remember doing a painting of all this farm equipment and getting a prize for it. I refused to have school dinners though, and I was the only one that did. They were very fond of dishing up cheese and potato pie and I couldn't stand that so I went home for dinner. I remember messing my pants quite a bit and when they ran out of pants they used to put me into girl's knickers. And I remember getting stuck in the mud and running home crying because I had left my 'Wellies' in the mud.

At Christmas we had a pillowcase each and our parents came down for Christmas. One of the most vivid memories I have is when my cousin went into the Navy and we had a big party. We children sat upstairs listening to them all. I was not bothered about the war, it was just like living at home because I was with the family and it wasn't like being away from home like others. The only time it affected me was when a plane came over and dropped its bomb in a field. I can remember having to be quiet when the 'News' was on because my Uncle Bill wanted it on, and you had to keep dead quiet then!

I can also remember little things like eating 'cow cake'. I used to love that stuff. It was bran and oil and vitamins and apparently lots of children in the war used to eat it. It was quite delicious and we used to eat it because you could not get sweets in the war, though I can remember getting 'Maltesers' at the beginning of the war. And my mother used to send us down big red juicy American apples.

We went home just before the Flying Bombs started and I remember that part clearer than when I was evacuated. Hearing them come over and then suddenly stop. And putting up the blackout. And I remember going down the air raid shelter on this particular night. Because we used to sleep in our beds indoors, usually, but this night we went down the air raid shelter, and it was just as well we did because next morning when we went indoors the wardrobe had fallen across my bed and I would have been under that.

JOAN MORGAN

I remember going to Redhill and being billeted on this young couple, Mr and Mrs Fuller, about a week before Neville Chamberlain made his announcement. I must have been about five or six. There was another young girl there too, called Jean. We listened to the wireless broadcast in the other room, and I think it was after the broadcast that they announced that they were going to test the air raid siren so that people would know what the difference was between an alert and the all clear. We waited for that and when it came we all had to get under the table and sit there. Mrs Fuller was crying her eyes out. We sat there until the all clear, and then it went again in the evening and we had to wait in the passage until the all clear came. That was about bed time. Mr Fuller must have joined the Army soon after because he was not around for too long.

I can remember having German Measles whilst I was there and my Mum and Dad came down. Mum took me home for a holiday because there was nothing much happening. While I was at home, Mrs Fuller wrote to say that she could not have me back because she had a little one of her own on the way. But she had found another billet for me down the road with another woman who had a little girl called Dorothy. So I went and stayed with them.

My new billet was opposite a tin chapel and they were very strictly religious people. On Sunday afternoons we had to go into the parlour and it had a green chenille table cloth on the table and an aspidistra in the middle. We were given an allotted chair to sit on and we had to sit there and listen to the Bible being read. After that she would go outside and get the tea and I remember that one time I was so bored that I got up and I must have started playing with the fringe around the chenille table cloth because all the fringe came undone and I was not very popular.

I cannot remember if that was the time I was sent up to bed, but I was always being sent upstairs to bed for being naughty and I was so annoyed because I seemed to be spending all my time in the bedroom and not getting my tea or supper that I pulled out all the drawers and opened all the cupboards and wardrobes, tipping everything all over the place. I stripped the bed and scattered the clothes everywhere. I used to stand at the window and look out and the boy next door called Gilbert used to wave at me because I was always spending my time in the bedroom.

My mother came down to see me. We had been asked to wear white clothes and a red, white and blue ribbon to school and to take a flag to wave because it was going to be Empire Day, but my mum could not get me one. Dorothy who lived at the house was dressed up to the nines and I think I resented her because she was treated better than me.

My mother tried to get me with Gilbert's family next door because there were six or eight children there, but his mother had already agreed to take another child and could not have me. My mother had intended leaving me where I was, but I made such a fuss that she took me home to London.

I vaguely remember being at home and going to school for a while. Then school was evacuated again. We went along to the school and I had a black cycle bag with straps with all my things in that and a pink label tied on me and I carried my gasmask in a cardboard case with a bit of string on it bumping against your bum as you walked along with it.

Miss Bowler, "Auntie" to seven evacuees in an Oxfordshire village, gives each child 6d a week for a savings stamp.

We all lined up in the playground with our teachers. We had to march around the playground two or three times, with someone carrying the school banner with Kelvin Grove School on it. Then we marched out of the gates and down Kirkdale with all the people on either side of the road with parents crying. I can remember women crying and there was a band playing as well. We marched down to Sydenham station and I can remember being absolutely bewildered by it. That is one very lasting impression of it all. We crowded on to the station and there were all these trains. They were pushing kids on to trains as fast as they could. As fast as one train went out the next one came in. Goodness knows how we managed to stay together. I was not with my teacher but we got rounded up afterwards.

When we got to Waterloo Station, I remember all the photographers with flashing lights and cameras. We got on to a train at Waterloo but we did not know where we were going. We got off the train at Yeovil and then we were herded through into warehouses or sheds at the station. As you went through you were given a tin of corned beef, and a packet of tea and something else, it might have been sugar. You had to carry these with you and these were for the people that you went to stay with. We spent the night in church halls and then we went in coaches. We went to Winkleigh and how on earth I managed to meet up with my teacher again I don't know but she was certainly there when I got to Winkleigh.

We went into the village hall and we sat on benches and people came along and said 'I'll have that one and that one' pointing to us. The Billeting Officer ticked the children off on the list as they were chosen, putting the addresses down where they were going. I was one of the last to be chosen, along with a girl called Molly Shepherd, who was wearing a lavender coat and lavender beret. She looked very genteel sitting on the bench. We went off with a Mrs Knight walking for what seemed like miles and miles, though it was not terribly far really. There were no street lights.

When I went out the back door the next morning the garden seemed to me to be one mass of colour and tall plants.

I don't think I was there for very long because my sister Hazel was soon old enough to be evacuated and my parents wanted us to be together, but Mrs Knight could not keep both of us. My sister was not quite five and she came down with my father. A billet was found for us with Mrs Parker who lived in a thatched cottage called 'Melduns.' She was a lovely woman and he was a Postman. I think we stayed there about a year.

Some soldiers took over the empty cottage next door and when my Father came down to see us at Christmas he stayed with the soldiers next door. Mrs Parker took in as many as she could for Christmas dinner. I can remember us and all these soldiers sitting round this table at Christmas dinner. There must have been about eight or ten of them. The Parkers kept chickens and they had killed two or three for Christmas dinner. I remember I had a watch for Christmas because I had learned to tell the time.

All the Christmas presents were exchanged at the table and I can remember the soldiers giving me presents like cards, paper book marks and hair ribbons, small things like that. There was one particular soldier I remember, he was a very handsome young lad, though he seemed quite old to me, and he kept teasing me. I cannot remember what he was teasing me about, but I remember crying and my Father being upset because I did not realise that I was only being teased. That Christmas really sticks in my mind.

I remember one very upsetting experience. There was a big black and white cat called Queenie and she had kittens and it was the first time I had ever seen new born kittens. But they drowned them all except one, which was kept for Mrs Parker's mother, and I was very upset.

It was lovely in the country, you could wander where you liked. There was not much traffic, just horses and carts. I think it touched something in me and I loved it there.

The school was in the village hall until something could be sorted out. It was jam packed with children sitting at long trestle tables on benches. There was only one teacher with children ranging from five years old right the way up to thirteen years old. She sat up on the stage reading aloud from 'Dombey and Son' by Charles Dickens. I can remember having to do some writing and draw a picture about 'Dombey and Son' but I cannot remember much about the story.

I had a teacher there called Mrs Evans who was Welsh and she taught us all to card sheep's wool and spin it. We used to go out and collect sheep's wool from the hedges. We had to make our own spindles. I can remember the lanolin in the sheep's wool.

We had a Christmas party there and whilst the tea tables were being laid the children were sent outside for a breath of fresh air. What nobody had realised was that it had been snowing and the snow was a foot deep and that is the first time I can remember ever seeing really deep snow. I made friends with a girl called Stella Trennigan whose father owned a farm. It was the first time I had ever seen cows being milked and I was allowed to try to milk a cow. I can remember playing in the hay loft. We used to slide down the hay, and one particular time I was wearing a new dress and I tore it from top to bottom, and we spoiled the hay too. I enjoyed being a child in the country.

Mrs Parker could not cope with my sister any longer because she kept soiling herself and was being difficult to train and we moved on to Torrington. Mrs Parker was quite willing to keep me but not my small sister. But my father would not let us be parted so we went to a hostel. There were about twenty children there. The Matron was a real martinet and we did not like her very much. She really was foul. She should never have been in charge of children.

I remember her telling us that we were going to have a lovely jam tart with real cream for our pudding, which was very unusual because jam was rationed. But it would only be for those who ate all their dinner. I usually ate my food but that day it was tripe and onions and I could not eat it. To this day the thought of tripe and onions makes me feel ill! I was sent off to school in the afternoon, without my pudding, and the tripe and onions was dished up again for me at tea time. I still could not eat it and by now it was all cold and congealed. I was sent outside to sit in the corridor with the plate of tripe and made to eat it. As fast as she made me eat it I was vomiting it up again but she still made me eat it. Everbody else was sent off to bed and one of the hostel maids called Betty came out and she kept nipping a bit off and giving it to the cat to eat. A lot of it disappeared but the Matron soon twigged what had been going on.

It was such an awful place to stay in that we used to dawdle back to the hostel from school. You could not call it home. The only freedom we had at that place was whilst we were in school. The children were in two or three different schools and so that we would not be late back, she used to come and meet us and we had to march in twos in a crocodile to the other schools and then all march on a 'route march' back to the hostel. After we had had our tea everybody had to get down behind our chairs on our hands and knees and for about half an hour we would have to have a Bible reading and prayers. It was like a Victorian workhouse. On Saturdays and Sundays we also had a 'route march' around the golf course. The old witch with her walking stick.

One particular day I had been naughty and was not allowed to go out on the walk because I had been sent to bed. The Deputy Matron had a dog which was not allowed near the children, but she let it come up on my bed to keep me company. When the old witch came back and saw the dog hairs on the bed she wacked me with her walking stick through the bed clothes until I cried. I complained to my Dad and I was found another billet.

My sister and I were no longer together, but we were in the same village. I went to live in an isolated cottage which was five miles from the town and three miles from the school. I was desperately unhappy to start with and I did run away. But I did not get very far, only a couple of miles because I did not know in which direction I should have been going and I could not remember where the railway station was so I gave up and went back.

My sister had been billeted in another isolated cottage which was near a hamlet about the same distance from the school. We both attended the school and we used to meet there together during the school day. The headmaster there was Mr Anear and he had a daughter Fleur. That was a lovely school I really liked it there because I was a bright child and he used to tell me that. There was an old turtle stove there and in the winter months we never sat at our desks we used to go and sit round the stove. I learned to play stool ball at that school.

I remember going to Sunday school while we were there. We had to go on a three mile trip to Sunday school. The vicar there was a nice man too. We had a competition once to draw Noah's Ark and I knew that my drawing was the best but I did not get the prize. It went to a boy called Teddy.

Domestic Science lessons, in the open air in Llangadock in Carmarthenshire, for girls of Mitcham Lane School, Streatham. 149

While I was there I went for the first time to a Gymkhana. I did not know what a Gymkhana was and nobody would explain what was going to happen. I expected to see lots of sheep because it was going to be held in the field behind the village hall where there was always a lot of sheep. It was the first time I had ever been in a marquee and there was a wild flower competition. The prize winner was the one who had the greatest variety of flowers. I can remember all the great cart horses with their manes plaited and three bells on a head-dress like a tiara. The fur around the hooves had to be brushed out and fluffed.

I can remember watching the blacksmith working at the forge and thinking how cruel he was for cutting the hooves and burning on the hot horse shoes. I can still smell that smell! At the Gymkhana the local foxhound pack came out to do a display. I remember going to the hound kennels afterwards, seeing all the hounds and being amazed that they all lived there. I had thought that the hounds belonged to different people and just came together in the pack.

We had to walk five miles into Torrington, the nearest town on Saturday mornings to get the shopping. If you were ill the Doctor came out to visit you in his pony and trap with the whip sticking up at the side, and that used to fascinate me. The postman used to take all day delivering letters and he always used to stop and have his Sunday lunch with us.

This particular place really sealed my love of the countryside. I can remember seeing adders and glow worms for the first time and finding wild raspberries. I remember the smell of wild garlic down by the brook. The whole area used to stink of onions. We had to go and collect the milk from the nearest farm in a milk container with a loose lid.

One of the things I always wanted to do was Maypole dancing but the 'vaccies' were not allowed to do it because that was for the locals only. It was the town tradition so I was never allowed to learn.

My mother sent me a parcel once with Imperial Leather soap and some oranges in it. I don't know where she got it because that was practically unheard of in the war. We hardly had any rationing where I was living. We had our own apple trees and were almost self-sufficient. We kept chickens and the eggs had to go to market but you were allowed to keep

some of them back and it was more than the egg ration. I had not heard of dried egg until I went home at the end of the war. I used to have a boiled egg for breakfast every morning before I went to school.

I grew up on egg custard tarts. Mrs Baker used to put black currants into the egg custard tarts too. We used to have sticky gingerbread and lardy cakes as well. We never had school lunch. We used to take our own lunch and we used to take bacon and potato cakes for our mid-day meal, and an apple. The bacon and potato cakes were made with belly pork because we kept our own pigs and killed one twice a year. I can remember learning how to salt down the pork in these huge earthenware containers. It was kept in the scullery and that was the meat for the winter.

We used to go rabbiting every Saturday morning. We each had our rabbit holes to watch with nets over them. The ferret was sent in and then you had to wait for the rabbit to bolt into the nets. We also used to chase the rabbits in the corn fields. When the men cut the corn the area in the middle grew smaller and the rabbits used to stay there and then run out.

We also used to go potato planting and then later on potato picking. The school holidays during the war were split up into a fortnight in June for hay-making. Sometimes, if you were lucky, you had a ride on the hay cart or on the back of horse. Then you went back to school until the end of August and beginning of September because the children were wanted to help with the harvest. We used to go 'stooking' the sheaves in the fields. There were six sheaves to make a stook and if they were stooked properly there would be a hole though the middle. We children used to have a whale of a time going right through the middle of the stooks. Until we got told off for knocking them over.

At Christmas time we used to go out with Mr Baker to a plantation to find a Christmas tree and we would spend a long time choosing just the right one to dig up. We made all our own decorations with flour and water and salt. You made the dough into shapes and then you had to bake it hard and then paint it. We also used to use shells too. You could always get on one part of the beach to find shells. Paper was in short supply so we used to make our own decorations with what we could

Children from Deptford Park LCC School, Deptford, evacuated to Haverfordwest in Pembrokeshire, sawing logs on the estate where they are billeted.

find. We had candles to go up to bed with and oil lamps downstairs but if you were doing something special, like sewing or something like that, you could light a second oil lamp.

I used to like playing with the shells, making patterns with them. I used to play with used match sticks too making all sorts of shapes with them. I got a lot of pleasure out of that, and doing jig—saw puzzles too.

We had an outside loo which was a bucket that had to be emptied and I used to sit out there and read the squares of newspaper that were put out there to use.

Sometimes when we went to school, we used to go over Gaten's Hill and quite often there was a dog fight overhead. That used to frighten me. There were hundreds of little quarry places there and I used to hide in one of those because I was afraid that one of the shot down planes would fall on me. That was the nearest we ever came to the war apart from seeing the Home Guard. The Home Guard used to turn out once a month on a Sunday afternoon and show their prowess to the villagers. One particular time they had found a high explosive bomb and they set it off to show everyone what a bomb sounded like! It made everybody jump! Everybody had been able to look at it beforehand and it was a tiny little black thing about six inches long. Shades of 'Dad's Army!'

We had a huge playing field and one morning when we got to school a lot of the boys were there blowing up white balloons. They told us that the American Airmen from the local air field had given them to them. One of the teachers came out and the air was blue! We younger children did not know what all the fuss was about, but I was told that these balloons were called 'French letters'.

When I had gone to Secondary School we used to have to go to school on a school bus. The driver was a very handsome man and I had a crush on him. He had a small stool and if you were good you were allowed to sit next to him. I was sitting on the stool and I saw an orange light down in the engine. I insisted that there was an orange light there and so the driver stopped the bus to have a look. He shot to the back of the bus and opened the emergency exit and very hurriedly bundled us all out of the bus. The engine was on fire! I was allowed to sit next to him for some time for being such a good observant girl.

Once, whilst I was sitting next to the driver I asked him what 'French letters' were and it really shocked him to think that such a good little girl would have heard of such a thing, particularly asking him that whilst he was driving.

My mother died near the end of the War and my father was injured by one of the first V2s that fell on Lewisham. He was blown five hundred yards down the road and very badly injured. He was sent on convalescence to Newquay in Cornwall. He was there for six months. We did not have any contact with him because he was so badly injured.

We were some of the later children to return home to London, because my father was afraid that he would not be able to look after us. When he married my step mother we came home. I could not take to London again. I could not stand it. I had become such a hoyden, a tomboy. I had learned how to lay a hedge and use a scythe and all I wanted to do was to be back in the country.

Joan Morgan and her sister.

London boys help out on the farm.

GLADYS MULHERN

Evacuation had first been suggested in 1938 when there was the first trouble with Hitler. My Mother and Father were quite prepared to come away with me with my school then. They brought a suitcase of clothes into school in case they had to leave hurriedly with us. Of course it did not happen and we quickly settled down again.

In my family there was my father and mother, my sister, who was Head of Cranbrook Terrace School in Bethnal Green and myself. My sister was a little older than me. During 1939 both my parents became ill with cancer. They had been such healthy people right up to then, so it was a very poignant time for us knowing that they were both so ill. Father was in and out of the London Hospital, and then we got him into a nursing home in Wandsworth. Mother was at home and able to get around although she was rather ill and attending the London Hospital as an out–patient.

Father died on the Monday of the week the War broke out. We tried to fix up the funeral but it could not be arranged before Friday, 1st September and that was the day that my school, Maryon Park Infants' School, was going to evacuate. Fortunately I had a very very good assistant Head Teacher, Miss Schofield, (we called her "Scho") and she was very capable. I said to her "Scho, you will have to carry on because I cannot come with you. I shall have to be at home until Saturday". So I did not actually go with my school. Miss Schofield took them and she rang me that evening to tell me where they were, at Cranbrook in Kent.

We did not know before hand where anyone was going.

We knew we would be able to take others away with us on evacuation as helpers as well as the teaching staff, so my sister and I knew we could take Mother away with one of us. My sister's school was not evacuated until Saturday, 2nd September. It was staggered a little bit, some schools going on the Friday and others on Saturday or Sunday. After my Father's funeral was over my sister and I discussed with Mother what was going to happen and it was decided that Mother would go away with my sister's school.

On that Saturday morning the three of us left the house, exactly as it was, we did not do anything to it at all. We had very good neighbours and we left the key with them and we just left our home, taking my mother who had just been widowed that week. It was an extraordinary time really, and my mother and sister did not know where they were going. They went to the school at Bethnal Green and I went up to town and got the train down to Cranbrook.

I think I realised what the children's parents were facing at that time. During the previous August we had on a number of occasions, gathered the parents together. I was particularly keen on this. I was the person who knew the parents best for I had been there for ten years at the Infants' School, when the war broke out. I had also had a lot to do with the parents whose children were now in the senior part of the school, as I had run Mothers' clubs and things like that for them over the years. So I got the parents together and talked to them about the evacuation, trying not to persuade them too much. I just had to leave them to decide for themselves, and I did realise what it meant to those parents to have to let their children go.

A large number of children went with our school and it was arranged in families, so that we did not separate them and they all travelled together. I heard from Scho the next day, that the little town had been full of excitement and how the ladies of the town had been there waiting to choose which children they wanted and deciding how many they could have. The billeting officer, Mrs Cheeseman was a very helpful person, and Scho and she got on very well together. Eventually they got all the children sorted out and sent to their various billets.

There was one funny story of a lady who saw two little twins, who looked angelic, and she thought she would like to have them. She said she would have "those two dear little boys", but we knew what those little twins were like, and so did she very soon! We had to move them shortly. They were lovely little boys but two little terrors! They were quite young. In those days we took children into school at three years old, even though it was not technically a nursery class. It was called the Babies' class and I used to take them the day they were three. So we had a lot of children under five, as well as the others.

Most of the children settled in very well and were most happy. They were very well looked after and I don't think we had many problems. Some of the children stayed on after the war and got very attached to their people. We had a rather bad diphtheria epidemic and one of the Junior children died which was very sad but there were no inoculations for diphtheria then. The children were very well on the whole and the country air did them good.

Evacuated children from Maryon Park School.

Gladys Mulhern in the country 1939.

When we first arrived in Cranbrook and we had a large number of children, we had to share with the Church school, in their building, so our children attended school part-time for a little while. It was a very lovely Indian summer in 1939, and we were able to have the children out of doors a lot if they were not in school, so we managed quite well. Later we were given the hall at the back of the Congregational Church, which was a wooden building and another decent sized hall called the Bull Room which was next to the George Inn.

We could not take any school equipment with us when we were evacuated. We only took our own belongings and our gas masks with us. After we had been in Cranbrook for about a week, Mrs Cheeseman the billeting officer, lent us a lorry which we drove back to Maryon Park School at Woolwich, and rescued as much stuff as we could from there. We were very disappointed because when we got there we found that the Auxilliary Fire Service had taken over the school and they had already rifled the cupboards, so we lost a tremendous lot.

Mrs Johnson was one of our Staff and she had a daughter, Joan, who was at the school. Mr Johnson was not a strong man, he was unemployed and he came with us as a helper. He was a very practical man so I got in touch with Kent Council, who were very good with supplies, and asked if they could obtain some leather for us. They did this and he mended the children's shoes. We were able to fix up a little room for him in the Congregational Hall that we were using as part as our school accommodation. He was there day after day working and doing a beautiful job, mending the evacuated children's shoes. You can imagine that they quickly wore them out, and this was how we used Mr Johnson as a helper and he was a great help.

After a while people drifted back to London and the children's numbers fluctuated. For the first year of the war very little happened and people just went back. We were near enough to London for the parents to come down to us to visit. Many of the children did go home for a visit and some did not come back again.

Eventually after two years, Miss Schofield had to be sent home and I was left there alone. There were about twenty-five children left then, of mixed ages. I used the Sunday School hall for my school and it was adequate. I had children from three years old up to eleven years old.

We stayed there until the flying bombs came and, although the town was not badly damaged, it was decided that there should be a new evacuation from Cranbrook of local children as well as the London evacuees. We started off just as we had from London in 1939, not knowing where we were going. We set off in the train and we got to a little village in Wiltshire, Great Bradley, near Trowbridge. I lived for a time with the headmistress of the church school there.

I stayed for only three months and then I came back to London in the middle of the flying bomb period. I arrived back in October, 1944. I went back to Maryon Park School and took over the Infant and Junior department of the school. Miss Schofield, who had been sent back to London, was teaching at another school and eventually she came back to Maryon Park School too. I was at Maryon Park from when I was thirty-four until I retired at sixty.

We were greatly helped by the local people in Cranbrook, and I enjoyed my four years there. I have been back several times to visit. I still see Mrs Stone who lived in a little cottage just across the road from us. She used to come in and look after us, clean our rooms and so on.

See Joan Pearce's story. She was a pupil at Maryon Park School.

NOTICE.

Plans for evacuation of School-children in the event of a national emergency.

The Managers have sanctioned the evacuation of the School, in case of need, in accordance with the arrangements made by the Government and the London County Council. It will be appreciated that exact details of arrangements in the receiving areas cannot be available beforehand; but the aim of the Scheme will be to ensure as normal a life as possible for the children.

It is anticipated that it may be possible to share a secondary school building—the local school having a three and a half hour session, and the London school a three and a half hour session. During the rest of the day the School Staff will organise educational visits, nature walks, homework classes, games and other activities. The children will probably be billeted in the houses of local residents, with whom the School Staff will maintain close contact, and every effort will be made to billet members of one family in the same house.

Extract from letter to Head Teachers from the Government.

Policeman and Islington child with sack, on his way to the West Country.

157

LIL MURRELL

I worked for a firm called Firman and company. They were wood merchants who made boxes for the fruit and vegetable markets like Covent Garden, Spitalfields and places like that. We also had a sack department where they made the sacks for potatoes, flour, and so on. We made sacks for Tate and Lyle for their sugar. So one half of the company was wood and the other half was sacks.

Our premises were on Morden Wharf, right on the edge of the river in Greenwich. It was opposite the Blue Circle cement works, and not far from the Blackwall Tunnel.

When the blitz started in 1940, our area was heavily hit. They dropped a lot of incendiary bombs, and some nights it seemed that most of London was burning.

One Monday we all turned up for work and our premises had been bombed. Everywhere was covered in water, the sacks were all burned, the wood was all burned. It was all inflammable stuff. The guvnor said that if we'd all like to help with the clearing up, then we'd open up again as soon as we could. So we cleared away the mess and opened up again. A few weeks later we got bombed again. This time the guvnor said, 'I'm not opening up a second time. We'll have to move out of London. If you want a job, you can come with us.'

So we moved down to Bexley and took over half of the Old Mill, which

Lil Murrell on evacuation while working at Firman's sacking factory evacuated to Bexley from Greenwich.

was an old water mill for grinding flour. A firm of corn chandlers, I think the man's name was Streetly, had the top half of the mill, and we had the bottom two floors. My guvnor dropped the wood side of the business, but we carried on with the sacks. We cut the hessian, made the sacks, and printed them. My job was to do the printing. We set up the printing machine in the mill. I printed the sacks with either W. Bruce or whatever, Spitalfields or Covent Garden.

If you had fairly long hair you had to tie it up in a scarf or a snood, because you could get it caught up in the machinery which could be dangerous. I used to wear bib and braces to work in as protective clothing. Nowadays, people wear denim jeans or dungarees in the street, but in those days they were only working clothes. You went to work in your ordinary clothes, changed when you got to work, and then changed again to come home.

About thirty of us stayed with the firm, including two office staff and one forelady. This was only a third of the people employed in London, so he recruited labour from the area, Welling, Sidcup and Bexley Heath. Two drivers were taken on, we had two lorries. They were brothers and lived right opposite the mill in cottages. The guvnor's son took over the works and we very seldom saw his father.

If there was an air raid at work and the warning went, you were supposed to go to the nearest shelter which was about a hundred yards away. It was at the back of the petrol station next door, which meant you went under the railway bridge and round the back of the petrol station. That was more risky than staying where you were. Most of the time, we didn't move, we carried on working.

The mill still had its water wheel, and the mill stream ran under the building. In the hot weather we used to paddle in it at dinner time. There was a farm behind the mill and we used to go and look at the animals. We also used the farm as a short cut to the railway station. It was much quicker than going round by the road.

I didn't move to Bexley, I commuted from home. At the very beginning we were taken by an open back lorry down the Rochester Way, as far as The Black Prince, and then into Bexley. After a while we went by train. We were given monthly season tickets, paid for by the company.

Lil's fellow workers from Firmans.

I would leave home at about seven o'clock in the morning, get a tram, or walk, from the Tunnel Avenue to the top of Blackwall Lane, then get a tram from Blackwall Lane to New Cross. I used to stand on New Cross station, in all kinds of weather, not knowing if the train was coming in or not, because of an air raid, or if I would ever get to work at all. We were supposed to be there at eight o'clock, but because of the difficulty with the trains, it was quite often about twenty past eight.

We finished work at five o'clock. If the trains weren't running, we would have to come home by bus. If it was icy or snowing the buses didn't run up Gravel Hill, so the only way to get home was to walk. If somebody stopped and said, 'Would you like a lift? How far are you going?', you didn't think twice about it, you just got into the car and they would drop you where it was most convenient. Of course in the wintertime it would be completely dark.

I did that journey from 1940 until 1946. The business never came back to London after the war. The old place is now a restaurant, called, of course 'The Old Mill'.

YVONNE NICHOLLS

I was at Prendergast School in Lewisham, and I was ten and a half when the war started. We had to wait at the school for about a week before we went. We had to take our cases into school every day and wait. Eventually, the go ahead came and that was on September 1st 1939, two days before war broke out. We were divided into squads and each little squad had to keep together. We all set off from the school in an enormous crocodile and we had to walk up to Catford and then we went from Catford Station.

The headmistress was Miss Franklin and she had about six hundred girls in the school aged between five and eighteen. Miss Franklin walked ahead with an enormous sandwich board with the school number on it which was H68. I have still got the label which I wore. All the way along, the mothers were waving goodbye. I shall always remember that. We felt quite proud of ourselves.

It never bothered me at all, going away. I was very lucky because my mother came with us as a voluntary, unpaid helper, and I suppose that softened the blow of leaving home. My father was in a reserved occupation and so he kept the house going while my mother and I were away.

At Catford station there was enormous excitement and no one in our group was crying. We were thrilled to be getting on a train and going to an unknown destination. We watched the map on the carriage wall to see where we were going.

They stopped the train at Lydd, which is in the middle of Romney Marsh and we got out. We were all taken into a field and we sat down. Nobody seemed to know what to do with us. Everybody was running around. There were far more of us apparently than had ever been expected. We just sat there for the whole afternoon. Then they came along with carrier bags of what they called 'iron rations'. A tin of corned beef and a bar of chocolate etc. We were supposed to keep them for emergencies but everybody ate the chocolate.

Then we were told that we were going to be split up. Some of us went to New Romney, some to somewhere else, and our little group got into a coach and we were taken to the Isle of Sheppey. We were taken to the village hall at Eastchurch. We stood in rows and had our hair looked at and our teeth inspected and most of us were found to be sane and healthy. People came along and picked us. They tried to keep brothers and sisters together.

Our little group were scattered about the island. Six or seven of us were put into the local vicar's car and came to an old disused holiday camp, which just consisted of chalets and a main hall where we were fed. We were put into a hut, which had a big hole in the side and the wind whistled through it all night. The next morning we played around in the camp and then we were moved to a post office at Warden Point, right on the edge of the sea. There was no schooling, we just played in the fields and wandered about.

Evacuees on Catford Station, September 1939. Note the barrage balloon.

When war was declared, on 3rd September, there was, almost immediately, an air raid warning. I probably saw the first shot of the war fired, because one of our planes, which was then unidentified, was fired upon when the warning went. I was looking out of the window of the post office, which is near the edge of the cliff, and I heard the guns go and saw the shells bursting in the sky.

In the end the whole school was reunited in Tonbridge where we shared the local girls' grammar school, and we were billeted in all the surrounding villages. In my first billet I was with my mother and another lady with her daughter. We were billeted on a Miss W, but we did not stay there for very long. My mother got very alarmed after a few days and said to me 'We've got to go', and she rushed down to the billeting office and we were moved very quickly. This lady, apparently had tendencies of 'liking' other ladies! Of course I knew nothing of that at the time.

We moved to a Miss Twort and her father. They were very generous and very kind. The first Christmas, they went away to visit relatives and they said that my father could come down and stay over the Christmas holiday. They did not really know us but they left the house in our care.

By now school was getting organised. It was all done on a very complicated rota system and we were not in full time education. We would go in on certain days, mornings or afternoons and the Grammar school girls would alternate with us. We had some lessons in church halls and we had to carry our books all round Tonbridge.

Many of the mothers went back to London and my mother was the only one left. She was attached to the local billeting office and liaised with them and the school, helping the children and their foster mothers. She did all this voluntarily, as part of her war effort.

There was not a lot of co−operation between the locals and the evacuees. Some of the local children used to shout at us and throw stones at us on the way to school and whilst we were waiting at the bus stop. I was really quite frightened of them, and if I saw a group of the local children I would dodge around a corner and go a different way.

Yvonne takes a ride.

Nevertheless, it was a lovely part of my life because I had always lived in the town and I just fell in love with the country. There was a freedom there which I had never experienced before and I have never lost my love of the countryside. My mum and dad bought me a bike. I palled up with another girl and we would go for miles on our bikes. All the signposts were down and we did not know where we were going.

There was so much war activity going on there. Soldiers used to be in the big Army camp on the Common and we would watch them on manoeuvres. It was all very exciting. In 1940 there were lots of soldiers coming through Tonbridge station from Dunkirk and everybody went down to the station to see them.

When the Battle of Britain started we had a grand stand view. There we were, evacuated for safety, and the Battle of Britain was taking place immediately overhead! I saw planes crashing, pilots baling out, and heard machine gunning. It really was an exciting time for a child. We used to cheer when an enemy plane was shot down, which is horrendous when you think about it.

I remember there was an Italian Prisoner of War camp nearby and we used to go along and just stare at them through the barbed wire. Our school was on a high hill above Tonbridge and it had extensive grounds at the back. Beyond that there was countryside, where they built the prison camp. We used to go through the hedge during our lunch time and see them. The Prisoners of War used to ask us to post letters for them, but how would a letter get from England to a foreign country during the war? They did not even have money for stamps or anything like that. We were terribly patriotic and we would not talk to them or smile at them because they were the enemy.

Tonbridge County School had big air raid shelters in the grounds and so when the air raid warning went we used to go into them. There was a system that if we were on the way to school when the siren went, we had to carry on if we were nearer to the school. But if we were nearer to home, then we had to go back home. Of course we may have been nearer the school gates, but we would always go back home if we could. The air raid warnings sometimes lasted all day, but we just carried on. I don't remember that there was much unhappiness and the girls settled down. But most of us, if we could, would go home to Lewisham at the weekends.

Eventually my father said that my mother and I were to go back home and we came back in August, 1940 so we were back in London for the Blitz. On 7th September, they set the London Docks alight. That was an unforgettable time indeed. I was really frightened when the bombing began in earnest. The people at our last billet wrote to ask if we would like to go back. So back we went and stayed for the winter of 1940–1941.

When the Blitz began to quieten down, we went back to London and this time we stayed in London until the end of the war. So many children came back that the others, who were left, were assimilated within the local school at Tonbridge. I went to school at Lewisham Prendergast School again, which was opened as a central school. Girls from other schools who had come back to London came to us and I can remember seeing many different school uniforms there.

I took my School Certificate Exam with my father's tin hat under the desk and just a blast wall outside the window. Buzz Bombs were literally going off all around us. At one point the blast from a Buzz Bomb blew the exam papers all over the room and we had to scramble on the floor for our papers. The invigilating mistress could hear the Buzz Bombs coming over and she stood there, looking very majestic, saying 'Down girls!' and we would get under our desks. Then, when the bomb had gone off, we would carry on writing.

When we left the school to go home we never knew whether or not our homes would still be there. We did not keep in contact with our last billet because so much was going on, and I did not think about evacuation any more, but I still have happy memories of Southborough and I often go there for a nostalgic trip.

*Eileen Owen (right, with flask) in the 'Spinster Express'
Torquay to London.*

EILEEN OWEN

In 1939 I was eighteen years old, living in Jerningham Road, S.E.4. and working for the Prudential Approved Society in Holborn Bars. A week before war was declared, the department was evacuated to Torquay, all the staff plus all the insurance cards and the ledgers in which health insurance cards were recorded. I think the furniture and records were moved by lorry. The staff, however, went by a special train from Paddington to Torquay.

Unlike children who were evacuated, there was a far greater age range in the staff, from eighteen year olds like me to some approaching retirement age. I suppose I was fortunate that I didn't have to worry about elderly parents or my house, but I was very tearful before I left. I was leaving my grandmother and, even more important to me at the time, my boy friend.

We were a happy enough crowd on the train. We were with office friends, section heads and senior staff. I recall that it was a beautiful day and the countryside looked green and pleasant.

On arrival at Torquay we were allocated bedrooms in various hotels. The records were unloaded in the large Victoria and Albert Hotel overlooking the gardens in Torbay, and across the sea. For a considerable while the work was chaotic, the ledgers being piled on the floor of the dining room, the cards in boxes, and we worked on trestle tables. Eventually things were straightened out and the sections found

The Prudential offices evacuated to Torquay.

themselves in bedrooms, lounges, and dining room. The one room that was not used was the bathroom because of the floor.

I and some friends were allocated a bedroom in the top rooms of the Toorak Hotel next to the Victoria and Albert, and spent some time in there before being moved to another hotel. Our meals were supplied. Eventually we were given a guinea a week for our board and encouraged to find our own accommodation. I found a private house in Chelston and stayed there quite happily for about a year.

For a considerable length of time a special train was hired for employees to travel to London for the weekend. This train became known as the 'Spinster Express.' After a weekend at home, I always caught the midnight train back to Torquay. I used to love rushing through the night, looking at the stars which, because of the lack of lighting due to the blackout, were so clear and bright.

The fact that we could go up to London every weekend kept the home sickness at bay, and of course we were with friends at work during the week. We all soon settled down to a regular life in Torquay. We went to concerts on the pier. I recall seeing a young Cyril Fletcher performing his 'odd odes'.

I bought a bike and on warm days would cycle off to the moors and scattered Devon villages. Swimming was another pastime, and after work some of us would get on our bikes and cycle off to Paignton, Babbacombe, or Anstey's Bay if we decided we were bored with Torbay itself. In the spring, there were wild daffodils to pick at Watersmeet and all the other wild flowers that grew in abundance. I can't say that we were an unhappy crowd once we got over the initial shock of being uprooted.

I eventually returned to London and worked in head office for a while before being called up into the A.T.S. in May 1942. Although I still write to a contemporary of mine who remained in the Torquay area, I have never been back.

JOAN PEARCE

I was nine years old when the war began. I went to Maryon Park School in Charlton and I was evacuated with the school. My mind is a blank where the departure is concerned but I have vague memories of the train journey. I was excited rather than sad. I thought it was a day's outing.

It was dark when we arrived in Cranbrook. We walked through a street and saw an outline of a building that amazed me — it turned out to be a windmill. My foster parent welcomed me with a Shirley Temple cut-out book and we had a parcel of chocolate, tinned milk and biscuits to give to her. I had a nice bedroom. Its wall was adjoining next door's bedroom. There was another evacuee there. I could hear her crying and I know I wondered why she was upset.

I think it was an old-fashioned house in very dark tones and there was a huge table dominating the room. The only noise was the ticking of a clock. My hostess had a grown up daughter who used to take me for walks with her boyfriend. I used to run ahead. I think he was called up shortly after my arrival. I was at that house for just three months, when my hostess broke her ankle and asked if I could be moved until she was well, but I never went back.

I was then put with the Fisher family, Mum, Dad, two girls aged nine and eleven, and a boy of seven. I stayed with them for the duration. I was an only child, so it was quite an experience being part of a bigger family. The house was quite small considering how many people used to stay there.

My parents and various relatives used to come and visit me. Lewis' Coaches had put on special coaches every week for parents to visit their children. In the winter, the coach always got stuck on Pole Hill and had to be pushed up by everybody. When the bombing was particularly bad, my family used to stay longer than just the weekend, sleeping anywhere. I know when the house was full of people, the three girls had to sleep in a double bed. In the winter we fought to sleep in the middle, and in the summer the opposite.

Joan as evacuee.

Members of the Fisher family.

The house was cold. There was not much coal, and it had to be put on a bit at a time instead of by the shovelful. One time it was so cold that the gold fish froze in its bowl. That winter I experienced sledging for the first time. We were very lucky, though, because the house was one of the first Council houses that had a bathroom. We had no hot tap and water was heated up in a galvanized copper with a tap to pour the water into a bucket. At bathtime the bath was filled up and the cleanest one was bathed first, then a bucketful of hot water was added for the next in line and so on. One time I scalded my foot quite badly when the handle of the bucket broke and water went over my foot. The last to take a bath was Mr Fisher, who was the local coal man.

At Christmas there were not many presents but they made it such fun. We used to go to the Fishers' grandparents' house, which was old with lots of little rooms. Instead of putting the presents round a Christmas tree they made it into a Treasure Hunt. As usual the food was marvellous and even in the 1940s their salad bowl was made into a work of art, decorated beautifully.

We were very self-sufficient. There were always fresh vegetables and fruit from the garden, and rabbits, chickens and ducks. Another new experience was seeing eggs in a nest with feathers still stuck to them. My job was feeding the chickens, boiling up all the potato peelings and kitchen waste and then putting bran in the mixture and squeezing it through my fingers to mix it. It was a bit hot sometimes!

Joan (second from right) and all the Fisher children.

We used to go for lovely walks to collect the wild grasses for rabbits' food. We collected it by the sackful. I used to like digging up the potatoes and beetroot. It was quite a miracle for a little Londoner to see this. My love of gardening now, I put down to this experience.

We all dreaded 'Pickle Onion' weekend when chutney, piccalilli and pickled onions were preserved. We all had to peel onions, do cauliflower chunks, and collect the tomatoes. Everybody cried except Mr Fisher. He sat for hours peeling the shallots and never had a moment's discomfort. Even the smell of the piccalilli 'brewing' used to make our eyes water. Runner beans were put into salt jars, and tomatoes and fruit were bottled in airtight jars. Eggs too were preserved in a special solution called isinglass. Jam was made, and that job was very pleasant, topping and tailing gooseberries and collecting wild blackberries for adding to the apples. Nothing was wasted. Even the rabbit skins were treated and used for gloves.

Our schooling seemed to be a bit haphazard. We were nearly always copying from books. We were taught in an old-fashioned chapel building with a black stove in the centre. Milk was put to warm around the outside of the stove in the winter. When numbers of evacuees decreased we were put in another hall over a garage, then integrated with the locals. I took my 11 plus exam in the local school and passed, but because I would have had to change my billet to go to Secondary School I decided against it.

I joined the Girl Guides, and I used to go to the local community hall to make sandwiches and peel potatoes for servicemen. We used to have a special badge for 'War Work'. We did the Church Parade March with the Home Guard and I carried the flag. I was very proud.

An aunt of mine used to come and see us and she insisted on wearing her 'London Gear'. She wore beautiful hats with veils, even for country walks. One day her beautiful hat got caught up in a bush and catapulted right over the top into a cow pat! However bad the bombing, she never came again.

The war seemed a long way away, but we did hear the German planes going over night after night and saw the glow in the sky in the London direction. We also saw the dog fights over fields and often heard the rat-a-tat of machine gun fire. One exciting time a parachute came down, and like 'Dad's Army' the Home Guard turned out. On just two occasions, whilst hop-picking, enemy planes did fly over us very low. Doodle-bugs, the V1s, began to get very frequent and our planes used to try and bring them down before they reached London.

Cranbrook began to be a very dangerous place and so we all had to move out of range. On D–Day I can remember wave upon wave of planes and gliders going over the house. The streets were lined with army lorries as far as you could see. My hosts became evacuees themselves and we went to Oxford to Fisher relatives.

I came back to London with very mixed feelings. The Fisher family came to my home on V.E. night to celebrate with my parents. We have kept in close touch ever since, which has been for over forty years. All the family are now married and I went to all of the Weddings. I last saw them just two months ago.

See Gladys Mulhern's story, as she was Joan's teacher.

The Fisher family in 1947 with their post-war baby.

JANE PEPPER

Perhaps unusually, my wartime recollections are of being at the other end of evacuee arrangements. My parents and myself (an only child) lived in a small three-bedroomed cottage in a Buckinghamshire village, and received evacuees in the earlier part of the war.

I was only four or five at the time, and while the evacuees went to the village school, I went off to my little private school a mile or so away - hence our paths didn't cross that much. But I do remember quite a lot.

First came Joan, several years older than me. An old photograph shows us together, me well dressed, fresh faced and healthy, contrasted with her ill-fitting clothes, thin little legs and unevenly cut hair sticking out from under a ribbon tied round her head but slipped askew. She was with us less than six months I think. She became ill with appendicitis and after the operation, her mother took her back to the East End.

She was followed by inseparable, unhappy sisters Pat and Jean, who clung together to ease the misery of homesickness. Pat had some sort of eye trouble which was only treated when she came to us, but this didn't prevent her from walking into a fence-pole in the twilight and knocking a tooth out.

After a year, their father yielded to their pleas to come home and came one Saturday morning to collect them. My mother remembers giving them their usual pocket money plus some extra as a parting gift, and

169

Jane at home in Buckinghamshire.

seeing them off the station. Some hours later a scandalised neighbour told her that she had just seen the children at a shop near the station with their father begging him to get them a comic. He was extremely drunk and shouting at them. Everybody concluded he'd done well in the local pub all day on the girls' pocket-money.

The general attitude I can recall, even from that early age, was that many of the London children were badly cared for back home, and that evacuation was an opportunity for them to be 'rescued'. To my recollection, however, there was only one London girl remaining in the village after a couple of years, and she was probably the exception. Her family abandoned her entirely, and she grew up as the beloved daughter of a large middle-aged unmarried woman with no family of her own, married a local boy in later years and brought great joy to her adoptive 'Mum'.

In general there was great solidarity among the London children while they were in the village. I remember hearing the whole group of them, in the light summer evenings, shouting and whooping as they ran about in the woods. My mother has told me how worried she used to get when Joan used to go off roaming with the others regardless of what was regarded in my home as the proper mealtimes and bedtime. She used to have to go up the hill herself, calling to Joan repeatedly to come indoors.

The expectation of children in the village school was that the boys would go to work on the farms, and the girls would go into domestic work. Hence, from about eleven onwards, the boys would tend the schoolmaster's garden and the girls would work in his house under his wife's supervision, for much of their time.

I wonder how the independent London children fitted into that scheme of things? Maybe that's why they went home so quickly!

Jane playing with Joan, an evacuee from London billeted with her.

MARGARET PHAIR

A bomb dropped on the shelter in our road. As a rule we would have been in there, my stepmother and me, but that night, due to the fact that my young sister wasn't well, we weren't, thank goodness.

Margaret, aged twelve, in 1939.

The war made very little impact on me, and I look back on being evacuated as an adventure. I was evacuated in September 1939 with my school. I was twelve years old and was put in charge of little Frank, who was about five. His runny nose and cries of wanting to go to the toilet kept me very busy. He looked like a walking rag bag, and his habit of sniffing all the time, drove me round the bend. I could forgive him all this, though, when he looked at me with his large brown eyes. He looked like a puppy dog.

I remember later in the year, at Christmas time, Frank took part in the school Nativity play. He was chosen to be Joseph. He did very well until it came to the bit where the 'Three Wise Men' offer the gifts, gold, frankincense, and myrrh. He started crying, and a teacher asked, 'What are you crying for?' 'Well,' he said, 'They keep making fun of me.' The teacher said, 'What do you mean?' 'They keep saying Frank's got no sense', he said, 'And I might have nits, but I haven't got myrrh!'

I was billeted with two spinster ladies. They were very strict, and I soon named their home 'Mustnot House', because of all the rules they laid down. A lively girl, like me, made them realise that this would not do, and things relaxed a bit. My natural exuberance got the better of me, though, and soon I was sent back to London.

As a result of this narrow escape, I was evacuated again, this time to Ely. I, as the last evacuee, was taken home by the billeting officer. She was the doctor's wife and lived in a large house bursting at the seams with knick-knacks from India. They had been missionaries out there when they were younger. Other occupants of the house were two students, a teacher, two boys from a 'posh' school, and a girl two years older than me, who was my sworn enemy.

Mrs Green was very good to me, and, as I was outgrowing my clothes, she helped me find 'new' ones from her good jumble, she collected this as a member of the W.V.S. I used to help her with some of her duties. I liked visiting her Mother and Baby centres, and have never seen so many toddlers getting on and off their 'pots' in all my life. I also helped in the house, making myself useful to the maids and the cook. I was paid sixpence a week for this.

I had a very nice Christmas 1940. I don't know where she got it from, but we had a real Christmas tree. It was all done up beautifully, and stood in the hall. We had a turkey on Christmas Day, at least I think it was a turkey, I never tasted one before. The children weren't allowed to sit with the grown-ups in the dining room, we had to sit at a special table by the window. On Boxing Day, the maid served up a bowl containing bits of turkey, all floating in this horrible stuff. I asked what it was, and Mrs Green said, 'It's curry.' It tasted revolting, so while she wasn't looking, I gently eased up the big bay window we were sitting by, and tipped the lot onto the ground outside.

Of course she looked across and said, 'Oh, you've finished it.' We all looked at one another and said, 'Yes Mrs Green.' 'Oh good, have some more.' she said, and rang the bell. The maid brought some more, and, of course we didn't dare throw it out the window this time, so we had to eat it. It was revolting!

My time spent with Mrs Green did influence me for the good. My years at school came to an end, and, when I reached fourteen, she got me a situation working for a farmer's wife, but the life was lonely and I returned to London. I wrote to her for a while and never forgot her. The Bible she gave me still has passages underlined by her at Bible class.

Margaret back in London, aged seventeen, in 1945.

173

JOY PLANT

We had decided that since Bonnie, my sister, and I wanted to be evacuated together, we would both go with the Hearnville Road School party. Bonnie was still a pupil there, and I had only recently left. A few days were spent in feverish preparation. Bags were packed, labels issued, and food bought and stowed away.

Every morning we tramped to school with our luggage on our backs, and every evening returned with the news that the time for departure had not yet arrived. This got annoying because we often had to refresh the food and clothes in our knapsacks, to have it ready for the following day. Those of us who didn't actually attend Hearnville Road School had a lovely time during those days. We used to sit in the playground and knit or read the whole day long.

At last, the day arrived, and we walked to school for the last time. We assembled in our different groups, and formed queues in the playground, with our banner denoting who we were held up in front. We then marched to the station. It was very crowded but, with great difficulty, Bonnie and I saw Mummy, and managed to kiss her goodbye before we passed through the gates.

It was very hot, and we had to stand all the time. One girl nearly fainted and was given a cup of water by a nurse. Many trains came through the station without stopping. They were all full of evacuees from other parts of London. Finally our train arrived and we all pushed our way inside.

At last we were off.

About two hours later, we arrived at our destination, Eastbourne. We were transported in buses to a school, and sat in the playground with beakers of lemonade and biscuits. A doctor examined us and then we departed for our new 'homes'.

As we passed out of the school gates, we were each handed a small carrier bag containing a tin of corned beef, a tin of condensed milk, one packet of sweet biscuits, one packet of plain biscuits, and a half pound bar of Cadbury's milk chocolate. The parcel was to be given to the people who were going to take us in, in case they hadn't got a supply of food in for us.

Bonnie and I were billeted at 24 Carlisle Road with two other girls, Pamela Gibbons, who was thirteen, and Pat Wall, who was eight. The place was owned by Mr Nicholls, a bachelor of about sixty, who lived with his two maiden sisters. Although the house was of considerable size, and a maid and a cook were employed, there wasn't really room for us all. Pamela and I slept on camp beds on a small landing outside the cook's bedroom, Bonnie slept on a camp bed at the foot of the maid's bed, and Pat slept on a divan in Miss Nicholls' bedroom. The only bright people in the house were Margaret, the maid, and Rose, the cook.

Two days after we arrived in Eastbourne, war broke out. The Prime Minister announced the news, and later we had our first air raid warning. We all trooped down to the shelter. This was a marvellous concrete affair with wooden seats, and water, heating and electric light had been installed. It even had a lavatory, there were two exits, the doors of which were fitted with rubber in order to prevent the entrance of gas, and inside was an air purifying machine. Evidently they were determined to resist the invader at all costs.

We were not happy in Carlisle Road. We were always hungry. Breakfast was just cornflakes, except on Sundays when we were allowed a boiled egg. We were given lunch at school, but it was not very nice and not nearly sufficient. Tea was jelly and two slices of bread. We had no supper at all, and yet the food cupboard, which was kept locked and guarded like a treasure chest, was full to overflowing. Rationing had not yet been introduced, so there was no excuse for us being so ill fed.

Joy and Bonnie with their Bingo prizes.

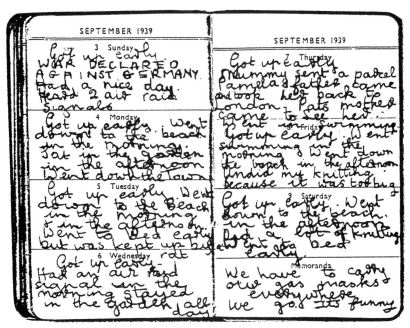

Joy's diary for the first week of the war.

All us evacuees were always treated as nuisances. Since I had no mirror, the cook used to let me do my hair at night in her bedroom. One evening, the elder Miss Nicholls informed me that I was wasting electricity. She also complained because I washed my hair, which wasted water. Pamela Gibbons stuck it for only a week, and then returned to London. Eventually, after crying every night in bed, I summoned up the courage to ask to be moved.

Our next billet was at Milnthorpe Court. We were desperately frightened and shy as a result of our previous experience, but Mrs Perry, our new hostess, did everything she could to put us at our ease. She was a widow with two children, Lilian, who at fourteen was a few months younger than me, and Forbes, who was seventeen. We hardly ever saw him as he was away at boarding school.

We were soon all one big happy family. Bonnie and I had a room of our own, with two beds, a wardrobe, a dressing table and even a washbasin with hot water. From our window we had a lovely view of the sea and Pevensey Bay. All summer we walked to school over the downs and we went for rambles to Beachy Head. Mummy used to visit us regularly, and we used to play 'bingo' on the pier. We won almost every time, and came away with boxes of chocolates.

At the end of May 1940, France capitulated, and rumours of a German invasion began to spread. The South Coast was no longer safe. On Monday 11th June, we were told at school that the following Sunday we were to travel to South Wales. I had fully enjoyed myself at Mrs Perry's house, it had been a lovely place to live in, but I was excited at the prospect of moving on.

The train was meant to leave Eastbourne at half past seven in the morning, but it seemed ages later when we finally departed. It was seven o'clock in the evening when we finally stopped at a small railway station, and were ordered out. We struggled up a narrow dusty road into the village. The place was packed with onlookers who stared at us as if we were strange objects that they had never seen before. We went to a school where we were given food and tea. Then a doctor examined our throats. We then sat on our luggage in the playground, trying to keep cheerful, although the smaller children got restless and refused to sit still. The sun went down and it began to get chilly.

Two hours later a group of us were marched up the road where we boarded a double decker bus. We were accompanied by Mr Thomas, the preacher from the village we were going to. He made us feel a little more at home. He taught us a few simple words in Welsh such as 'barra' for bread, and 'mennin' for butter. We firmly believed that Welsh was the only language used, and that leeks were always served at a meal. Mr Thomas said, to our relief, that they didn't eat leeks every day and that some Welsh people didn't even like them.

We arrived in a village called Nantygroes, and drew up at the village school. The place was crowded with people, and the task of disposing of us to our homes began. This part was horrible, I felt just like an animal being bought at a sale. I was told that Mrs Evans, the wife of the schoolteacher, would be my foster mother. Bonnie was put next door with Mr and Mrs Lewis.

They were farmers and had a great deal of land around our houses. A vegetable garden was laid out at the back of the house, at the bottom of which was a pig sty and a lavatory. All the drinking water came from a pump in the garden.

The next day, we went to school and were given one of the classrooms for our own use. The small children there couldn't speak any English, and were immensely interested in us. They followed us around the playground and stood and stared at us whenever they had the chance.

One of our first tasks was to copy 'The Grace Before Meals' in Welsh, from the blackboard. We sang this before our dinner every day. One afternoon, we all wrote an essay entitled 'Our First Impressions of Wales'. After about a week, I was transferred to the secondary school. I hated the first few days, the chief reason for this being the fact that it was a co-ed school. The boys teased me unmercifully, they pinched my books, wrote caustic comments on my papers, and copied my Cockney accent.

Mummy came down to see Bonnie and me during the summer holidays. We went to all sorts of places, even as far away as Llanelly. Daddy wrote and told us that the first big air raids in London had begun, and that lots of people had been made homeless in one day. When Mummy had to go back, I was very upset, especially as I knew she might be in danger. On September 1st we remembered it was the first anniversary of our evacuation. The war had already lasted a year!

All the water came from the pump outside.
Joy and Bonnie took turns to fill up the buckets.

Joy was fostered by the schoolmaster of the village school.
here he is with his wife and two daughters. Joy is on the right.

16ᴬ Hildreth St₁₁
London SW₁₂

Dear Jay,

Now please don't worry too much about me. I'm taking great care of myself. Stick to your job & that will make me happy. If you pass through, it is all I have worked for.

Now here is my news. Today at 12-45, we were Blasted. First a bomb in Oakmead Rd & then, one in Culmore Cross. Every window is out & I'm so sorry to say your lovely room is the worst in the house. Every bit of ceiling down & walls all busted. We had packed away all ornaments & covered up everything. It has been one alert all day long so I had to keep running to shelter. Tomorrow if there is an all clear I'll go up & rescue all your school things

Joy's mother writes to her from London.

In August of the following year, Mummy decided that we should leave Wales and both go to Windsor, where my own school, Clapham County Secondary School, was evacuated. I was, of course, sorry to leave all the friends I had made, but I was thrilled to be going back to London. I could hardly sleep for excitement. Mrs Evans gave me a parting gift of a primrose yellow nightdress case, which I still have.

The moment the train drew into Paddington Station, was the happiest of my life. Bonnie and I thought everyone talked very Cockney, and for a long while afterwards we talked with a decided Welsh accent. We certainly saw some difference in our house. It had been blitzed in April, when incendiaries fell on the roof and completely burned out the kitchen.

The Campbell family in Wales, 1941.

♀ 卐 -Boo! Boo! Boo! ♀

5 SATURDAY (125-240)
Haile Selassié restored, 1941

Got up late. Absolutely horrible today — poured with rain the whole time. Worked all day — at my Environment file — an awful lot of work to do. Finished my "Xmas Tree" jumper — it looks nice.

South Germany & Austria are to surrender unconditionally to the Allies tomorrow — Only Norway & rest of Germany left now — hurrah!

6 Sunday (126-239)
Rogation Sunday

Got up late. Worked all morning and afternoon. Finished my Divinity play & did my English grammar questions. Spent the evening making a nice cotton frock for the doll I made. Also helped to make a life size guy of Hitler which we are going to burn on Victory Day.

Announced on wireless that Churchill is to speak on Thursday & V·E day will probably be before then — I just can't believe it.

HURRAY!   **7 MONDAY (127-238)**   CHEERS!
Rogation Day
Bank Holiday, Scotland

Went to Coll: SPECIAL V.E DAY ANNOUNCEMENT — ALL GERMAN RESISTANCE IS AT AN END — VICTORY WILL BE ANNOUNCED AT 3 p·m TOMORROW. All houses are decorated with flags. House at corner has coloured lights on — ever so pretty. Bonfire on waste land.

8 TUESDAY (128-237)
Rogation Day   also Victory Day.

VICTORY DAY — It's all over — no more bombing or blackout no more sirens or doodlebugs.
Had a lovely time celebrating. Had a tea party in the street — blanc manges, jelly, iced cakes and pop. Played games afterwards. In the evening we danced round the bonfires and watched all the fireworks. Floodlighting!! Danced until 12 o'clock — Red the Edge all the way up Bwlch Rd. Finally crawled into bed feeling more dead than alive — music still blaring away

Joy's diary for the last week of the war.

DYMPHNA PORTER

We had been preparing for evacuation for many months prior to the outbreak of war. A large amount of time in the summer term at school was spent in rehearsing for air-raids. School was a large London County Council School for all ages, divided into Junior Mixed and Infants and a Senior Boys and separate Senior Girls Department. It was situated in East Acton in the Borough of Hammersmith and served the children from two large council estates, Old Oak and White City.

I lived on the White City Estate with my mother and father, my older brother Desmond and my younger brother Brian and sister Maureen. My parents were Irish immigrants who had come to England in the 1920s looking for work. My father was a painter and decorator, but work was not plentiful and he was frequently out of work. Consequently we were very poor. The richness in our lives came from my parents desire that we should be well educated and they taught us to love literature, music, took us to museums and, when they had the money, to the 'pictures'.

I was nine years old in 1939 and in the top class of Old Oak Junior School. I liked school very much and resented the time spent away from lessons in the improvised air-raid shelter. These 'shelters' were converted classrooms with the windows bricked up — dark and airless.

We had been issued with gas masks early in 1939, and each time a mock air raid took place in school we had to march to the shelters and put them on. I hated this, the only consolation was that we were given wine gums to chew whilst wearing the gas masks. Sometimes we would sit for more than an hour doing nothing, to prepare us for the 'real thing'.

I was only vaguely aware of what was happening in Europe, but I did know that Adolf Hitler was an evil man. In the summer holidays of 1939 we had to make regular visits to school to be briefed on what would happen if evacuation should occur. We were put into groups of about thirty pupils with one teacher and a parent who would be accompanying the school. My mother had decided that she would come with us.

Crowd of kids waving as they board train.

At five o'clock in the morning on Friday 1st September, the Powell family trudged from 125 Westway to the playground of Old Oak School. We each carried our own carrier bag of clothes — we did not have suitcases in those days. We were each allowed to have one toy to take with us. I took my china doll, Mary, whom I loved very dearly, and which I still have.

When we arrived at the school, the teacher in charge of each group issued us with a luggage label which we had to pin on to ourselves and another small carrier bag of provisions as we did not know when we were going to get a meal.

By six o'clock, the playground was filled with hundreds of children, many with weeping mothers clinging to them. I was quite excited about leaving London and although I was sorry to be leaving my father, I did have my mother with me. My younger brother Brian and I thought it was all a great adventure and planned many things which we would do when we got into 'the country'.

Buses soon came and took us to Paddington Station. I had never been to a big railway station before and was astounded by it. I remember the enormous glass roof which I was to see many more times during the course of the war — sometimes in its bombed state.

Paddington was just thronged with children from schools all over London and we were bustled on to a train. My group got split up from the remainder of the school in all this chaos and we eventually arrived in a village called Box in Wiltshire, with a school from another part of London.

On arrival at the village we were taken to the village hall and told to stand in family groups. The Billeting Officer was frantically trying to keep brothers and sisters together so that they would not be split up in their billets. The village women were wandering around the hall, surveying us and trying to pick 'nice' looking children, as we were indeed a motley crew.

We seemed to be standing around for hours, rejected because we were too large a family. Eventually, a lady with a very posh voice came over to us and remarked that we looked a clean lot and that she would take us.

The house we were taken to was not far from the village hall. It was adjacent to the village church. It was enormous. I can remember thinking that it looked like Buckingham Palace. It was in fact the Manor House of the village, called Box House, and our benefactor was the Hon. Mrs Shaw-Mellor.

I had never been inside such a beautiful place before. I had only read about such places. I looked around in wonder at all the space and the magnificent things. Mrs Shaw-Mellor told us that we would be living in the servants' quarters and that my mother would be in charge of us.

We were given one large bedroom for all of us and we were to have our meals in the servants' hall. This was a very large room with a long table, because there were fifteen servants.

Brian and I decided to explore the house and play hide and seek, but were soon reprimanded and told in no uncertain terms that our place was definitely 'below stairs', and that we were not to wander from the servants hall.

The first meal which we had filled me with awe. Eating with so many people, strange food, using a napkin for the first time, it was too much. I cried myself to sleep that night, clutching Mary.

On Sunday 3rd September we all sat around the servants' table with the radio switched on. At eleven o'clock in the morning Neville Chamberlain announced that Britain was at war with Germany. I can remember vividly the young house-maids, chamber maids, and parlour maids bursting into tears and burying their faces into their crisply starched white aprons. I asked my mother why they were crying and she told me it was because their boy friends would have to go to war. My mother was crying also and I held her hand.

That night, before we went to bed, we had a rehearsal for an air raid. This time the air raid shelter turned out to be the most magnificent accommodation. Box House had acres of grounds and the shelter had been built underground far away from the house. We had to walk for what seemed like miles through an underground tunnel until we reached some beautiful rooms. These were elegantly furnished, again with designated areas for the servants and us. I didn't mind going into this shelter. We were allowed to play ludo for the duration of the mock raid.

With the chauffeur's children in Box, Wiltshire 1939.

Because of the influx of evacuees into the village, the village school was unable to accommodate us and so the evacuees were given the village hall. We were divided up into six classes, all in one room. There were few books and nothing to write on and so most of the lessons were given orally. School was very boring. I was due to sit my 'scholarship' (or 11+) that year but nobody seemed to bother with things like that. So I missed out on going to Grammar School at that stage. I was very disappointed.

Just before Christmas of that year, my mother gathered us all together in our room and told us that she was going back to London to look after my father who was very lonely. We were sad. Mrs Shaw-Mellor said that she could not keep us without my mother to look after us and that we would have to find another billet. It was impossible to find anywhere to take four children and so we were split up. Brian and Desmond went together as did Maureen and I. The houses we went to were very different from Box House.

They were next-door to each other in a terrace with two small bedrooms, no bathroom and an outside toilet. The landlady was kindly and very deaf.

At Christmas time Mrs Shaw-Mellor visited us to bestow gifts. I got a dolls' tea set and had great fun with Mary. However, I missed my mother and wanted to return to London.

I had by this time made friends with a girl called Dorothy from another London school. For her Christmas present, she had got a small bicycle. She was unhappy also. We plotted together to cycle back to London. Late one night in January 1940 with snow thick on the ground, I crept out of the house and met Dorothy at an appointed place. We took turns to pedal the bicycle whilst the other one sat on the saddle. We couldn't make it up Box Hill and had to push. Miraculously we rode for nearly six miles, to Chippenham, when we were stopped by a policeman, who talked to us kindly and returned us to Box. I was smacked for this and not allowed out to play for a whole week.

The early months of 1940 passed by without any invasion or air raids and so at the end of the summer term we were all overjoyed when my mother said we could return to London. She came to fetch us and we returned on the train to Paddington Station. It was lovely to be home and I was looking forward to going back to Old Oak School again.

Unfortunately there was a great teacher shortage, either because they were evacuated or because they were in the forces, and so school could only be in half day sessions, one week in the morning and the other in the afternoon. I spent much of my free time in the local library, reading and writing on projects.

In September we experienced our first real air raids. In the small garden of our house we had an Anderson shelter, half under ground and very different from the one at Box House. We all slept in this shelter because most of the raids occurred at night and we needed that security. The people next door to us wouldn't have a shelter built because it would spoil the garden and so at night they would come and share ours. My father built bunks in the shelter where nine of us slept.

There were many catch-phrases around during the war and at this time one particular one caught my imagination — 'boosting morale'. I didn't really know what this meant but on looking it up in the dictionary I decided that all the neighbours living around us needed their morale boosting. Bombs were dropping all around us, the noise from the guns

Children clambering into an Anderson Shelter.

based at nearby Wormwood Scrubs was deafening, food was short and there was little light relief. I thought they needed entertaining and so I formed a concert-party.

There were four of us, myself, Eileen (my best friend who lived next door) and Brian and Maureen. My elder brother disdainfully declined to participate. We used the initials of our first names for the name of our club, Dymphna, Eileen, Brian and Maureen — in order of seniority — and we became the DEBM FOUR.

We would invite the neighbours into my house in the early evening before the air raids began and regale them with singing and dancing, piano duets and funny jokes. Whether we achieved our aim is uncertain, but there were certainly some smiles on the neighbours faces as we cavorted unashamedly.

It was after one of these 'concerts' that the air raid siren sounded and we were hustled into the shelter, when suddenly there was the most horrendous crash and the shelter shook. It was some minutes before anybody could venture outside to see what had happened. The roofs of our houses had been blown off and walls partly demolished. A high explosive bomb had fallen on the church just three hundred yards away. We were all scared, but my mother was devastated. She panicked and said that we must immediately be re-evacuated. She did not even have time to consult my father, who at that time was working for the Rescue Service, digging people out of bombed buildings.

We hurriedly put a few clothes into a bag and walked to Paddington Station. There were no buses or tubes as it was in the middle of the night. It was a long way.

Emergency services had been set up at all the main line stations for emergencies of this kind and there were few formalities to be gone through. My mother simply registered us with an official and we were soon bidding yet another tearful farewell to her. We were herded on to the train with hundreds of children from all over London. There were no friends from our own school and we had no idea where we were going. The train seemed to be making an endless journey. At one stage I remember passing the sea and my heart jumped in eager anticipation at the thought of being able to swim, as this was one of my hobbies. But we turned inland and rattled on for several more miles.

Boot repairing class for Mitcham Lane School, Streatham, at Llangadock, Carmarthenshire.

Eventually we came to a halt. We had arrived somewhere and disembarked from the train. I remember thinking, 'It is 30th September 1940, I don't know where I am and I have no mother or father.'

We were taken by buses to another village hall. This time there were no welcoming ladies to select us. The glamour of being host to evacuees had worn off. The reputation of evacuees from London had been smeared by reports that we were dirty, unruly and dishonest, and nobody wanted us. There were, however, a few kind souls left and my sister and I were taken to one. My brothers were left behind in the church hall.

It was very late at night when we were introduced to our new family. They were an elderly couple with one grown up daughter. At first I couldn't understand what they were saying as they spoke with a funny accent. They told us where we were. We had come to St Columb Minor, a village about two miles from Newquay, Cornwall. My geography of the British Isles at this time was abysmal and I had no idea where this was. I asked whether it was near London and was told it was about two hundred and fifty miles away. This appalled me.

My sister and I shared a bed in a small room. We clung to each other that night. Things looked brighter in the morning when we were able to explore the house. It was quite a large house by our standards, with five bedrooms. Like most houses in this area the family did Bed and Breakfast for summer visitors. It was soon evident that we were taking up one of these valuable rooms and we were moved into the attic.

On the first Sunday morning we were there, Maureen and I were asked if we had been confirmed, so that we could join the family for Holy Communion. I had, but said that I couldn't take Communion because I hadn't been to Confession. On learning that we were Roman Catholics the family were horrified and said that we couldn't stay. I had began to quite like it there and begged to be allowed to join them for Communion without going to Confession. Eventually they agreed. Off we went to Church for the 8 a.m. Holy Communion Service. At 11 a.m we returned for Morning Service, at 2.30 pm we went to Sunday School and at 6 pm we went to Evensong. This was to be the patten of my Sundays for the next five years.

I had been billeted with a very religious family who were the pillars of the church. 'Uncle' was a churchwarden, 'Aunty' the leading light in the Women's Guild and 'Aunty Joan' was the organist and choirmistress.

When the Roman Catholic Priest who had accompanied the evacuees heard that I had taken Holy Communion in a Protestant Church, he came to the house and informed me that I would never be allowed to take Communion in a Roman Catholic Church again and I was excommunicated. I was only ten.

My indoctrination into the Church of England soon affected me. Within weeks I was reciting by heart the Apostle's Creed, the Nunc Dimittis and the Magnificat and I quickly knew almost every hymn number in the Ancient and Modern Hymn Book as it was my task each week to put the hymn numbers up on the board in Church.

Brian and Desmond, meanwhile, had had great difficulty in finding billets. Nobody wanted boys. They were split up and Desmond very soon returned to London as he was fourteen and able to leave school.

School for the evacuees was once again the Church Hall. There was a very nice Headmistress in charge of us and on looking back, I realise she tried to put as much variety into our lessons as possible. In addition to English and arithmetic we had sewing, music, play-reading and poetry. This I enjoyed.

She also introduced out-of-school activities, one of which was Recorder Club. I quickly learnt to play and she gave me a recorder to keep and asked me to play the hymns in morning assembly. I still have the recorder.

It soon became apparent that two hundred and fifty children having lessons in one room was not educationally beneficial and so the Parish Council allowed us to use other venues in the village. We were divided into classes and I spent one year having lessons in the Methodist Church and another year in the Bethel Chapel.

As many evacuees began to return to London and Plymouth and numbers became fewer, the handful of us who remained were absorbed

186   *Children from Woodmansterne Road School, Streatham, in the Village Hall at Farmers, Carmarthenshire.*

into the village school. This was conducted on very rigid and Victorian methods in a Victorian school building. I was quite bright and always top of the class, but I was bored and not being stretched. I spent much of my time reading and writing stories and helping younger children.

The highlight of the week was when the Mobile Library van came to the school and I was allowed to act as librarian. I enjoyed doing this and I also got the first pick of the best books.

There were no school dinners provided in those days and, for five years, each weekday my lunch consisted of a threepenny Cornish pasty which the local baker used to bring around on a tray. I could really have eaten a fourpenny one ! Some days these pasties were horrible, with gristly fatty meat, but on other days when the butcher had no meat the baker would use corned beef instead. I much preferred these.

On most Saturdays, Maureen and I were given sixpence each and had to walk the two miles into Newquay to have lunch at a British Restaurant. These were canteens set up by the government to help people to supplement their rations. I hated the food.

If my mother had sent us some pocket money we would go to the pictures, otherwise we would wander around the shops or go to the beach.

The one delight in living in Cornwall was the sea. The beaches were magnificent and there were lots of coves and caves to explore. I also learnt to surf. I used to watch people surfing on the big Atlantic rollers and envied them as I didn't have a surf board. Then one day I found an old ironing board on a rubbish heap and realized that its shape was similar to a surf board. I stripped it of its outer covering and found a lovely wooden ply wood board underneath. At last I had a surf board. The other children in the village soon copied my idea and there were many angry and perplexed mothers who could not explain the disappearance of so many ironing boards.

The people I lived with had relatives who owned a farm and in the school holidays I would spend many days helping to pick potatoes and to harvest and I even learnt how to milk a cow. It was hard work on the farm but I enjoyed my days there.

All signs were blanked out when invasion was feared.

187

The house where Dymphna lived in Cornwall. Notice the Bed and Breakfast sign in the window.

In the summer months, Aunty and Uncle would have visitors in for Bed and Breakfast and an evening meal. I had to do a lot of work for them, changing beds, cleaning rooms and preparing vegetables. I was envious of Maureen who did not have to do these chores, but was allowed to play as she was much younger. I was always glad when the summer season was over.

On Sundays we were not allowed to play games and there was one awful year when Christmas Day fell on a Sunday and so the toys and games we had been sent had to be put away. I thought this was very hard.

In the dark winter evenings we were allowed to play games like draughts and ludo and then 'Monopoly' came on to the market and this was great fun and occupied many hours.

Towards the end of 1943 we returned to London for a short period. There had been few air raids and my father by now had been drafted into the army, and my mother was lonely.

It was nearing the time when I would be leaving school as I was almost fourteen. I did not want to leave school and reported this at my leaving interview. I could not go to Grammar School as I had not taken the Entrance Examination and so I was sent to Hammersmith Central School. These schools do not exist now. They were a form of interim school between Grammar and Elementary but with a vocational bias. I was put into the commercial stream learning shorthand, typing and book-keeping. I was not very good at it and I hated it. By now I had decided that I wanted to be a teacher, but it was a goal not within my grasp.

I was secretly overjoyed one night when my school was hit by incendiary bombs and burnt down. Air raids had become frequent again and my mother was anxious for our safety. She had been offered sanctuary at the home of my father's army friend in a small mining village in South Wales. I refused to go, but Maureen and Brian were bustled off to Paddington yet again. The beautiful glass roof had by now been destroyed and I began to look on Paddington as a scene of departure and rejection.

If two strong men are available to handle the shelter, the quickest and most effective method is to turn the shelter on its side and knock up the ends with a hammer.

FIGURE 5A

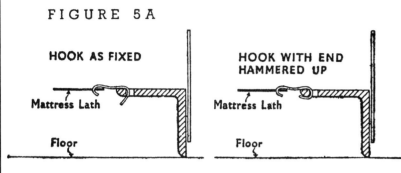

HOOK AS FIXED

Mattress Lath

Floor

HOOK WITH END HAMMERED UP

Mattress Lath

Floor

seventh stage

Put the side and end panels over the studs.

Get inside just before the last one is put into place, and fix the four hook-and-eye fastenings as shown in Figure 7. You

FIGURE 6

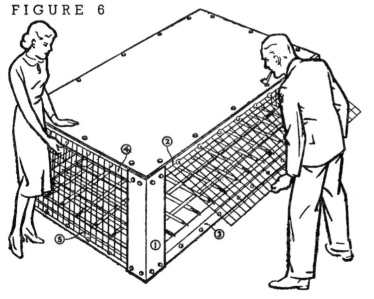

will notice in the illustration that the eyepiece is fastened to the last wire of the end covering; the hook-piece, however, is

My mother and I visited Maureen and Brian on some occasions. They were learning Welsh at school and had already acquired quite strong Welsh accents. I felt estranged from them.

Back home at Westway we had abandoned the outside Anderson shelter and were now in possession of a Morrison shelter. This was a strong metal cage which could also be used as a table. One night my mother and I were asleep inside it, when suddenly we were blown right outside the house into the garden still inside the cage. A 'doodlebug' had dropped nearby.

This time my mother insisted that I could no longer stay in London, that Brian and Maureen should be returned from Wales, and that we should all return to Cornwall. This we did. Maureen and I went back to Aunty and Uncle but Brian had to be found another billet.

Because I was fourteen now, I could not go back to school and so I had to find a job. I became a shop assistant in a small village shop. I did not find this very satisfying. The headmistress who had given me the recorder was still in the village and she took a great interest in me.

One day she came into the shop with some exciting news. The Cornish Education Authority were looking for potential teachers to supply the demand which would be needed when the war was over. They were going to set up a school for fourteen and fifteen year olds, educate them, and then train them as teachers. Selection was to be by interview. I was recommended by her to go for interview.

Excitedly one morning, dressed in my best dress and hat, I got on a bus to go to Truro, where the interviews were to be held. I obviously impressed them at the interview and I was selected. Unfortunately there were not enough other candidates of the right calibre to form the training school. There were only four of us in Cornwall who were selected.

However, it was decided that the four of us could be absorbed into the local Grammar Schools. I could not believe my good fortune when I entered Newquay County Girls School for the first time. I expected it to be like all the schoolgirls story books I had been reading; things like 'Upper Fourth', 'prep' and 'lab' had become a reality.

My big disappointment was that I could not wear the uniform. My mother felt it was too expensive, especially if, when the war was over, I was transferred to a London Grammar School and would have to have another uniform there. I felt very conspicuous being the only girl without uniform. I found the work very difficult as I had not been taught subjects like algebra, trigonometry, physics, French and chemistry. I worked very hard and spent all my leisure time studying.

One thing I was very good at was athletics and games. I was soon in the netball team and was selected for three events representing the Middle School on Sports Day. I was very excited about this as I had not done anything publicly before. I had hoped that Aunty and Uncle would come to see me but they were not interested and felt that I was wasting valuable study time on such trivial pursuits.

However, Brian, my staunch ally and proud of his sister, played truant from school and came to watch me. I won all my three events: high jump, hurdles and 100 yards. I had now the Middle School Championship and was presented with a magnificent silver cup.

Brian and I proudly walked home from Newquay clutching the cup. When I arrived at the house I was severely reprimanded for being so late and was sent to bed without any tea. I was told that the cup could not stay in the house. When Brian returned to his billet he had been locked out and had to spend the night in a garden shed. When he went to school the following day he was caned for playing truant.

Our glorious day was shattered and we longed to go home.

We began to sense from reading the newspapers and from grown-ups' talk that the war was coming to an end. Suddenly on May 8th 1945 I heard the church bells ring for the first time. The war was over and we could go home. There was great rejoicing that day. We did not have to go to school and the whole village prepared for a big party in the evening to be held in the Recreation Ground. The party was to be preceded by everybody joining in the Floral Dance down the village high street. I had been taught this dance at the village school, but never imagined how lovely it would be to be bedecked with flowers and invited to dance by Richard, a boy I had admired from a distance for a long time. It was one of the happiest days of my life.

Soon after this we left Cornwall for ever, bidding fond farewells to those who had looked after us. I had mixed feelings about them but was very grateful for many of the things which they did for me.

When we returned home, there was a big welcoming party in Westway and I felt that being an evacuee was something quite important.

I corresponded with Aunty and Uncle for many years afterwards. They came to stay with us in London, and years later I returned to St Columb Minor with my husband and baby daughter, to 'show them off' and to let them see that I had become a successful teacher.

I learnt many things during six years of evacuation but one thing above all others — I know I could never voluntarily part from my children under any circumstances.

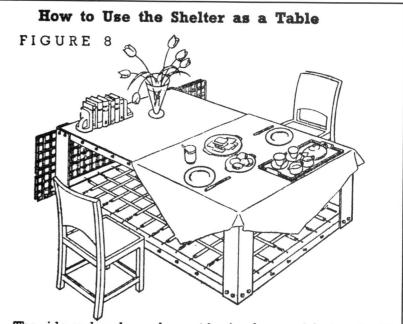

How to Use the Shelter as a Table

FIGURE 8

The side and end panels must be in place and fastened with the hook and eye fastenings, when the shelter is in use as such. To use it as a table, or to make the bed, the panels can be removed.

SHIRLEY PUGH

We were living in Liverpool, and the day war broke out, I heard the announcement on the radio and went to play out with my ball against the house wall. I was eight years old and I lived with my father and mother, my grandparents and a baby sister. I asked mother if I could have a label and go on a train and be an evacuee. She said she would see to it, so a week or ten days later, she and Grandma saw me off at Lime Street, on the school train bound for Denbigh in the beautiful Vale of Clwyd. As I had not yet attended the school I didn't know the other girls, but I soon made friends.

From the station we had to walk up a very steep hill to the church hall where we sat in a circle so that the locals could choose us. The local dignitaries such as the Mayor, the Town Clerk and the bank manager had first choice. I was lucky enough to be chosen by the doctor's wife. She only lived round the corner in a very fine house and introduced me to the doctor and their son David, a boy of my own age.

Next morning I found my breakfast cooked by a maid, Myfanwy, and so it was every day, and she made me eat cereal, bacon and egg, toast and marmalade, before I went to school. It was more than a mile to walk and I had to walk home at lunch time and then home at night - it did me no harm and I still like walking!

Quite early in 1940, we were taken back to Liverpool. Many children had not had as happy an experience as I had, and most were homesick. When the school year came to an end in July we were encouraged to continue to attend school, but a programme of dance, singing and drama took the place of lessons. We had frequently to take shelter when the sirens sounded.

The doctor and his wife continued to keep in touch with us and asked my parents to send me back to them in Denbigh. When they learned that my mother was expecting, they told her just to come, with my sister and the new baby (which turned out to be a brother) and they would find us somewhere to live.

So the rest of my war years were spent very happily. I attended a Welsh

Shirley on Evacuation.

council school and passed to the Grammar School. As far as I was concerned there were only two alarming happenings. A bomb was said to have landed in a field outside the town and one day a company of small, yellow-faced, slit-eyed soldiers wandered into town. We thought it was the Japs but they were Siamese.

My father came to stay every third weekend when he had a Saturday off. I didn't quite realise how my mother must have felt, on her own with three children, far from her parents and her husband. I didn't know that sometimes, when I was tucked up and asleep in bed, she heard the German planes flying overhead, in from the Irish sea, heading for Liverpool and Birkenhead. The baby was not very strong and had a deformity of his feet which was later corrected. I helped Mother by wheeling him out a lot in the pram.

When I returned to Denbigh on 3rd September 1989, people asked about 'the baby'. I said, 'Oh, David? He'll be fifty next year!'

LORNA PYKE

About three days before war broke out, our refugees arrived. My father had telephoned his bank manager in London, and suggested that his wife and three children, aged four, six and eight should come and stay with us in North Devon. We lived in a rambling old Georgian house surrounded by fields, with orchards and woods beyond the garden and a tennis court.

My mother and father were used to peace and quiet as I was the only one. The young family brought laughter, noise and cheer to our house. We took ourselves off for picnics, and the shadow and dread of war and all its consequences was shouldered by our elders.

The days were golden and sunny and, one day, joined by some young neighbours, we went to the fishponds and woods to play 'tag'. We hoped the landlord, who was fierce, would not be around. A Scottie dog accompanied us, and having first put our picnic baskets under the humpback bridge, and the lemonade bottles to cool in the stream, we played around the pine trees.

Suddenly, the dreaded landlord was spied, walking down the field adjacent to the bridge. We all hid under the bridge, clutching the Scottie dog. The landlord stood on top for what seemed like ages. Finally he said, 'Come out! Leave immediately!' We slunk off to our own domain, where everyone soon recovered their spirits. My father subsequently received a nasty letter concerning our trespassing. 'One more thing I could have done without,' he said.

London children evacuated in style to a stately home.

When war was declared, nobody knew what would happen. The young mother and her children felt very isolated and out of touch down in Devon. There was an atmosphere of tension and fear, although everyone tried to remain falsely cheerful. She decided to go back to her husband, and they left us. I was sad to see them go, but three days after that, I was called up, and went to Bovington Camp in Dorset.

Meanwhile people were being evacuated from London in large numbers. We had two cottages which were commandeered for families arriving in our area. They were adjoining the garden and in an orchard. They were of the 'two up, two down' variety, with a cold sink in the scullery, a large black cooking stove, and an outside 'privy'.

The evacuees hated the isolation. It was two miles to the nearest pub and shop. They kept their coal in the cupboards, and were lacking in any sort of hygiene, using their bedroom floors as the 'loo'. When my father asked to inspect the cottages, he retreated under a torrent of abuse. They left after a short period, bored to tears by the peace and quiet, and missing their neighbours on their London streets.

My uncle and aunt, who lived in Putney, had two small girls, aged six and eight, who were evacuated with their school to Cattistock in Dorset. Uncle Raymond and Aunt Molly missed them very much. When they came from London to visit the children, they invited me, then stationed at Sherborne, to tea one day.

We first went for a walk to warm ourselves up, not having much in the way of heating during the war. It was wet and windy, and we returned and sat around in the little sitting room of the pub where they were staying. The little girls were shy, and my aunt cuddled them on her knee. My uncle was full of jokes, but everybody knew that this treasured meeting would soon be over, and the heartache of separation would start again.

Back in London, a bomb dropped right next door to them. Everyone in that house was killed, and my aunt and uncle, next door, found themselves suspended over the space of what had been their home. Their possessions were blown down the street, and Aunt Molly's fox fur was wrapped around a lamppost. They were homeless, and had lost everything, but at least they knew that their little girls were safe, and that they were right to have had them evacuated.

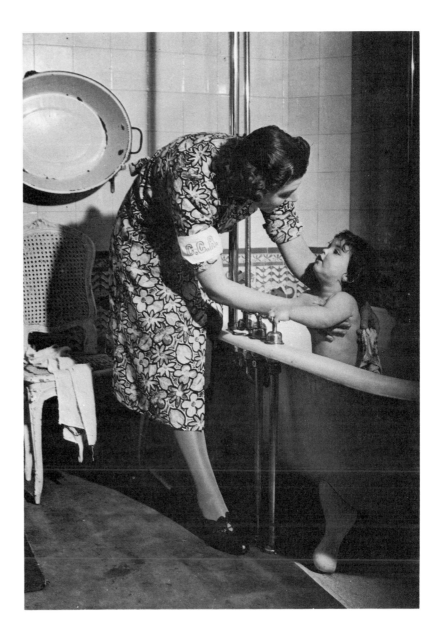

Bath time at Waddesdon Manor for London evacuees.

Mrs Liddell, headmistress of Hugh Middleton Infants School, Farringdon Street, explaining the evacuation scheme to children and their mothers. 26th August 1939.

ETHEL ROBINSON

A woman had come to the house and said I was to go round to the school and give them the children's particulars for evacuation. The day my children were evacuated I was all up hill and down dale, I did not know what I was doing. I had to give them all their separate clothes because we did not know if they were to go separately or together. Terry was four years eight months, Peggy was nine or ten and Joyce, twelve. They had their tags tied on and they each had their little cases.

We had to walk to Canonbury Station. I picked up Terry and walked along with him. He was a ton weight but I did not care. When we got to the station one of the women came up to me and said, "You are going to let him go, aren't you?" I said, "Of course, why?" She said, "Well, the way you have stuck to him all along, we thought you were going to change your mind!" Well as long as my children were safe I did not worry about myself. That is why I let them go.

When I came back home, in all the kerfuffle about getting them off, I found I did not have a key to get indoors. I had to go to the lady next door and see if I could get over her wall. I had to break a window to get in and then I just sat there and had a good old cry. Then I thought "Well it's no good crying, I've just got to get cracking", but I did not know what to do, I missed them so much. I had to go round to the school to find out where the children had been sent and I learned that they were at Reading, in Berkshire.

Ethel Robinson's children Terry and Peggy.

I did not wait to see the children's hostess because if I had seen her I would have made a big fuss and I did not want to get the albino lady into any trouble. She told me that nobody liked the hostess at all around there because she loved her drink and she used to go out regularly and get drunk. The albino lady, Mrs Eastall, wanted to keep the children and so she did. She looked after them wonderfully, and when it was their birthdays she would make a cake and have other children in to have a party for each one. I was very pleased about that.

But Peggy did not like being away very much. She had a little fairy cycle but it did not have any brakes on it and one day she put Terry on the handlebars and went tearing up the road. She stopped and saw a Military Policeman standing outside this place and she went up to him, it was a good thing she did, and she asked him where London was. She thought London was only up the road. He looked at them and said "Oh, you look very tired to me. I think you had better come in and have a cup of tea." So they took the bicycle in with them and they were treated very well.

Of course, meanwhile, Mrs Eastall had missed Peggy and Terry, and had got so worried that she went to the police. They contacted us of course and we had to go down to Reading Police Station. When we got there they had already found them from the Military Police, but neither of the children wanted to leave because they had had lemonade and lumps of cake and were having a good time.

We took them home after that, there was a lull on at that time. I got them into school in London but they did do a bit of truanting. One day, my husband went to the library, which was across the road from us, in Holloway Road, and as he went in he saw our two children over the road. They had not been to school. When he asked them why they were not in school they said they had a holiday! I took them back to the school and it turned out that they had not been to school for a week. They had left in the morning with their milk money and came home for their dinner at the right time.

When the bombing started again, Peggy and Terry were evacuated to Berkshire to stay with a Mrs Easthall, and Joyce went to Somerset. They did like it in the country really because there was so much space to play in and they stayed there until the war was over.

They had been away for some months and one day, when my husband, Ted, came home from work — we were picture frame makers — I said to him, "This house seems like a tomb, it is so quiet". So we decided to go down and see the children. We had a motor bike and side-car and we went to Reading. We found the children were with a woman who did not care tuppence for them. I could not find my three children at the house at all. Apparently the woman had gone out and left my children sitting on the door step. There had been a violent storm and another lady, down the road, heard them crying. She was an albino lady and she took them into her house. She was a marvellous woman.

IRIS SHARP

I was just eleven years old in September 1939, my brother, Michael was seven and my sister Valerie was coming up to her fifth birthday in October. It seems very young, when you think about it now, to be parted from our parents. It must have been dreadful for them to have to make the decision, but I suppose the Government made it for them, telling them they were saving the Nation's youngsters. It is quite a thought, isn't it, that parents were persuaded not so much because THEIR children would be safer but because THE COUNTRY'S children would be safer. I wonder though, whether we were so safe when you think about some of the places children were sent to.

I went to Sandhurst in Kent, which is on the Sussex/Kent borders, and planes were going overhead all through the Battle of Britain. We were in the hop fields whilst they were going over, watching the vapour trails in the sky and dog fights going on, though it did not mean much to me at the time.

Sandhurst was a lovely place, however, and in many ways we were very, very lucky. There were we three children, another family of three and another child whose mother came with her. So there were seven of us children, living in this very large house. I think the gardens were what impressed me most when I was there, they were so beautiful. I had never seen such well kept gardens, all owned by one person. The house was owned by an elderly lady, Mrs. Hodges, whose late husband had been a Church of England minister. She showed us some beautiful vestments that she had embroidered with gold threads, some years before. One of the grandchildren was there as well, Miss Sally, with her Mademoiselle.

The sitting room was ours and we ate and played there. Mrs. Hodges had her meals in her own room and lived in her private area. We did not actually become part of the family. There were three maids. There was a parlour maid, a cook and a housemaid there, and there were a couple of gardeners. The cook cooked our food, of course, and it was brought into us. Mrs. Lucas or Mrs. Long used to do most of the trotting backwards and forwards, and most of the washing up was done by the maids. Mrs Lucas used to help too but I do not think she was expected to do too much. The maids seemed to have taken in this huge number of people willingly. They were a nice group.

I remember the milk used to be delivered in a big churn and then put into jugs on a tray. They did not have fridges but the cellar was very cold. The jugs were filled up for early morning breakfast, early morning tea for Mrs Hodges, and anyone else who happened to be staying. The big jugs were for the evacuees' breakfast and tea. These jugs were all put on a big tray and the Parlourmaid carried it down the stairs to the cellar. I remember, on one occasion, there was a terrible scream and a bang and all the jugs went everywhere. She had trodden on a frog as she went downstairs! The cellar was damp and cool and the back door was right by the entrance to the cellar steps, and I suppose this thing had hopped in and down the steps. That was goodbye to a lot of jugs and a lot of milk and the frog as well.

Just down the road from where we were was a group of about six cottages. There was a Mrs Smith and her daughter Pat, who lived there. She was a wonderful lady. Her husband was in the Army, he was at Dunkirk, and her daughter, Pat, was about my sister's age. She made us very welcome. She was always available if someone wanted a shoulder to cry on or some comforting was required, like a sore knee to be bandaged.

The Army trucks used to go through the village, past the Sandhurst Cross, and half of them used to hesitate at the top of the hill right by the cross and Mrs Smith would come out of her house and say 'Got time for a cup of tea boys?' and she would make a pot of tea for them out of her

Evacuated children at Waddesdon Manor in Buckinghamshire.

meagre rations. She would take in their washing and have it ready for them. If they were going on manoevres or something, she would take in their towels and things for them and she would have it all ready for them when they came back. Of course some of the village frowned upon this little bit of help, but she said, 'If somebody is doing that for my Fred then that is all that matters. They can talk, they can say what they like. I only hope someone is doing the same for him.' She felt she was doing her bit for the war effort.

Mrs Smith died some years after the war, but every year, in the Spring, she would go out and pick primroses and send a box of them to my mother. Her husband remained friends with us for years afterwards. He moved to Dartford and he used to come up to London and see me every five or six weeks and have a chat about old times.

Other than Mrs Smith's daughter, Pat, there were no other children nearby. There were no other houses nearby either, really, but there was a farm up the road and there were some apple orchards. We were allowed to walk through the apple orchards and we could eat anything that we liked as long as it was on the ground. They were delicious apples and even though they were windfalls we did not have to worry about them, they were lovely. I remember seeing cob nuts on trees for the first time, green first of all and then brown. We'd break them open and eat them.

We had this big sitting room downstairs and a huge bathroom, one of the biggest bathrooms I have ever seen, with the bath in the corner. We were allowed the five attic bedrooms around at the back part of the house, and from there we could see the kitchen garden. A large part of the garden was made over to us to play in. I remember being very impressed with the dahlias, especially one huge one. There was a peach tree growing up one wall which caught the sun. One of us, I don't remember which one it was, climbed up part of it and snapped a branch off. Gosh, we made a run for it! There was also a lovely piece of the garden, known as the primrose walk, and in the Spring of 1940 I can remember, vividly, the sight of hundreds and hundreds of primroses out. I can particularly remember taking my parents, when they came down to see us, through the gardens to see it.

The lady with the 'only daughter' eventually went back to join her husband in London and another lady called Mrs Long came down. She had two grown up daughters, one of whom was a diving champion who used to give diving exhibitions before the war. Mrs. Long was a kindly lady, and she looked after us very well. She also became very attached to the lady of the house and when Mrs. Hodges eventually thought she could not cope with evacuees any longer, Mrs. Long stayed with her to be her companion. The war started many friendships which lasted for years.

We had about a three quarters of a mile walk to the village school. There were problems in getting my little sister to and from school, because she was young and her little legs found the walk pretty hard going. I devised games to make her get to school in reasonable time. Of course, the 1939/1940 winter was a very bad one and we did not go to school for about three weeks and we thought that was fantastic. The Headmaster, Mr Bowling was a wonderful man, very caring. He divided his school up very evenly. The younger ones were incorporated into the classes with his own village children. But the bigger ones were shared between the school and a Methodist hall about another quarter of a mile away. We had a week about, one week we would be in school and the next we would be down in the Methodist hall. There was an old harmonium there which we were forbidden to touch, but of course we did touch it.

In the June of 1940 I was moved to Snodland because the schooling I was getting in the village school was not up to standard. I should have changed schools in the September that we were evacuated, but I had stayed with my brother and sister, who were now going back to London. The lady that I went to in Snodland was horrified that she was getting such a large evacuee. Because I was tall and I had an enormous appetite, she found feeding me hard going. I remember on one occasion she had her sister and her husband there and we were having Sunday morning breakfast. I picked up my fourth slice of bread and looked up to see my hostess mouthing to her sister, 'That's four pieces of bread!', and feeling mortified that she was criticising my appetite. I had always eaten well at home and in my previous billet. She found, soon after I arrived that she was going to have a baby, and so a few months later I was moved on to her husband's brother's house. They were a nice family. They had two children and they looked after me very well and made me welcome. They were very ardent Methodists, and it was three

Evacuees read letter from home.

8th June, 1946

To-day, as we celebrate victory, I send this personal message to you and all other boys and girls at school. For you have shared in the hardships and dangers of a total war and you have shared no less in the triumph of the Allied Nations.

I know you will always feel proud to belong to a country which was capable of such supreme effort; proud, too, of parents and elder brothers and sisters who by their courage, endurance and enterprise brought victory. May these qualities be yours as you grow up and join in the common effort to establish among the nations of the world unity and peace.

George R.I

times a day church. Mrs Eastwood was a beautiful dress maker. She used to sit in the evenings at the sewing machine. On Saturday evenings she would work until the dot of midnight and then the sewing would go away because she did not believe in doing anything like that on a Sunday. She did not do any cooking on Sunday either. She would cook elaborately on Saturday morning and that did for a cold lunch on Sunday as well. Mr Eastwood was a lay preacher. We were given religious books and pamphlets to read on Sunday and sent three times to church.

I persuaded my mother that it was necessary for me to come home to London every other week end, and I used to get on the train from Snodland on Friday afternoon after school, singing all the way home if there was nobody else in the carriage with me. Of course it meant that I was at home for some of the raids but it did not matter to me, I was just glad to be home. My mother worked in the Arsenal in the cordite factory to start with and I remember being horrified one time when I came home to find that she was yellow from the cordite. She used to have to have extra milk ration to counteract the yellow. Then she became a bus conductor on the London Transport buses for four and a half years.

About 1970, my sister and I decided to have a nostalgic trip down to Sandhurst. We got off at the coach stop, where we had always got off, and we walked up through the village to the green, with the clock tower on it, looking at all the houses and remembering the people. When we got up as far as Sandhurst Cross, we peered into the front drive and walked about half way up. Then our courage failed us, and we walked back out again. We went off to have a look round Bodiam Castle and then we went back to the Cross again and this time we walked back up the drive again and decided to knock on the door. There was a Mr and Mrs Whistler living there and we explained that we had been evacuees there and said would they mind if we just walked around the garden. They said, 'Oh do by all means and when you've seen all that you want to see, come and knock again and have a look around the house.' Any way we walked around the garden and then came back to the house. It was big, but not as big as my childish mind had remembered. They took us up to the attic bedrooms which had been our bedrooms but it had all changed. I have always liked the country and I am sure it first stemmed from being evacuated to the lovely countryside around Sandhurst.

Message from King George the Sixth to the children.

SHEILA SHEAR

Not the least of the traumas which World War II brought was the evacuation of Londoners to safe areas in the country. To be suddenly uprooted from one's home environment, family and friends was very frightening to all, but especially to young children.

Following two abortive attempts to leave London, one in 1939 the other in 1940, each time taking only our nightclothes and sabbath candlesticks, my parents decided in the height of the Blitz, January 1941, that we had taken enough of nightly bombing and shelter life and that they, my sister Myrtle, aged four, and myself, aged nine, should try once more to leave London for safer surroundings. We travelled to the small town of Chesham in Buckinghamshire, suggested by my father for no reason other than he had been evacuated there for a short time as a young boy in the First World War.

We arrived at the billeting office early in the afternoon and were told to go across the road to number 26 Blucher Street, where a bachelor named Harry Mayo had agreed to take in a family of evacuees. With trepidation we knocked on the door and were surprised when the door was opened directly into the living room, no hall or entrance at all. We introduced ourselves and Mr Mayo invited us in and showed us around the house.

There was the small room we had just entered, which led into another of similar size which then led into a scullery. Mr Mayo said we could occupy the front room which was furnished with an antique circular walnut table and four chairs, a pair of Victorian 'Mother and Father' chairs and a love seat — I was too young to appreciate the beauty of this furniture. To my delight there was also a piano in figured walnut with gold candelabra and a matching stool to hold music.

Mr Mayo would use the second room and we were to share the scullery, which had a grey stone floor, a gas cooker and a cream 'Butler' sink with running water, but alas it only produced cold water. There were no facilities for hot, no bathroom and no inside toilet. Mr Mayo would keep to his own in the front of the house, my parents and sister would share another in the back, and for me, a luxury I had never previously enjoyed, a room of my own. It was very small, only a bed and a chair, but for me it was magical to have this privacy for the first time in my life. The thrill of looking from my bedroom window onto the garden and beyond to the lovely park and dairy farm brought an excitement I shall always remember. Later, in the summer, I found that if I leaned far enough out of my bedroom window I could pick apples off the tree, and although they were sour cooking apples, they tasted like nectar to this 'East End' evacuee.

There was no lighting or heating in the bedrooms and we undressed and did our nighttime reading by the light of a torch when we were lucky enough to be able to buy torch batteries. In the years that followed we were to become familiar with the smell of a paraffin heater, a luxury we only enjoyed when we were ill, and aside from that dressed and undressed in bitter cold in the winter months. Downstairs was lit by gas mantles and my father, a B.B.C. News addict, was devastated to find that Mr Mayo did not possess a radio. He promptly brought a set that was run on accumulator batteries and it became my regular weekly job to take these batteries to be topped up. So we introduced Mr Mayo to the delights of 'Music While You Work', 'Saturday Night Hippodrome', 'Worker's Playtime', 'ITMA' and the many, many wonderful programmes that became such a large part of our lives during those stressful years.

The rent for this house was 12/6d per week and Mr Mayo thought that my parents' offer of 7/6d towards this was far too much, but was persuaded to accept this contribution, although he never felt comfortable about it.

Very soon my sister and I began to call our host 'Uncle Harry'. He appeared quite elderly to us, but I realize now he was then in his late fifties. Over the years which followed we became his family, he became our beloved uncle, and we were proud of the way a single gentile man and a traditional Jewish East End family learned to live together in such difficult and trying circumstances.

At Passover Uncle Harry ate matzos, the unleavened bread which Jewish people eat for this week long festival, on Sabbath he enjoyed 'kneidlach' a delicious matzo meal dumpling in chicken soup, which he insisted on eating with a knife and fork and not with a spoon as we had always done. He even fasted with us for 25 hours on Yom Kippur because he thought it would be unfair for him to eat when we were not permitted to. The fast is difficult enough, but alas on one occasion he began his with bacon and so suffered an unbearable thirst all day, but stubbornly refused to give in and waited to break his fast with us on some more conventional Jewish cooking.

At Christmas it was our turn to join in and with much excitement we accepted invitations to join with Uncle Harry's family for Christmas Supper.

Food rations had been stored and food points saved to provide enough to give us all a good meal and for the first time Myrtle and I were introduced to the traditions of mince pies, Christmas puddings, Christmas trees and home made Christmas crackers.

We played games, sang songs and danced the St. Bernard's Waltz, Military Two-step and The Lancers, it all seemed a long way from the constant air raids, bombings and shelter life we had left behind.

As we evolved into our daily life we learned much about each other. Uncle Harry was a talented amateur artist and painted country garden scenes and vases of flowers which he copied from the covers of chocolate boxes. His pride and joy was a copy he had painted of the 'Laughing Cavalier', we were fascinated watching him and learning the mysteries of mixing oil paints and the care needed to paint in watercolours. He introduced me to the joy of looking at paintings and my family have several of his, which they treasure.

His shaving routine, which took place in his downstairs room, was a daily ritual. He used an open 'cut-throat' razor and sharpened it on a leather strop, lathered his face and then carefully scraped off his beard. Myrtle and I watched with awe, afraid to speak or move in case we distracted or jogged him and very relieved when the razor was washed and placed in its little plush velvet box until the next day.

If the sun was shining and we were not at school, Uncle Harry would take a day off work from his job as a furniture upholsterer and he, Myrtle and I would go on a picnic when we would collect berries, fir cones and wild flowers to press when we got home. He spent hours reading to us and helping us with our school homework and on special days let us read from his set of encyclopaedias.

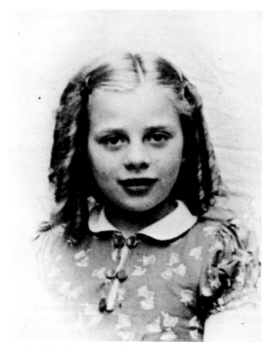

Sheila Shear, nee Ripps, aged ten years.

He encouraged me to learn to play the piano and, in the early days, supervised my practice hours with patience and tact. Sometimes he gave us his sweet coupons when the ration was two ounces per person per week, and every Friday he gave us 6d each pocket money. This practice continued until the week I was married in June 1953, by which time I was twenty years old and the pocket money had increased to 2/6.

We learned to love country life and were happy at school, but constantly concerned about my grandparents in London. When the bombing worsened they began to visit us for short breaks and Uncle Harry would insist that he slept on the floor downstairs to give them the luxury of a good night's rest. He became the greatest of friends with my Grandmother and Grandfather — Mamma and Zeida, although they spoke very little English and he no Yiddish, and he showed no surprise when my very orthodox Grandmother arrived with her own pots, pans, crocks and cutlery because she didn't trust us to be kosher enough for her requirements.

We joined in all traditional local events, fairs and garden fetes and all wartime fund-raising efforts such as 'Salute The Soldier Week', and then, in May 1945, it was all over — Victory in Europe. We joined the singing, cheering throngs 'round the war memorial in the centre of town, but returned to find Uncle Harry crying — unhappy because we, his family, would soon be returning to our own house. We promised to stay until school started in September and assured him that he would always be our dearest friend, whether we lived with him or not — so began another era of our friendship.

Sheila, aged twelve, and Myrtle, aged eight.

With mixed feelings we returned to London and from the first week Uncle Harry began a pattern of visiting us every Thursday. Always a bad traveller, he would journey by train from Chesham to Baker Street and often walk from Baker Street to our home in Tulse Hill, South London, a distance of some eight or nine miles, but never, ever complained. Myrtle and I would rush home from school, always anxious to see him, and on my Father's return from business, dinner was a lively meal exchanging the week's news and gossip, and together looking through the weekly 'Bucks Examiner' which he always brought with him. After dinner we would pack him a bag of home — made cake, bread pudding and anything else we thought he would enjoy, and 'en famille' we would escort him to the bus stop for the return journey to Baker Street.

He was an honoured guest at my wedding and thoroughly enjoyed the synagogue service and traditional Jewish meal and festivities which followed, as can be seen on the treasured photographs in my album. Following my marriage yet another pattern evolved, now he visited my parents' home for lunch and tea and they all came to my home for dinner, something from which he derived as much pride as my parents.

About every third year Uncle Harry came to London for the express purpose of buying a new hat; and the entire family would accompany him to the local Dunn's Hat Shop where he would take ages choosing a new hat which looked exactly the same as the one he was discarding — a dark brown trilby.

As the years passed and he was ageing he visited us less frequently, once a fortnight, then once a month, and during his last few years only occasionally when he would stay overnight, but contact was maintained by long and frequent letters, which he wrote with a steady hand in spite of advancing years and failing eyesight, and occasional visits to Chesham from me and my family.

From my first year of marriage I sent him a food parcel every Christmas, and immediately after the Jewish New Year and Yom Kippur in the Autumn I would begin to collect food for 'Uncle Harry's Christmas Hamper'.

Each week I purchased a few items and I had many embarassing moments in shops and supermarkets on meeting my Jewish friends when paying for tins of ham and spam and pork — all explanations sounded feeble. The hamper grew larger each year containing, in addition to tinned foods, biscuits, tea, chocolates, sweets and jam, of which he was passionately fond. As we raised our own family, handkerchiefs, socks, ties and small gifts made at school were added from them — Christmas 1975 was no exception and the hamper was larger than ever.

In January 1976 Uncle Harry's nephew telephoned to inform us that just before Christmas Uncle Harry had been run over by a car on his way to visit his neice in hospital. The injuries were fairly minor, but after two weeks of being unwell Uncle Harry had died that morning, he was 94 years old. He had always said that he did not believe in the church, he was not even sure that he believed in God but he was without doubt the truest Christian I have ever met.

My mother and I travelled by train to Chesham for the funeral — the town seemed smaller, the hills not so steep as when I was a child, and memories came flooding back.

Uncle Harry's family welcomed us, knowing we shared their grief and had arranged for us to travel in the first car and sit in the front row in the chapel. It was difficult for me to believe that I would never see Uncle Harry again, he had been an important part of my life for so many years.

The Vicar's moving eulogy reminded us that all people who reach a great age have 'Quantity of Life' , but that Uncle Harry's life had also

had great quality, and then it was all over, no more talking, no more flowers, no more Uncle Harry.

We returned to his nephew's home for tea and, as is customary on these occasions, the talk was of the past and the life we had led as London evacuees in Chesham. Then we were driven to the station and travelled home by train to London — we would never return we had no reason to. The following day my mother, sister and I each received a letter from Uncle Harry's Solicitor with a small bequest and an accompanying letter — the letter read:

'A very small token of my very great affection'.

Celebrating VE day in the country.

204

RENEE SILVERMAN

One day, when I was ten, we were told at school that we were all going to have to go away from London, not with our mums and dads, but with any brothers and sisters that we had. I had a brother who was two years younger than me and a sister who was eight years younger than me — just a little baby, so she couldn't come with us.

We had no suitcases, so our mums packed our clothes in a pillow slip and put string round the top and pulled it so that it looked like a rucksack and you had that on your back. You all had gas masks in little boxes, so you had one string hanging on one shoulder and the other string hanging on the other.

When we got on the train, some of us were crying and some laughing, lots of noise and lots of confusion. We got off the train at Windsor, which is not very far from London at all, but then it seemed a very long way from home, and we went into a hall. I can remember it so clearly, it's like it happened yesterday. If you were with your brother or sister, they tried to find you somebody who would take you together. So we walked along the street and the lady and man who were in charge of us knocked on a few doors and asked, 'Can you take three children? — can you take two? — do you want a boy? — do you want a girl?'

It was very frightening because we didn't know these people. We were only little and we didn't know who we were going to stay with. Well, most people wanted to take one child, so those of us who had brothers

Renee Silverman, nee Hersh.

Harold and Renee.

and sisters got left to the last. Eventually, a lady said that she would take my brother and me and she took us into the house.

She had a boy who was then about fourteen and he was very spiteful — he was a horrible kid — I don't think it was that he didn't like us, but he didn't want two strange kids coming into his home and sharing his life. He wasn't really very nice. They had an aviary in the garden and there were hundreds of tiny little budgerigars and canaries and that was his hobby. He bred these birds and he would not let us go anywhere near it.

My brother was only eight years old and he did miss his mummy and daddy a lot, but he was really quite a naughty little boy, and every time he did something naughty, I used to get into trouble. When he had been naughty and he didn't want to get told off (nobody ever smacked him), he used to pack all his things back into one of these pillow cases that was his kit bag and say, 'Right, I don't want to stay here anymore,' and walk out of the street door. They'd go after him and everybody had to run round looking for him. They couldn't let him go in case he got lost or something happened to him.

He remembers how he felt so unhappy, especially when he first arrived and the boys he was going around the village with took him to the sweetshop. He remembers they were all leaning over the glass-topped counter, looking at the sweets, with their hands on the glass top, when one of the boys said to the shopkeeper, 'He's a "four-by-two",' pointing at my brother. The shopkeeper said very angrily, 'Get your hands off there — I don't serve "four-by-twos".' My brother didn't understand what was meant by this and only years later realised it meant, 'He's a Jew'.

We wrote to our mums and dads and told them where we were living. After about two or three weeks, mums and dads used to come to see their children and they would come on a Saturday or a Sunday, whenever they could. And we went to school there. They gave us a school building that they had emptied out especially for the evacuees. We had our own London teachers, so that was good. We recognised everybody and we had all our own friends, so that was rather nice that we could keep together like that.

Well, no bombs fell in London for a long, long time at the beginning of the war, and as the time went on, more and more mums and dads took their children home. My dad came one day and said, 'Well, there's no reason why you should be here. There really isn't any bombing and we're going to take you home.' Of course, we were really pleased. We wanted to get home as soon as we could.

Then we lived in London at home and we went to school and all the windows in the school were pasted with sticky tape to stop them from smashing inwards in case the bombs started and the glass shattered. One room had been all reinforced with wood and concrete in the school, so that if there was a raid while you were there, you could go there for shelter. We lived in a big block of flats and on the ground floor, a room had been reinforced in the same way. We weren't home very long before the bombs did start to come. So, for a little while every night, we had to go downstairs to the shelter and I think I spent lots and lots of nights just reading and reading and reading.

We stayed in London until the doodlebugs started. I had an uncle who lived in Luton where it was thought no bombs would drop because it wasn't a very important place then, so my brother and I went to Luton and went to school there. A few weeks later, my mother and sister came and took a little flatlet not very far from where we were. They were only a short bus ride from us, and that was nice. My sister, who was five, went to school in Luton, and she remembers that when they had scripture lessons, she had to sit outside the door on the floor with a book, because the teachers said, 'Your scripture is different from ours.' She always thought, 'I wish I could hear about it.' She felt awful sitting on her own.

I played hookey from school for six weeks, and nobody knew I wasn't there because the teachers didn't know who the kids were. We were told to go to a school and if you turned up, you did, and if you didn't, you didn't. School was a church hall with very long trestle tables and each table was supposed to be a different class, so each had a teacher. All the tables were next to each other and one was learning Sums and another was learning Nature Study and another was learning English, so it was all a terrific muddle.

Renee, Harold and Jean Hersh back in London 1945.

There was no register, so no-one would ever have known if I didn't go to school. I went for a while, but then I got bored, so I used to get on the bus as if I were going to school, and get off at the Town Hall, which was also the Library, and go to the British Home Stores. At that time, they used to sell loose crisps — you could buy a quarter of a pound or just two ounces, and for two ounces, you got a great big bag, because of course they didn't weigh very much. I would go to the park and sit on a bench and read, and when I thought it was about time to be going home, I would take the books back to the library and get on the bus. The lady I was staying with never, never knew that I played hookey from school for six weeks. She still doesn't know, even though I write to her every Christmas. And I don't know why I went back. I suppose I thought that one day someone might come knocking on the door, but nobody ever did. I believe I got most of my education reading those books rather than going to school.

ERIC SMIDMORE

Like thousands of other school children, I was evacuated from school on the 1st September, 1939, a Friday, two days before war was declared. There were six coaches, each filled with fifty children from our school. We went to Darenth, just outside Dartford, which now seems a strange place to get away from the bombs!

Five of us including the teacher were billeted in a very large house belonging to a Justice of the Peace. It boasted a cook, a maid, a chauffer and gardeners. After about a month, we were transferred to the village. My younger brother and I were in one house and my older brother and a friend in a house nearby.

On September 3rd, when war was finally declared, we were all in Church. The siren sounded but the vicar, who was hard of hearing, carried on with his sermon, wondering, I expect, why the congregation was leaving! I remember running across the fields afraid of being bombed. When the 'all clear' sounded, not understanding the different signals, we ran faster!!

After three months away all was quiet at home and our parents let us go back. It was some time in 1940 that a second evacuation took place, but this time parents took their children to a London station, we went to Kings Cross, where teachers organised groups of children to go further afield.

Outside the J.P.'s house. Left to right: Johnny Winch, the schoolteacher, Norman, Jack and Eric Smidmore.

We went to Cambridgeshire, to a farm in a small village. When we arrived at the village school, the local people came along and chose the children they wanted to live with them. As my brother and I were a 'pair', a farmer took us together. We were excited at the time, I remember, to be going to a farm, but after a while this wore off.

Although we were not physically ill-treated we were very strictly brought up. We had to go to Church four times on Sundays. The farmer's wife said that we should call her 'Mum' seeing that she was looking after us. Food was always on our mind, as we never seemed to get enough. After a while three other boys were billeted with us. There was a wash house attached to the main house where the laundry took place and this served as our bath-house. A wood-fired boiler heated the water which was then transferred into an old tin bath by ladle. We kids were scrubbed there once a week.

Dear Mabel and Reg,
I thank you for your letter, and 1/-.
I hope you are keeping well.
Norman has been placed in my class, so that Johny, Norman and I sit to-gether.
He is quite a good reader and speller. I expect he takes after his big brother.
We played a match on Saturday and won 15 goals to 3.
We are playing again Tuesday morning and again Saturday afternoon.
I am making full use of the pads Reg gave me.
Well, we do not need anything excepting for Wellington. We must have them because of the mud and puddles on the way to ~~school~~ school.
I think Norman will make a good football player when he grows up. You ought to see Eric he takes a couple of minutes to get ready, then he spits on his hands and runs up to the ball and misses it.
Well, thats all I have got to say cheerio
love from Jack ×× and Johny and kids ×××××

Jack Smidmore writes home.

We had chores to do on the farm; early morning milking and 'mucking out' the sheds. School holidays were non-existent as far as we were concerned. We cut cabbages, sugar beet, and did potato picking in all weathers. We were paid a small amount of money, which we never got in our hand. It was 'saved' for us and when we needed clothes it was used to buy these. At night we were allowed out to buy our supper, one pennyworth of chips, and sometimes we used to buy half a loaf from the kindly village baker. I often wondered what he thought of us, buying bread to eat in his shop at night. But he never told anyone about it and we were grateful for this. It was often drummed into us all that we would not be eating as well as we did had we stayed in London.

Every Saturday we were allowed to go to the pictures in the town, about five miles away. We looked forward to this, especially in the wintry weather. At least we were warm for a few hours. I cannot remember being allowed to sit in the house whatever the weather, only to go in for meals and to sleep. We were either at school or working on the farm, and we were not able to go in until certain times. We used to climb over a locked barn door on the farm and sit in the hay that was stored there, to keep warm until it was time for bed. It was a good hiding place.

Down on the farm.

The Smidmore brothers helping out in the gardens.

Quite a few evacuees were posted to the village and the usual feuds took place between the locals and the Londoners. Even at school the resentment was present, my brother being regularly caned for lateness even though he was doing chores for the farmer before school. If any misdeeds happened in the village, the Londoners were blamed. We rarely saw sweets and on one occasion when we were given our ration coupons the village shops had sold out, or so we were told!

I remember, at the age of eleven years, helping a calf to be born by tying a rope to its legs and pulling it out. I also watched a pig being slaughtered, which was illegal without permission, in the war. It all helped our education, I suppose, but looking back we would sooner have stayed in London. One and a half years of evacuation came to an end, when our mother decided to bring us home. I suppose there were some good times but although there were some friendly villagers, the evacuees did 'band together'. As it happened, when we did come home, the real air raids started so we did not really miss anything.

See Irene Swanton's story. She is Eric and Norman Smidmore's sister.

ENA SMITH

Norman and Eric Smidmore wearing suits they bought with money they earned on the farm.

Eric and Norman Smidmore talk about their evacuation experience. Norman is telling how the school master caned him for stealing walnuts. The brown stains on his fingers gave him away.

On Sunday, 3rd September, 1939 we were told to assemble at Charlton Manor School, South East London. I had four children: Beryl was seven and a quarter, John was five and a half, Peter was not quite four and Irene was nine months old. I was going with them on evacuation.

We lived in Weyman Road near Charlton Manor School. We had to get up at five o'clock in the morning and be at the school at six o'clock. While we were having breakfast there was a knock at the door. It was an air raid warden to say there was a chink of light through the pantry window — and war had not been declared then — so we had an argument!

We had to take one change of clothing, one blanket and a gas mask each, that is all we were allowed to take. We walked from the school to Charlton Station which was quite a way. I had taken a very large pram with the two youngest children in it. When we got to Charlton Station there were lots of children, all with labels on, and parents assembling there. Then the train came in. We had no idea where we were going and I did not know what to do about the pram. They found room for it in the guard's van.

We arrived at Tonbridge Station and from there we got on green buses to take us to High Brooms. Just as we arrived at High Brooms there was an air-raid warning and everyone scattered. Some of the helpers took the two eldest children, and they told me to go with the two youngest to

CONTENTS

	Page
GENERAL MEMORANDUM	1
Description of the Small Child's Respirator ...	1
Description of the Baby's Protective Helmet ...	3
The Choice of the right Protective Device ...	4
INSTRUCTIONS FOR USE OF BABY'S PROTECTIVE HELMET	6
INSTRUCTIONS FOR USE OF SMALL CHILD'S RESPIRATOR	7

July 1939

the cottages that were just opposite the school. The rooms were full of evacuees. Then the all clear went and a Mrs Barefield came over to me and she said, 'Will you stop with me?' I think they were all worried as to whom they were going to get, you know. I said to her, 'Well, I've got four children,' and she said, 'I'll go next door and see if they will take two of them.'

It was a little Victorian terraced cottage and it had two rooms and a tiny kitchen downstairs and two or three bedrooms upstairs. It was decided that we would stay there. On the first night there was a loud bang from next door and John had fallen out of bed. As it was next door, I could do nothing and I could hear him crying. I saw a light come on so I knew something was being done.

We survived there, but there were nine of us in this little cottage and it was a dreadful squash. Eventually Mrs. Barefield had decided that the two children next door (John and Beryl) should come in with us so there we were, husband and wife and their two children and me and my four.

It was the poorer people in the majority of cases who were willing to take evacuees. Of course the money helped, but I think they were more aware of our needs and they were marvellous to put up with us as they did. I think both sides felt a bit hard done by. We because we were not in our homes and able to live the way we wanted to, and they because they had to put up with a great crowd — being billeted on you. Imagine suddenly having to put up with a family of five — Just think of the noise!

I remember when we had been there a little while, Peter wanted to go out and play with the other children in the street and he came back in with a large bump on one side of his head. I put some arnica on it and he was frantic to go out and play again. A little later on he came in with another bump on the other side, and I thought, 'Oh dear, everybody is so rough down here!' Eventually, I wanted to get us somewhere else together but it was not possible. Peter, Irene and I went to quite a nice little place in Prospect Road, Southborough and the other two, John and Beryl, went to another house in Southborough. I went to see if they were getting on all right. The woman came out with a great big knife. Their bedroom was up in the loft and all those children had had to eat was potatoes. It was really dreadful and so I took them back with me.

We moved to a flat over the Co-op shop, which was absolutely mouse-ridden. You never saw anything like it, there were mice everywhere. The room we went into had got greasy marks all down the walls. The woman there came to me with a tray of crockery, but everything on it was cracked. I told her I was not used to cracked cups, and things improved a little bit. It was dreadful though. They had a bathroom which they never used — never used the bath — so I had to bath the four children in a tin tub before the fire. Later on she used to ask me to go in for a cup of tea with her and she used to say to her son, 'Don't give Mrs Smith a cracked cup!'

I discovered that I knew the District Nurse there from Blackheath. Her mother was ill and eventually, when her mother died, she asked me if we would like to go to live with her in another house in Prospect Road. It was terribly cold in the Prospect Road house. There was a huge bathroom which was absolutely freezing. There was a geyser that spluttered and bubbled and exploded with an awful noise. Peter was frightened of that and thought it was going to blow up. We did stay there for some time. I was very worried about Beryl's education — she was coming up for eleven. My sister had returned to Shooters Hill and so it was arranged that Beryl should go and stay with her and go to school in London.

Peter contracted scarlet fever and he was in hospital for a very long time. When he came out of hospital, Freda (the District Nurse) had decided to sell her house and they gave us another old ramshackle place. It had gas lamps in it, and an awful lot of old furniture.

Many people went back to London even in the first weeks. We stayed considerably longer, but when we came back, the raids were still on. I remember turning over the settee and putting two of the children under it for shelter. We had an Anderson shelter in the garden but it was full of water and we could not use it. We then had a Morrison table shelter in the dining room and we used that. I used to put the children in and put the wire round it. It was pretty grim during that period.

The Smith children at Prospect Road, 1941. nephew, Beryl and John.

The Smith family picnic on Southborough Common.

PETER SMITH

One of my first memories is getting up in the dark and sitting by the French doors, eating our breakfast. There was a knock at the door and an argument.

I can only remember a little about the first house we stayed at. There were false teeth in a glass and just up the road there was a shop on the corner that sold penny kites. We sometimes went there to spend our Saturday morning pennies. But John knew a shop, behind the High Street, where they would sell you four liquorice shoelaces for a ha'penny and we would eat our liquorice walking back. Then just about where the school was, near the church, was a shop that sold a first class ice cream for the other ha'penny.

There was a place where we went for our haircuts. You used to have a haircut for fourpence and if you sat still he would give you a ha'penny back. I don't suppose I often got it back. The older two went to school just over the road and I went there occasionally, being looked after by Beryl when my mother had to come up to London.

I remember the garden at Prospect Road, with Victorian tiles in it and at the back was a cowfield. The cows came into the garden one night.

Later, we stayed for a while at a cottage. I remember that ramshackle cottage very well. There was an old pear tree at the bottom of the garden and the pears just dropped off into a kind of mush. We were

John and Peter Smith at Prospect Road, Southborough, 1941, showing off their new caps.

there for the Battle of Britain, and you could see the planes overhead in the sky and the guns going. I remember watching the 'dog fights', seeing aircraft on fire and others crashed, and the parachutists coming down.

There were a lot of nice things about being evacuated, especially the space. We could go down Dog Kennel walk and on the heath and to the woods. We used to go out to collect chestnuts in the autumn. I remember picnics on the heath and tobogganing and a pond with frogs. We happened to be walking near when they were leaving the pond in their millions, and you could not help but tread on them, there were so many. I remember seeing snakes too. Oh yes, there were lots of advantages for children.

We came back to London whilst the raids were still on. When we travelled on the Southern Region railway all the windows had their own little blinds. When you got to a station you could not tell where you were. It was unlit, and as like as not you would get out at the wrong side! You had to open the door and jump out very quickly so that you did not show a light.

There was a 'humdinger' of a raid the first night we returned, and my mother put us under the sofa. I remember using the Morrison shelter. It was quite a good table, but it was very awkward, as you could not get your knees under because of the wires round the edge. You were supposed to leave them up to stop any debris coming in during a raid. We used to get in at the far end. I remember once there was a Doodlebug coming straight towards the house. We heard the engine stop and we all fled into the table shelter, but Dad stayed at the window and we all shouted at him to get in! We had our windows blown out several times. We used to go out and collect shrapnel after a raid.

Some time towards the end of the war there was a gathering at Greenwich Town Hall and all the children of the borough were invited along. We were given two second-hand toys that had been contributed by the children of Australia. I remember coming back with a book that had a dog on the cover from a boy who lived in Cunnamulla, Queensland. That was wonderful. We had food parcels too. I remember when a ship went aground off the Norfolk coast, and it was carrying oranges. The oranges floated ashore and we were sent two crates of them by our Norfolk relatives. We used to take them to school and give them to everyone.

Government Evacuation Scheme

A B C D according to answer

Registration of children under five. May, 1939.

Place of Registration

Name of school THE CHARLTON MANOR L.C.C. (J.M.) SCHOOL HORNFAIR ROAD, S.E.7. GREENWICH

Party No. X 1216

A.
①

Name and Address of Mother	Surname—Christian Name(s)
	SMITH ENA
Address	19 WEYMAN RD

Names and Ages of Children Under Five	Surname	Christian Name(s)	Age Years	Age Mths.
	SMITH	PETER	3	6
		IRENE		5

A	Does mother wish to go with above children ?	Yes or No YES

B — Mother wishes children above to go with

Surname	Christian Name(s)	Mrs. or Miss
	YES.	

Address

C — Mother wishes children to go with party from :—

D — Mother wishes to withdraw the following children from school and take them with her or send them with the person named above

Names of Children		Name of School from which they will be withdrawn
Surname	Christian Name(s)	
SMITH	JOHN	CHARLTON MANOR
	BERYL	CHARLTON MANOR

Signature of Mother .... E A Smith

Signature of Registrar .... E. M. Clark

COPY TO BE HANDED TO MOTHER TO KEEP UNTIL EVACUATION TAKES PLACE.

MILLY SQUIBB

I was about twenty four years old in 1939, and I had four children. When war broke out I was down hop picking in Kent. We were in a place called Bell Common and we did not realise what it was all about because we had no wireless there. We learnt from the local pub that we all either had to go home or stay where we were. We decided to go back home, and we came home and stayed there for the first year because there was no bombing.

We were living right near the railway station in Bermondsey. I was born in Dockhead near Tower Bridge and I had lived there all my life. We used to sleep under the railway arches when the bombing started. We stayed sometimes in what they called No.3 Arch, Bermondsey, in St. Thomas Street, quite close to London Bridge and it got bombed. It was one of the worst bombings in that part of London. There were over a hundred youngsters killed there and a lot of them were never found. It was a landmine. It fell on No.3 Arch and when you look back on it, under the arches was one of the worst places you could have gone.

We got bombed out at least five times, well blasted out really, more than bombed out. There was a big tea warehouse near us called George Payne's and they got burnt down. The heat smashed all our windows, so we had to move out. Then we moved into Tooley Street, into a block of flats called Vine Street Buildings and we got bombed out of there too.

The Sunday they tried to burn London was the worst night of my life.

From then onwards I decided to send the children away. I sent three of the children, Maureen aged seven, George aged five and Lennie aged nine and I sent them to Newhaven. I wanted them to all stay together. The woman they were staying with took a dislike to my little boy and she made his life hell.

My eldest girl phoned home one night and she said, 'Mum, Georgie's run away'. Of course I left the baby with my mum and we went down to look for him. We found him with a woman just up the road. She knew what was going on and she took him in. He was friends with another little evacuee boy that was staying with her and he told her that the other lady was cruel to Georgie. She used to make him go without his food, and she'd send him up to bed with no dinner.

It was bad enough having a war on and the children having to go away from home, without having people picking on them. We brought the three children back to London. We had to come back by train and we had to stop two or three times on the way home because of the bombing. It was awful.

Then I had my baby, Michael, and when he was about seven or eight weeks old we went to Wales, a place called Llannelly in South Wales. When we got there, they put us in a place and there was a nice white table cloth on the table and forks, no knives, just forks and spoons, and a massive big plate of brown and white bread and butter. We thought we were going to have a meal because it was Sunday dinner time. But do you know what we had? Cockles! They had been down to the beach and picked them that morning and that was our dinner and that was something we never had at home. I always managed to make a meal of a pound of sausages for fourpence ha'penny, and a couple of onions or two penn'orth of pot herbs and make a blooming good stew out of that lot.

I knew the food was not good enough for the money that the woman was getting paid to look after us so I went down to the billeting office on the Monday morning and they put me in a house with a man who had just lost his wife. He had two sons, and they were all at work down the mines. I cooked and cleaned and looked after them and the children. I stayed there for a year and it was fantastic. The man was quite upset when I came home. Because my husband was taken ill and as things were quieter in London, we all came home.

A MESSAGE FROM THE MINISTER OF HEALTH

TO PARENTS WHO HAVE EVACUATED THEIR CHILDREN

MINISTRY OF HEALTH
WHITEHALL, S.W.1.

[handwritten facsimile of the letter reproduced in print on the right]

A Message from the Minister of Health
to Parents who have Evacuated their Children

Ministry of Health
Whitehall S.W.1

You are among the many fathers and mothers who wisely took advantage of the Government's scheme to send their children to the country. I am sorry to learn that some parents are now bringing their children back.

I am writing to ask you not to do this. This is not easy, for family life has always been the strength and pride of Britain. But I feel it my duty to remind you that to bring children back to its congested towns is to put them in danger of death or what is perhaps worse, maiming for life. You will have noticed that the Enemy is changing his tactics.

He is now concentrating heavier air raids on one or two towns at a time, leaving others alone for the moment.

Nobody knows which town he will attack next. So don't be lulled into a false sense of security if your home district has been having a quieter time lately.

Remember that in April over 600 children under sixteen were seriously injured in air raids. So keep your children where they are in the reception areas.

Don't bring them back even for a little while. This is your duty to the children themselves, to the A.R.P. Services in your home town, to those who are working so hard for them in the country, and to the Nation.

Please read this message as the sincere words of a friend both to you and the little ones.

Yours Sincerely,
Ernst Brown, June 1941

The Government urges parents to leave their children in the country.

Serving food to shelterers in a London Tube Station 1940.

Back in London, we slept in the shelter of course. One night we were down there and I wrapped up Michael in a blanket and put him on the bunk beside me but in the night he rolled off. He was not hurt because he was well rolled up and just bounced on the floor. We were at home when the Buzz bombs started and I was waiting in Peckham High Street, I had done some shopping, when one went off.

Then we went to Liverpool. The house we stayed in was beautiful on the outside, but when we went inside! She was an elderly person and she used to play a lot of bridge and whist. She said, 'You can have the blue room.' I will never forget that blue room! Out the back there was a little kitchen for us to use. I had never seen anything like it in all my born days. There were cobwebs everywhere, in the saucepans and everything. I like a bit of soap and water. Cleanliness is next to Godliness, my mother always taught me, and I had to set to and clean it all up. I had been there for three days when she asked me to have a whist game. They were all in this front room and she was all for top show. Everything was lovely in the front room, but beyond that was filthy.

I did not like it there and neither did the kids, so I said 'Right we are going home'. I had a big old-fashioned black pram and I packed it all up with our clothes and I put it in the railway guard's van. Unfortunately the train got bombed. We were all right and we got home safe but the pram never did.

When we got back to London, I had to go to the Women's Voluntary Service and fetch some clothes because the kids only had what was on their backs. We were allowed to pick out two of everything that we needed, and I have never forgotten the W.V.S. for that. Three months later I had a letter from the railway people to go and pick up my property. The pram was all buckled, but the things were still inside it. They were all wet and mildewed and we could not use them any more. I had to go to the W.V.S. to get some more things and they gave them to me. A lot of people had to do that because they lost everything in the bombing.

We used to go down the Underground in Borough High Street and we used to have our beds on the floor all in a row. We used to try to pick a warm corner, so we did not get any draughts from the passage ways. They used to run the trains every night on the Circle Line for the kids to have a ride. One night I lost one of my children, Pat, and it was two hours before we found her. We did not let her go riding on the trains again.

IRENE SWANTON

Evacuation came to pass for me soon after my second daughter was born at the British Hospital for Mothers and Babies, Woolwich. Her birth on the 1st May, 1944 at 9 pm interfered with the 9 o' clock broadcast that the Nursing Sister was more interested in. She complained that I might have let her listen to the news as the Prime Minister was speaking. I therefore knew that things were happening on the war front, but at that moment in time, I could not have cared less.

I returned home, and, now with a family of two, tried once again to live as normally as possible, dodging the bombs and eagerly awaiting the news that we would soon be invading Europe and hopefully the war would come to an end. I remember ironing on the glorious 6th June, 1944, listening to the wireless and hearing John Snagge tell us that, 'D-Day has come.' It gave us such a lift and extra hope that all would soon be well.

Unfortunately, it was not that easy. We still ducked into the Morrison shelter at night and during the day when things were rather heavy, but about a week later, we had a dreadful night. The shocking noise that seemed to go on for ever, and was inexplicable at the time, was the first indication of Hitler's secret weapon — the most frightening experience of the V1s or Flying Bombs.

The attacks of these terrible weapons were more ruthless and harder to cope with because of the tremendous numbers being sent over and the

Irene Swanton, nee Smidmore, and her brother Eric.

Irene and George Swanton, with their children Jennifer and Gillian.

unknown pattern of just where they would cut out and destroy buildings and people. My difficulty was trying to get the children in the shelter. Our Morrison was in the garage adjoining the house and it seemed I was always in the middle of bathing or feeding them when the siren went. Before its wailing note had finished, the rattle of the V1's engine would be heard. I prayed it would keep going until I had both baby and toddler into the safety of the shelter. As I ran, the flying bomb could be seen quite clearly, flames spurting from its tail, and I felt reasonably safe until the next noisy and evil bomb went overhead.

My husband, who was serving with the RAF ground crew in Cumberland, admitted to being so much safer away from it all, but worried, like thousands of others, for his family's well-being. His Commanding Officer, hearing the announcement of the advent of the V1s, suggested he looked for accommodation for us in the village and gave him leave to collect his family. So we evacuated from London to Millom.

We stayed at first with a family of four, husband, wife and two teenage children. Like many young evacuees, my experiences were often tinged with the harshness, unfriendliness and, often, greediness of others, although being older helped me to cope a little better.

Since I had two younger children, extra rations were permitted, but the man of the house was a selfish bully, always demanding extra bacon, butter and milk from his timid wife, so our ration books were used to his advantage.

My mother, bless her, must have queued for hours and even days to send us a box of fruit, yet some of this was taken by the son of the house in spite of the box being in my bedroom. I suppose shortages cause longings for the unobtainable, and there were many more incidents, but since we were safe for the duration, what did it matter!

See Eric Smidmore's story. He is Irene's brother.

220

PAT TAYLOR

When evacuation became necessary my mother told my sister and me that we were going to the country 'to try it out' — just for a couple of weeks. I preferred the idea of going to my aunt's in Australia, but this was not to be. I was to go, with my elder sister, to Kent. We hadn't ever been away from home before . . .

On the morning of departure we assembled at Woolwich Dockyard Station, with our boxed gas masks hanging round our necks with a piece of string, and I believe we carried brown paper bags with an orange and some food. We didn't know where we were going, and we didn't want to go. I certainly didn't want to leave my home for the unknown.

We left by train from Woolwich Dockyard Station and went to Snodland in Kent, and were transferred by bus to a place called Birling, where we assembled at the village hall. We thought, from what people said, that it was Berlin! Later, we were taken as a large group along the country lanes, by a local warden. He knocked at each door and asked the occupier whether they would like to take in any evacuees, and how many. Time passed and it was getting dark. Some children were left at farmhouses and had a lovely time. The woman (where my sister and I, and a school friend of hers, stayed) agreed to take three girls. She was a wizened old lady. Her husband was a ruddy faced man who always wore corduroy trousers tied under the knees with string. He went off every day with a shotgun to catch rabbits, which was what we seemed to have for dinner most days, except for Monday when it was bread and cheese and pickles, because Monday was washday. With rabbit stew we always had swede, which was the first time I had ever tasted them, and I didn't like them.

She rented a pair of tiny cottages next to the pub in the village of Ryarsh, where the 'London' bricks came from. As it turned out later, it was right in the trail of the bomber planes. The cottages were exceedingly small after our Victorian London house, and full of furniture and other clutter. In the scullery were housed a large assortment of wild birds, but very pretty. We had to sleep, three in a bed, in the adjoining cottage, and I had to sleep in the middle because I was the youngest. I didn't know the other girls. It wasn't my school so I knew no one. We had a jug and ewer on a washstand. We were given a half-filled water-bottle at night, which the three of us were supposed to use for washing in the morning! If we wanted the toilet in the night, we had to go out, cross the pub yard (full of beer crates), go through a gate, walk down quite a long path, passing several aviaries of talking magpies on the way, to a cubicle, inside which was a bucket underneath a wooden seat-top.

At school we learned some different songs from the ones we knew in London. I preferred the London ones like 'Linden Lea' to 'Shenandoah'. The school had two classrooms; my teacher, also the headmistress, was very kindly, although she looked rather fierce, and seemed

Pat Taylor and her sister on evacuation.

Girls from St. Georges C. of E. School, Battersea. Open air sewing lessons in Pembrokeshire.

eccentric. I also liked her because at Christmas as a prize she had selected some large wax crayons for me, so I now had something to draw with. Outside the school there were walnut trees. We could collect the nuts if we were early for school. Part of the school garden was divided into small personal-gardening strips, which reminded me of graves. For some of our lessons we had to go to the village hall, which was a tin hut. It was bitterly cold. There was a valor lamp for heating, and every morning we had to run round the hall before starting lessons, supposedly to get warm. We sat at individual flimsy card tables. If the siren went we had to crouch under these tables with our gas masks out of their boxes and ready to put on. We also had to knit socks for the seamen on four needles which I found a bit difficult at first.

It was a very cold winter. I was very thin and undersized and I felt the cold badly. One day a teacher (from my sister's school) came to ask what kind of clothing we felt we needed. I said a pair of gloves. 'A pair like mine?' she said, which were a pair of fur gloves. 'Yes please!' I said eagerly, I was somewhat disappointed when she returned at a later date with a woollen scarf, which she said I could wrap around my hands. It was quite nice; soft and pink with a fringe on the ends.

One day, a Sunday, the school congregated and we went up the hill to skate on a frozen pond. It was bitter. I felt so miserable that I eventually went home and knocked on the latched door to be let in. The woman refused because she said it was healthy outside. Just like when I developed German measles and she told me to go out in the sunlight and the spots would disappear. Every time I wrote home to my mother I said that if she didn't come and get me I would come home.

I had one joy, that in the village there was a huge old elm tree. I could climb up inside, and at the top there was a bench seat. Sometimes I would call out to people and imagine they would wonder where the voice was coming from. I have been back years since and it has gone. The cottages have been converted into a rather elegant house.

One day we evacuees decided to clean up the cottage where we were staying. We took up the matting only to find a quarter of an inch of dirt underneath. When the woman saw what we were doing she was horrified. Another time we decided we would like to read in bed as we were sent to bed so early. So went to the village stores and asked for lots of cardboard boxes, which we cut up to fit each small pane of glass in the window. Because of black-out regulations no light was to show at night. Our endeavours and delight was short-lived. The warden could see the chinks of light through our cardboard squares and promptly paid us a visit! The woman told us off!

Christmas arrived and everyone was invited to a large party in Snodland. We had balloons, everyone received a present and such a nice man got everyone singing, and everyone enjoyed themselves.

After Christmas I was transferred to my sister's school in Snodland. We were taken there every morning by coach, driven by one of the village farmers. Here I was able to learn algebra. I couldn't understand geometry, and I wasn't allowed to join the French class because I hadn't already done any French. This was a great disappointment to me. We had cookery lessons, well I had two — each time making bread buns. I had two housewifery lessons — and each time I had to scour out tin baths with 'monkey Brand' and kind of block 'Vim' used for cleaning. Some girls played 'mother' to large celluloid dolls.

We lunched at school. That is we took sandwiches. Always we sat in the same place. I sat opposite a local girl called Ada. She disgusted me. She chewed with her mouth open, and I saw all the masticated bread being turned into a sludgy pulp! It turned me sick but at the same time I felt just a tiny bit fascinated.

On my birthday I wanted to celebrate — something. I decided to run all the two and half miles to the nearest town and back, in the rain to buy two doughnuts to share with my friends. I had to be back for mealtime.

My mother paid me, or us, one visit during this time. A friend had driven her down. Was I delighted. She never forgot how when I went to greet her, I leapt into the air, hitching my legs around her waist and hanging on to her shoulders. It was as much as her seven stone could take. My sister and I were taken for a car ride to Maidstone, and we laughed at a motorcyclist hurtling along at great speed — we called him 'flying legs'. In the car we were doing seventy!

By this time the pair of little cottages were gradually filling up with other people, two boy evacuees, who were allowed to sleep in the next

Taking cover.

bedroom of our otherwise empty 'sleeping' cottage. Then a woman and her little boy came and then a pregnant woman from Scotland, and the old woman's grandchildren were dreadful. We had different sittings for our meals.

I think my mother had seen enough. It wasn't long after that, that she decided we should return to London. How relieved I was! Most probably my sister too.

It was good to be back in London, even with the bombing. Twice our doors, windows, complete with frames, were blown in. It was only then that for two nights we slept in the shelter, The shelter was so cramped. I bought myself a tuppenny packet of digestive biscuits and put them in a cocoa tin to keep them crisp. These were for an emergency.

I watched dogfights in the sky. I collected sackfuls of shrapnel in quite large pieces, on average about five inches long by an inch wide. The council blacksmith opposite told me that if I collected enough and gave it to the council they would present me with a four inch model spitfire. I saw the fire in the Arsenal when people said that the cordite factory was alight. My mother found part of the fuselage of a German plane, complete with a motorised switch, which my sister promptly dismantled and ruined. When the V1s first came, I thought they were noisy low flying planes, with courageous pilots. One almost dropped on our house but the wind turned and carried it two streets away. I went indoors to tell my mother and just as well I did, as the garden became littered with panes of glass and huge lumps of concrete. Fronts of houses were torn out; twisted iron bedsteads hung from exposed floors. With the first bombings the streets looked as though a giant has spilled great sacks of flour over every street.

It was only when the warden came to attach green metal pieces to our gas masks, to prevent gas entering the masks that I became terrified. I ran into the bedroom, locked the door, and hid under the bed. It took me back to the beginning, when I had first been fitted with a gas mask. They smelled awful, they looked awful, and they were frightening. I had resisted trying one on. My two favourite teachers had taken me to the art room and tried to force one on me, and those memories of terror remain with me to this day.

GLADYS THOMAS

During the summer of 1939 I was teaching at Calvert Road Junior Mixed School in Greenwich S.E.10. It was a very happy school, with children and staff very friendly and harmonising well, and I think we thought we would go on for ever. There were rumblings of troubles in Germany, trenches and shelters were being built in the streets of Lewisham and occasionally the wail of practise air-raid sirens could be heard. Even packets of railway tickets and gas masks came surreptitiously and were packed into the cupboards, but somehow we thought this didn't concern us. Nobody would be crazy enough to start another war. People were just exaggerating about this crazy man Hitler, and we just carried on. The summer holidays came, and off we went to Exminster without a care in the world. What a lovely summer it was, with long sunny days and seaside trips by train. Then out of the blue at the end of August came the announcement on the radio: All L.C.C. teachers were to report back to their schools on the Thursday. I couldn't believe it. Back I had to go.

On the Friday I went to school. There we were given identity cards, gas masks and allocated our own particular group of children, ten or twelve as I remember, and a voluntary helper, and told to report at the school by eight o'clock on the Saturday morning. I went home and how empty it seemed. Things could never be the same again, and they never were. It was like being in a nightmare; it just couldn't be true.

On arriving at school the next morning we were all too numb to say much. The children were too dazed even to cry. With their identity labels, gas masks, lunch bags, holding on to their brothers and sisters, they looked so vulnerable. They had said goodbye to their mums and dads outside the school. We didn't know where we were going, what was going to happen, or if we should ever see Calvert Road again. Actually I never did.

At a quarter to nine, a number of L.C.C. trams pulled up outside the school. On the pavements were the mums and dads. In front, with their backs to the pavements, were a number of policewomen clasping hands and making a barrier so that the mums and dads couldn't push forward. We marched out with our pathetic little groups and filled the trams. There was barely a sound. The trams glided off and took us to New Cross Station where we were guided to the right platforms.

In a few minutes the big steam train puffed in and we boarded it. I remember that carriage clearly. It was one of the old-fashioned sort, upholstered in red with its own lavatory, and there was I with ten children whom I didn't really know, not being in my own class, and a helper. Off the train went into the unknown.

We soon realised from the countryside that we were going through Kent into Sussex and eventually the train pulled up at Hastings.

At last one could sense a shiver of excitement — as it was the seaside — but there was not a lot of time for emotions. We were met by some very capable ladies who ushered us into motor coaches and took us to what I think must have been a Church Hall. We were given refreshments and then started the billeting.

Of course everyone wanted a pretty little girl. These were soon allocated and in the end we were left with the not so pretty poor cockney boys in their woolly jersies — ill-fitting jackets and thick trousers and their hair with a donkey fringe across the forehead. Their would-be hosts were, of course, those with big houses who had said, 'We'll have a couple of children if they are not all taken.' So the little boys from the back streets of Greenwich landed up lost and bewildered in grand houses with baths and dining rooms and big gardens. I was billeted with a Hastings teacher. Off we went in various directions, having been told to meet at Lower Street School the next morning, Sunday.

*Gladys Thomas with her teaching colleagues
from Calvert Road School, Greenwich.*

On the Sunday morning we all met in the Hall of Lower Street School, the school we were to share during our stay in Hastings, children, helpers, teachers just talking about our billets. The radio was switched on and we listened to Neville Chamberlain telling us that we were at war with Germany. There was a long apprehensive silence — then the air-raid siren went — we just sat, horrified! Some went out and put handkerchiefs in cold water — to use if Gas Bombs were dropped. Nobody spoke, then the All Clear went and there was a huge sigh of relief — then excited talking. Our evacuation to Hastings was started.

Mothers and babies were due to arrive on the Sunday afternoon. We took lessons one week in the morning session — and one week in the afternoon. When not teaching, we went for walks on the beach, over the downs, and swam. Some children returned home as it was the phoney war. Nothing much happened to remind us of war, apart from the blackout, or seeing the young men (who were to be our saviours in the Battle of Britain) doing their physical training on St. Leonards Sea front.

JUNE TILLET

I was evacuated in about October 1939 from All Saints School in Blackheath. I was nine years old. That day, I went to school, with my little case, you could only take a certain amount of clothes, and gas mask and they put our labels on us in the classroom. I remember standing there with my sister and my brother and all the class, getting ready to leave.

We marched down the road with Miss Harris, she was my teacher. We walked across the heath to Blackheath station and got on the train. Of course we didn't know where we were going to. Mum and Dad came to the station and waved us off. I was excited. I'd been on a train before because I used to go and see my gran at Waterloo, but I wasn't all that used to it.

We arrived at Bexhill. I can remember the teacher standing there, and all us children waiting to be billeted. A woman said that she wanted two sisters, and my sister, Rema and I were chosen together. Her name was Mrs Page. Fortunately, we had a lovely billet. Some weren't so fortunate. It was a big shop, a 'Freeman, Hardy and Willis' shoe shop in Devonshire Road.

Mr Page was the manager there, and our bedroom was the top left hand side room over the shop. The shop had all oak panelling, and there were all strips of carpet down the shop, with a polished floor in between. Also

17th June 1940. London evacuees re-evacuated from London station.

there were lots of little wooden footstools. It was all brass outside and they used to clean all that. It looked very smart. Mr Page always wore a suit and he had two girls for staff. They used to wear green overalls with 'Freeman, Hardy and Willis' on the front.

We were allowed to play in the shop in the evenings. Mr Page used to say, 'Be very careful when you open the boxes, don't mark the shoes when you put your feet in them.' We took it in turns to pretend to be the assistant or the customer. We used to say, 'What would you like madam?' 'Oh, I'll have a high heeled pair of black shoes, thank you.' And then we'd go up the little wooden ladder to get the shoe box. They were beautiful shoes wrapped in tissue paper. We used to think it was marvellous.

There was a 'speaking tube' in the wall and it used to make a whistling noise. When Mrs Page wanted us to come upstairs, she would whistle down to us and we used to put our mouth to it and say, 'Yes?' and she would say, 'Alright you can pack away now, it's teatime.'

She was very nice, she used to give us nice food that we'd never tasted, like mincemeat balls. My mum never used to make anything like that. We used to think they were lovely my sister and I, we'd never had them before.

It was lovely in Bexhill, we used to go down to the beach and in the sea. Mrs Page used to take us to the pictures now and again. I thought it was wonderful to go to the pictures with her. And we used to play with her baby, David, a little boy six months old. He used to have 'Virol', and she used to put his 'dummy' in it, and when she was out of the room, I used to dip my finger in it. I used to say, 'Ooh, isn't it lovely,' hoping she wasn't going to see me.

Mum used to come down and visit us about once every few weeks on the Maidstone and District Coaches. They used to stop on the front, and if she wasn't on it, we used to get so disappointed. We were only little. Mum came down to see us for the Christmas we spent down there. That was very nice.

We were down there for a year, but then they started to put barbed wire up on the sea front, because of the threat of invasion, and Mrs Page got quite frightened, being with the baby. She decided to go back to Kidderminster, which was her original home and my mother said that she'd have to bring us back to London. I remember when we were saying goodbye Mrs Page cried. I can see her now, she wore glasses and had her hair drawn back.

When we came back the blitz was still on. A lot of schoolchildren were re-evacuated to Wales, but we didn't go. In fact we practically lived in our Anderson shelter for most of the next five years.

I never saw Mr and Mrs Page again. Apparently he went in the Royal Navy, and she wrote to my mother to say that he'd been killed in action. It must have been terrible for her, she was only about twenty-six.

I've been back several times to see the shop. It's still there. It's been modernised, of course, the front's all different but I went back a few years ago and it was still 'Freeman, Hardy and Willis'.

17.—Clothing.

Besides the clothes which the child would be wearing, and such should include an overcoat or mackintosh, a complete change of clothing should be carried. The following is suggested:—

GIRL.	BOY.
One vest or combinations.	One vest.
One pair of knickers.	One shirt with collar.
One bodice.	One pair of pants.
One petticoat.	One pullover or jersey.
Two pairs of stockings.	One pair of knickers.
Handkerchiefs.	Handkerchiefs.
Slip and blouse.	Two pairs of socks or stockings.
Cardigan.	

Additional for all—

Night attire; Boots or shoes; Comb; Plimsolls; Towel; Soap; Face-cloth; Tooth-brush. *Blankets need not be taken.*

Head teachers are at liberty to utilise material during needlework lessons, for the making of clothing, small bags, towels, etc., for the benefit of the children, particularly those whose parents are poor. Such articles, except those sold to pupils or otherwise disposed of to pupils in accordance with regulations, should be regarded as official property.

18.—Food.

All adults and children should carry sufficient food for the day of evacuation. Suggestions for children's food follow:—

Sandwiches (egg or cheese).
Packets of nuts and seedless raisins.
Dry biscuits (with little packets of cheese).
Barley sugar (rather than chocolate).
Apple; orange.

No access to the beach.

ANITA TRUMAN

The months leading up to the Second World War did not make a big impression on me. I was an eight year old little Jewish girl living in the East End of London. However, I do remember snippets. I remember hearing about Moseley and his Black Shirts, about their marches in the East End and the violence involved with those marches.

I remember listening to the wireless every Saturday lunchtime (we called it 'dinner time') with my family — my mother, father, younger brother, and myself. Each Saturday there was a programme about what was happening in Germany. The one thing that stands out in my memory is hearing how the Germans made old Jewish men crawl around on their hands and knees, forcing them to eat grass like animals. That was the first time I had ever heard the expression 'Schweinhund' (pig-dog) and that was how the Germans were taunting the old men.

I remember hearing about a man called Chamberlain, and I well remember the phrase 'Peace in our time'! Everybody was talking about it and I remember how happy the grown-ups were that there wasn't going to be a war. But they were wrong.

I remember trying on my gas mask at school for the first time, and being taught how to use it. It was all quite fun, but I also knew that it was serious. From that day on until the end of the war I never went anywhere without my gasmask.

On 31st August, my father came home early and brought with him two white canvas haversacks (something like the ones sailors use). My mother put a few items of clothing in the haversacks for my brother and me. They had a list of the things they had to pack. Everything was ready and then my father remembered that he had forgotten to buy an 'indelible pencil' (what on earth could that be?) He went out and came back a little later with the pencil. He wet the point in his mouth and proceeded to write our names on the haversacks — Anita Greenberg, Arnold Greenberg. It came out a mauve colour.

We were all up early the next morning because it was the day Arnold and I were going to be evacuated. It all sounded wonderful. We were going into the 'country'. We would see cows and sheep and trees and flowers. These things weren't exactly in abundance in London's East End.

At about nine o'clock we all started off on foot for Stepney Green Station. On the way we saw lots of other little family groups going in the same direction.

The station itself was really crowded and we had to queue to get in. We were given buff-coloured name tags to tie on to our coats. Some of our teachers were waiting for us on the platform and this is where we said our 'good-byes' to our mummies and daddies. There wasn't a lot of time because we were ushered onto the waiting train by our teachers. I wasn't sad or unhappy — in fact I was quite looking forward to the adventure. Someone must have done a wonderful job of brainwashing me. I didn't cry then, but now, fifty years later, I do shed tears when I cast my mind back and remember.

We didn't know, and neither did any of the parents, where we were going. My mother and father had drummed it into me that my brother and I must not be separated. My brother was six years old and I was the big sister.

The train finally arrived at a place called Windsor. We were taken to a church hall and there we were given brown carrier bags with string handles. Inside we found sandwiches, a cold drink and a bar of chocolate. We were in a big hall and there were lots of children.

Anita, above and to the right of the teacher, in the class of 1939 at Stepney Jewish School.

After we had rested and eaten we were all taken on a march down a very long road. I think it was called St Leonard's Road. Along this road there were rows and rows of houses and outside each house stood the housewife. As we walked along, the housewife would say 'I'll have a girl', or 'I'll have two little boys', etc. It was a long walk down St Leonard's Road. All the children in front of my brother and I had been swallowed up and were already in various houses. Now it was our turn. Mrs Taylor said, 'I'll have the little girl.' When I heard that, I grabbed my brother's hand and refused to go. I said, 'My mummy said that we must stay together,' and Mrs Taylor agreed to take both of us, Arnold and me. She had only one spare bed, but that didn't matter - we were only little children and could both sleep in the one bed. And so we took on our new status — we were now Evacuees.

Mrs Taylor took me into the front room and sat me at a desk and asked me to write our names down on a card. She then gave me some writing paper and asked me to write a letter to my parents giving them our address, and letting them know that we were all right.

During the previous year, 1938, I had been sent to a children's convalescent home in Broadstairs, where I stayed for seven months. I thoroughly enjoyed my stay there, and I think this helped to make me a very independent little lady, and well able to cope with the situation in which I found myself. However, this was not necessarily the case for my little brother. The first night we were there, he wet the bed and this went on for a number of nights.

Two days after our arrival in Windsor, on a quiet Sunday morning, I was playing in the street outside the house when I heard, for the first time in my life, the wail of the air-raid sirens. All the people came out of their houses into the street and just stood and listened. Nobody spoke. The sirens rang out that morning throughout the country and signalled the beginning of hostilities between England and Germany. In other words, the beginning of the Second World War.

As an eight-year-old child, I had romantic notions of war, and imagined men on horseback fighting each other with swords. I wasn't a bit frightened and in fact kept a look-out up and down St Leonard's Road for the rest of the day to make sure that I didn't miss anything!

Anita, aged seven.

Anita Truman, nee Greenberg, in her Brownie uniform, 1939.

Our schooling was a bit disrupted. One week, the Evacuees went to school in the morning and the local children went in the afternoon. The next week, the local children went in the morning and the Evacuees went in the afternoon, and so on.

About two weeks after our arrival in Windsor, my parents came down to visit us on a Sunday, and in fact they visited us every second Sunday for the whole time we were in Windsor. My brother and I used to go out with them when they arrived at mid-morning and spend the whole day with them until it was time for them to return to London. They could see that we were well looked after, and I am sure they returned home feeling easier in their minds.

But all was not absolutely wonderful. I became rather quiet and withdrawn. The Taylors seemed to prefer my little brother to me and I felt it.

One Sunday, when my parents were not due to come, I took my brother out for a walk. I don't remember how far we walked, but we came to what I thought was a park, and I could see horse-chestnuts lying on the grass under the trees. We had learnt, in our short time in Windsor, the value of conkers, and I was hoping to get a tenner. Someone called out to us and when I looked up I could see about six people sitting at a table having tea. I realised that this was not a park, but the private grounds of a large house. The people beckoned to us to come over to them. They asked us who we were and when I told them that we were evacuees, they were very kind and one of them offered to give us sixpence (about 2½p in today's money but worth a lot more in those days). I didn't know very much about money as there was never much of it around in our house. I refused the money and repeated what my mother had instilled in me, 'I mustn't take money from strangers.'

I realise now how very vulnerable we little children were. My brother and I were lucky. We didn't come across any unkindness, but I know that this was not so in the case of many evacuees.

I remember that I was always late for school. There was no real reason for it. Mrs Taylor always got us ready in good time. I blamed it on my little brother, saying that he walked too slowly, but in truth it was just as much my fault for dreaming on the way to school.

One Sunday, my parents brought one of our grown-up cousins to visit us. My cousin, Ann, had the remedy which would enable me to get to school on time. If I repeated the following all the way to school I would never be late again:

Left — left — had a good home and I left;
Right — right — serves me jolly well right.

I don't remember whether it cured my lateness, but I certainly had to be nimble footed at the change over between 'left left' and 'right right"!

I do remember that our teachers sometimes took us for walks in Windsor Great Park, and we all used to sing as we walked along. Songs like, 'Run Rabbit, Run Rabbit, Run, Run, Run', 'Underneath the Spreading Chestnut Tree' (with all the hand movements), and 'South of the Border, Down Mexico Way' stand out in my mind.

Mr and Mrs Taylor had a son aged twelve. One day he asked if he could look at my head. When I asked him why, he told me that he had heard that Jews had horns! That was my first brush with anti-semitism, although I didn't realise it at the time.

Five months after we arrived in Windsor, in February 1940, my brother became ill with a bad bout of flu. My parents decided to take him home with him so that they could look after him themselves. I made such a fuss about being left behind that they took me too. After all, nothing terrible was happening in London. A few days after we returned to London, my parents received a letter from Mr and Mrs Taylor, informing them that we could no longer return to their home. It didn't really matter because, as I have already said, nothing much was happening in London — and that is how my brother and I were in London during the blitz!

But that is another story . . .

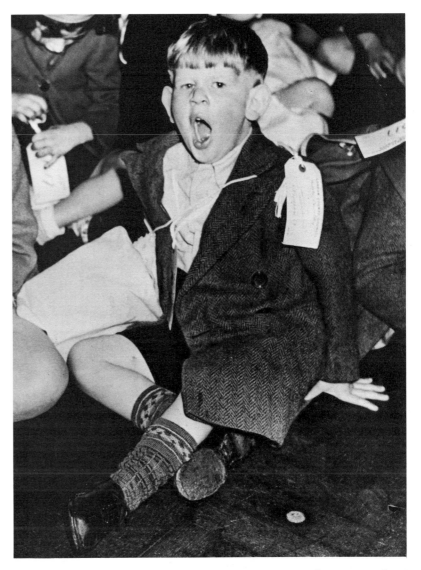

Small boy, from Myrdle Street School, waiting to be evacuated.
1st September 1939.

235

OLIVE TUCK

It was January 1940 and my mother was taking me to a nursery somewhere in Camden Town where I would stay for a day or two before being evacuated. I was nearly four years old and mother had been telling me how I would go to stay in a nice house in the country and she would come to visit me quite often. I was being 'sent away' because I had been looked after by a child-minder who was rather deaf and had used me to listen for the air-raid siren and so at that very early age I had a nervous problem and couldn't bear noise around me in case I missed hearing the 'warning'.

I remember I had on a navy blue reefer coat with the usual label in my button-hole, I was clutching a Mickey Mouse Annual and had my gas-mask slung across my chest.

I was taken to a village called Box in Wiltshire and I remember the Billeting Officer, Miss Pike, a very sensible tweeds and lisle stockings lady. I don't think anyone chose me to live with them, because Miss Pike took me to a family who made it clear that they didn't really want any 'Londoners' but very reluctantly took me into their home. The next few weeks or months (I'm not sure how long I was there) are a blur of misery. I remember being smacked a lot and having to spend a long time each day sitting on a chair with my finger on my lips (children should be seen and not heard).

The next thing I remember is mother coming to visit, the smell of her perfume, lots of kisses and cuddles and being moved to another placement. This couple had no children of their own, adored little girls and for a year or so I was blissfully happy with Aunty and Uncle. Uncle worked on a farm and I remember the smell of cow manure on his boots when he came indoors on a cold winter's day and took his boots off by the roaring fire. I remember the laughter as I went through his pockets looking for the 'treat' he may have brought for me — a comic 'Chick's Own' or 'Rainbow' or perhaps a sweetie or even a rosy apple. I remember mother coming to visit there. It must have been hard for her to see me so happy with my foster-family and I remember going to the station with her and waving good-bye. I am not sure how long this happy state lasted, but I remember starting at Box C of E school and walking there with some other children each day. It must have been about one and a half miles each way, but I can never remember it being a hardship. It all ended when Aunty fell down the stairs and sustained a serious back injury which meant she could no longer care for me.

Thus I was moved to my third and final placement. This too was a childless couple and Uncle was as soft as butter, whilst Aunty ruled the house with a rod of iron. It was at this point that I really began to miss my mother and father and listening to 'Children's Hour', I would burst into tears when Uncle Mac told us all that Mummy and Daddy were thinking of us. This Aunty kept me very clean and made me dresses on her sewing machine, but I can never remember her giving me a kiss or cuddle. She was a super cook and I was well fed, but I had it drummed into me that this was all done for ten shillings and sixpence per week. My mother told me in later years that she often sent extra money down for me, but I was never told about this.

Aunty had quite a temper and when I displeased her she would shake me hard and bang my head against a window-box she had in her conservatory. Why didn't I tell mother about this when she and my father visited? Because Aunty told me that if I did they would take me back to London and I would be killed by a bomb, and if they didn't she would hit me again when they had gone home. So I used to pretend that everything was fine and cry myself to sleep when they went back to London.

It wasn't all bad. We went for long walks in the country. Aunty used to take me into Bath on market day and we would buy lardy cake as a treat. Uncle liked pike fishing (I think to get away from Aunty) and would sometime take me on a Sunday to a place called Christian Malford. I think he was terrified of her and spent a lot of time saying 'Yes M'dear' and 'No M'dear'. She made him wear a white apron to eat his meals. My sister who is five years older than me came down to see me in 1948. My parents had left me down there when war ended as they were carving out a career for themselves as publicans and assumed I was happy there. Anyway I told my sister how unhappy I was. She told Mother when she got back to London and within three weeks I was back in London with my family.

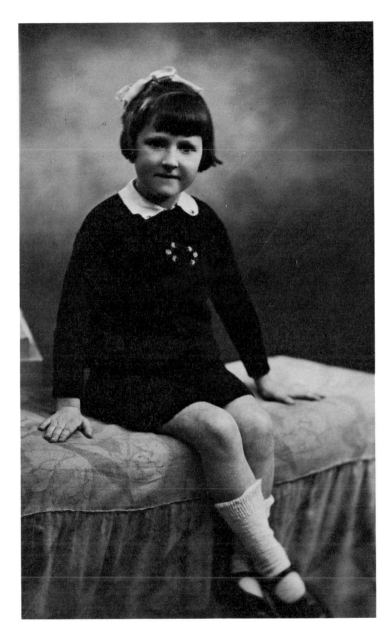

Olive Tuck, nee West, 1941.

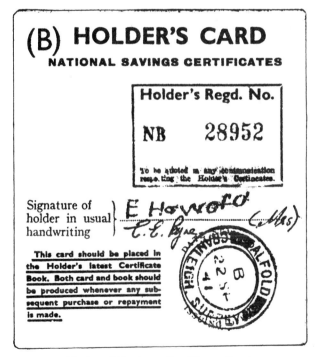

National Savings Certificate Card.

MARJORIE WALKER

I was nine when war broke out. I was evacuated with my two sisters. We went to Lancashire and we were put in this mill owner's house. It was a bit exciting at first but then I was crying because I wanted my mum. My sisters were younger than me, and they didn't mind so much. We all cried a bit at first but then they accepted it philosophically, which I never did. I just kept crying and crying. I wanted to go home to my mum.

I slept in a room with my sisters. They kept us all together because I was always crying. Eventually I would have had my own bedroom, a thing I had never had in my life before. At home I slept in a room with about four or five of us. And the food up there was marvellous compared with what we got at home, but even that couldn't compensate for the loss of my mother. In fact, I felt guilty that I was eating all that lovely food and my mother was probably having just the food we always had at home. After dinner, which was fish on a Friday, I always thought of my mum just having rice, and cheap rice at that, and I just wanted to come home. I felt guilty, I was getting that I suppose, and she was getting nothing.

The place itself was so utterly different, all that grandeur in the mill owner's house, so beautifully furnished, but I just wasn't interested. Our house in London wasn't furnished anything like it was up there. It was a mill owner's house, and it was furnished just beautiful. All that grandeur I suppose. But I don't know, I just wasn't interested, I just wanted my mum.

I posted letters to my mum without stamps on and covered in tears, asking her to come and take me home. Everyday I wrote a letter on any scraps of paper I could find, and put them in any old envelope without stamps or anything. I just posted them to my mum, saying, "Please come and get me." They tried to talk me into staying but it was no good, I just wouldn't stay. I wasn't naughty, I was just miserable all the time. My two sisters were very happy there and stayed, but I just didn't want to stay away from my mum. In the end she had to come up to fetch me and take me home because I was so unhappy. I stopped at home after that.

When I got home we did go back to school, but the sirens kept going and we had to keep going down the shelter, and half the time nobody went to school anyway. Our school wasn't bombed, but the planes used to come over Bexley on their way to London, and they would drop their bombs if they had any left, mostly incendiary bombs and land mines. It was such fun and so many things were happening, you didn't realise how awful it all was, how many people were being killed.

Growing up during the war, I saw things happen that no children had ever seen before. I've seen houses being blown up, especially in the docks, and burning buildings, and getting out of the station in London and the station was actually on fire. It wasn't frightening because we were all so young, we didn't realise what was happening. Now I would be terrified, but then it was just something different.

Mrs Shepherd with her seven children in a double air raid shelter.

MICHAEL WARD

I was on the list for evacuation to Canada and had an embarrassing medical (at eight I had tried my sister's nail varnish on my toes!) but the sinking of a passenger ship with children on board put paid to that.

I went to Hampshire to stay with my grandparents. I remember being found to have nits on arrival. Horror of horrors in my grandparents' fairly comfortable house! Of course, I had picked them up on the train from Waterloo, or did I perhaps get them at school and my mum hadn't noticed? Washing with vinegar and plastering with Morgan's Pomade was the treatment. I remember wandering the silent autumn lanes in heavy sea drizzle causing vinegary water to run into my eyes.

On one such walk I heard a loud 'clump' and seconds later a German Heinkel bomber passed over below cloud level at no more than three hundred feet. It had dropped its last bomb near New Milton water tower, killing an old lady, before heading home across the Needles and the Solent.

Then I went home for the blitz. In 1944, I lived on through the V1 raids that have been described many times. We watched them from the school grounds and lay with bated breath at night when the engines cut out. The worst seemed to stop above our house and hit our school, destroying the cycle sheds!

In 1944 the first V2 rockets fell and I was evacuated soon after to Bungay, Suffolk with other Romford children. My worst experience was standing around while other children were picked out for billeting. I was left over, and taken eventually under sufferance by a Mrs Lines who already had one boy.

Later I was taken by a Mr and Mrs Leeder of 2 Flixton Road, Bungay, (her son was the mayor of Diss) where I spent a happy year, mostly on the USAF 8th Air Force Bomber Base at Flixton. I am still in touch with the widow of a B24 Liberator pilot who flew S-Sugar.

An abiding memory is of the Christmas goose catching fire in the oven and the night a flying bomb (V1) came over. Mr Leeder was out in the outside loo and watched it pass by, like a comet with a flaming tail, while Mrs Leeder, her two sons and us evacuees sheltered in the Morrison shelter. Mrs Leeder was beside herself with panic — calling, 'Will, Will', but we two old hands took it all in our stride!

MAUREEN WELLER

I was thirteen years old when war broke out; the age when, having read a schoolgirl's usual quota of 'boarding school stories', the anguish of the reality of leaving home was overlaid with the exciting prospect of boarding school adventures in store. Thus, for most girls of my age, fiction had in some way prepared us for evacuation. In 1939 I was attending a south-east London grammar school. A safe refuge in the form of a vacant boarding school premises was allocated to us; the location was the south coast. In many ways the transition from day school to boarding school was easier in war circumstances than in peacetime, for although we faced a new strange life away from home, we did so in the company of our own friends and teachers. The port town we moved to was very pleasant and sufficiently accessible to home for our families to visit us.

However the disastrous events at Dunkirk completely changed the complexion of the situation. Our safe location was now vulnerable to enemy attack from France and another evacuation was hastily planned for us. I have blurred but painful memories of our journey to North Wales. It began at dawn and involved about eight hours by train followed by what seemed an endless coach journey, throughout which we existed on but a few sandwiches. This time we were to be billeted with local families so a new apprehension was added to our ordeal.

My friend and I were last to board the coach so by the simple laws of distribution we were last to be handed over into the keeping of our somewhat reluctant foster parents. By now it was dark and we were climbing from the coach outside four terraced cottages standing in isolation halfway up a Welsh mountain. Mr and Mrs W. had been 'volunteered' to take one evacuee, so with hindsight one can appreciate their feelings to receive double their expectation. Unfortunately this showed clearly on their faces, so arriving brought us little relief of comfort. This sensation of being strangers in a foreign land was reinforced by Mr and Mrs W's asides to each other spoken in Welsh. Any detailed recollections of the remainder of that long day were obliterated by total exhaustion.

The light of the new day fully revealed our new circumstances and Mrs W's unrelenting forbidding expression, which we later discovered was permanent. She delivered one jug of hot water for washing ourselves to the bedroom, which we shared. This was the only hot wash of the day and had to be carried out without room heating, whatever the season. It was not only heat, but also water which was in short supply. We discovered that its source was a tap shared by all four cottages situated in one of the front gardens. 'Water Lugging' quickly became part of our daily routine. Water closets were therefore still a thing of the future and reality consisted of a primitive privy in a draughty wooden hut at the end of the garden by the vegetable patch. This constituted an agony of dilemma when the need to use it came in the middle of the night. We had been provided with a chamber pot for this purpose, but embarrassment was the ultimate deterrent, equalled only by the scariness of a solo journey down the garden path in the dark.

Downstairs there were two rooms, the kitchen/living room where everything happened and the parlour which was forbidden territory except for declared special occasions. We were completely unprepared for the bathing arrangements in a tub in front of the kitchen range, demonstrated without warning by Mr W. He came home from work one day, took off his outdoor clothes and then continued to remove the rest. We fled to our bedroom, but have often since wondered how this uncommunicative couple would have dealt with the situation if we had stayed.

By now I was fourteen and developing the obstinacy of adolescence. This streak was never more active than on Sundays when Mr and Mrs W. required us to go to Chapel with them. This ritual, among all those recently new to me, was the least congenial. There was a sensation of being irreversibly sucked into the strange ways of unknown powers. All else I had suffered, with or without protest, but chapel-going was where I took an intransigent stand, as also did Mr and Mrs W. They would do their part in the war effort by accepting two London evacuees. They would put up with the inconvenience and all the problems. But they would NOT keep a heathen under their roof.

So once again I was moved, ironically thanking the Lord for deliverance from Mrs W! My new billet in the valley was, by contrast, considerably more liberal and certainly more welcoming; in fact, a most agreeable place to wait for the war to end.

Maureen's sister on sandbag hill.

EILEEN WELLS

It was from South Bermondsey station that we first started out. I remember all of us children standing along the platform with our name tags pinned onto our coats, along with this cardboard box which carried a most frightful object called a gas mask. The box had a string through it, so you could wear it over your shoulder, and we were all very scared and I suppose looking back now, a bit excited as to what was going to happen to us.

My mother and father and little sister had come to see my younger brother and me off, and they were telling us to be brave and not to cry as we were going to the country where you could pick apples off a tree, and eat lots of them, and that we would grow into big children, and that the next time we saw them we would nearly be as tall as they were. Then the announcement came that all parents were to leave the platform so that the teachers and helpers could get us on the train. I can still remember my mum and dad waving to us, and they were crying, which then brought on the tears with my brother who was screaming for them.

When we were at last settled on the train, I looked out of the window, and saw a very funny looking thing in the sky. It was a large silver balloon that looked like a sausage with a little tail on the back. All the kids were buzzing about, looking and asking what it was, and that was my very first glimpse of a barrage balloon. Looking back now, it was that balloon that helped us on our journey into the unknown. It took our minds off our parents who we had left behind. And then we had a surprise, we were all given a cardboard box containing some fruit and cake and some bars of chocolate.

We finally arrived at Lancing in Sussex and had to walk off the platform two by two, holding each other's hand. We walked all the way through the town to the local school, and then we were sectioned off in our different age groups, or into family groups of brothers and sisters. There were a few people there who were going around looking at us, and then they started to pick and choose, but there were more children than there were foster people. After some of the kids went, the rest of us were told to sit on the floor. They came around with some lemonade, and it seemed like ages. We were then told to get up and go two by two, hand in hand out into the playground.

Then we had to march round the different roads, knocking at people's houses to give us temporary accommodation. Looking back now, there wasn't much kindness about in that particular part of Sussex. They really did not want us snotty London kids upsetting the rural charm.

I remember walking up very posh roads and drives, along with the billeting officers. We were somewhere in the middle of the long file because it never seemed to get shorter. As the officers approached the doors, they were either told they didn't want us, or they made out they were out, but we still went on. Finally, it came to our turn to be either taken in or turned down. I never forget it was a Mrs Bullivant whose house they knocked at. It had a big conservatory, and we had to go round the back before she even spoke to the officer. After speaking to each other for a while, she agreed that she would take the boy, but she did not want the girl. She did not like girls. It was then that I spoke up and said, 'My Mum said that I was to look after my brother, and that we wasn't to be parted.' I was told not to be silly, as it was only for a little while, but I made such a fuss, that somebody else was taken in.

Well we finally got our billet, in Tower Road, and it was to be the most scary and awful experience. It was with a certain Miss Fluitt. She was a very old spinster, a retired schoolmistress. She was a little person who used to wear this grey dress with a white collar all the time. The night times were the worst. In our bedroom was this very old dark wardrobe with a marble washstand to match, and this very old bed with a carved headboard with faces on it. The room had bare boards which were polished, and a rug either side of the bed.

Billeting Officer in Mrs Holdsworth's cottage in Kingston Blount, helping her fill in subsistence forms while her charges look on.

When it was bedtime, she used to come in and sit in a rocking chair which was at the side of the bed, and sing us lullabies, which was the most awful noise you ever heard. What with her and the creak of the chair on the floorboards, we were petrified. It was alright for my brother, it was my side she used to sit by. I used to put my head under the bedclothes so I wouldn't see her. Then her singing would stop, and then I would get brave and take a peep out, and there she would be, just sitting there staring. She was like a witch, she even had a little beard.

One day, I think it was a Sunday, she said that she had made me a frock out of an old dress of hers. It was the most awful thing you ever saw, it had big mauve and brown flowers on it. She made me put it on, and then she paraded me around before her neighbours, telling them what a pretty girl I looked. I must have looked a terrible mess. I even had to go to church with her in that frock, and to complete the outfit, I also had a little straw hat, goodness knows where she got it from. I still recall the embarrassment I felt that day, even my young brother laughed at me.

Another awful time we had while we were there, was when Miss Fluitt bought some cakes for tea. She had invited two of her spinster friends. We were told that we were to be on our best behaviour and not show our bad London manners. It all went very well until it came to each taking one of the cakes. The ladies chose theirs, I took mine, and there was a chocolate cake left. My brother wouldn't take it, he didn't like it. I offered to change, but she wouldn't hear of it. That cake, by the way, was put on the table for a fortnight until one of us ate it. It was me in the end. I told the lady in the sweet shop about it, because we were so unhappy there and so frightened, and she must have reported it, and we were taken away to another billet saying that she was a little too old to be looking after children.

Mr and Mrs Moorman were our next billet, at 'The Nest', Myrtle Crescent, They were a Canadian couple who had been in Sussex on business and were unable to get back to Canada, so had to stay in England for the duration of the war. It was a very nice place. We used to call the man Uncle Eddie. Unfortunately he died while we were there, and Auntie Ethel couldn't look after us, as she went to stay with friends.

So we had to move once more. There were several temporary stays after that, not very happy ones. One I particularly remember is where me and my brother each slept on a Maxwell's laundry basket within a recess by the fireplace, which wasn't very comfortable to say the least.

Mr and Mrs Fisher were our final billet. That could have been a lot happier if it hadn't been for their children, John and Jean. They were horrid to us, always getting us into trouble. Yet when our parents came down to see us, they were as nice as pie because our Mum and Dad used to save their sweet coupons and bring us down what sweets they were able to get at the time, or any other little treat, and those kids got treated the same. After their visit, we used to see them off at the station. That used to be a very tearful farewell. I used to have a terrible lump in my throat that used to last for a long time. Then we used to arrive back at the house, and those horrible kids would make fun of our red eyes.

Just to show you what horrors they were, one day Mrs Fisher made a pot of macaroni cheese, which she left on the fender. There was a kitchen range she used to cook on in the living room. Alongside the fireplace was this sofa which we were sitting on. John came along and knocked the pot off the fender. It ran everywhere, all over the blue rug, which was in front of the fireplace. Who got the blame? Us of course. We were made to scoop it up, back into the pot. It looked terrible, there was hairs from the cat in it and blue streaks of dye from the rug. Me and my brother had to have it for tea. She said she couldn't afford to waste it. They never had it though.

That incident, I believe, was the last straw. It made us so unhappy, I went and bought a letter packet, in those days for twopence, and two penny stamps out of my pocket money of sixpence. I sat in the 'rec', the recreation ground, and wrote just six words, 'WE WANT TO COME HOME *NOW*.' Within the next day or two, our Dad came down to take us home, telling our foster parents that they missed us too much to leave us there any longer.

Evacuees' tea time.

EILEEN WOODS

I was four years old when the war started. My sister was fourteen and my brother was eight. They were evacuated with their schools, Joan to Highbrooms and Bernard to Hawkhurst in Kent. My mother and I were taken to Maidstone. My earliest memory was of sitting in a car while being chosen by the ladies who had agreed to take in evacuees. My mother had been a nurse and a house mother in an orphanage before her marriage and after a few weeks she volunteered her services to the local authority. She had to leave me and I was sent to a billet in Groombridge. The family was very kind to me even though I remember wetting the bed! They understood it was because I was missing my family.

In the meantime my mother was given the task of setting up a 'Sick Bay' for evacuees. The local authority was at Tunbridge Wells. They acquired a large bungalow 'Chez Nous' in the village of Speldhurst. Mother's job was to organise and run the home so that, should an evacuee fall ill, he or she would be sent to 'Chez Nous' where mother would nurse them and when they were well they would return to their billets again. The inevitable happened. I caught chicken pox and was duly sent off to the sick bay. When the doctor came on his visit he looked at my medical chart and remarked on the coincidence that my name was the same as the matron in charge of the home. 'Well that's because she's my daughter,' replied my mother, and told him that I was billeted at Groombridge. 'Not any more,' he said, 'she's staying with you now.' And I did for the rest of the war.

The village was right in the thick of it as there was an ack-ack unit based there. They used to fire at the enemy planes passing overhead on their way to and from bombing London. I clearly remember watching the Battle of Britain being fought in the skies above us.

We had a very large Morrison shelter in the dining room and you could always tell when there was going to be an air raid, even before the sirens were sounded, because our cat and our dog would come charging in from the garden and make straight for it, or for the bathroom which had the bath always full of water — they were our 'early warning system'!

After a raid, we used to love going out into the garden to collect shrapnel and silver foil strips that were dropped in order to upset the radar systems.

Our dog Rover was a beautiful black labrador retriever. He used to love taking us children to school and was very protective towards us. One day I came home from school expecting him to rush to greet me as usual but there was no sign of him. As I was searching for him my mother came and broke the news to me that she had volunteered him to the army. He became a war dog sniffing for land mines in Belgium and France. I was heartbroken.

One night my mother saw a plane (which was making an awful noise) come down in the woods at the bottom of our field. So at first light, she went to look for survivors. She phoned to report it and said she could find no trace of the pilot or the crew. She was told that there probably wasn't a pilot and to say nothing to anyone and someone would come to investigate. Soon we were visited by lots of VIPs and 'top brass'. It turned out that we had had one of the very first 'Doodle Bugs' and it had missed our home by just a couple of hundred yards!

On another occasion, the vicar called on us and asked if my mother would attend the funeral of a German airman who had been killed in the locality. She was a little reluctant as he was an enemy. The vicar pointed out that he was also a mother's son and maybe a husband and father and it was a Christian thing to give him a decent funeral. She agreed, and so did many other villagers, because the funeral was well attended and there were many flowers I remember. He had a simple white wooden cross on his grave and I used to put wild flowers on it from time to time.

Eileen in the play Dick Whittington. Eileen is to the right of the fairy.

*Eileen and some of the boys at Speldhurst,
with Peggy the dog in 1941.*

Eileen, end right, with fellow evacuees.

I enjoyed my school days in the lovely little village school. (I wonder if they still dance round the Maypole as we did.) I won a prize in a competition organised by the local education authority. We had to paint or sculpt anything to do with the war. Some of the paintings were magnificent with the boys' imaginations running riot! I made a warship out of grey plasticine and it was good too — my prize was a half crown National Savings stamp.

We were sent some sweets from America. The teachers had to share them out amongst us, I think we had about four each, and we thought they were wonderful. Another time somebody brought some hand-made rag dolls to 'Chez Nous' for us girls, which had been sent from America for children in hospital.

By now the sick bay no longer took in sick children and instead my mother had children who needed extra care as they were rather backward or difficult.

We regularly went to the pictures at the Ritz in Tunbridge Wells, but first we'd go into Maynards sweet shop next door for our week's sweet ration!

During those trips we saw very many of Archibald McIndoe's 'guinea-pigs', walking wounded, as East Grinstead Hospital was so near to Tunbridge Wells. I know that I was often very frightened at the sight of them and tried very hard not to show it as I knew they were very brave men. They were always allowed to go to the front of the queues at the cinema and rightly so.

By the end of summer 1944 with the advent of the V2 flying bombs it was decided to transfer my mother's services to Nottingham, a safe area. We went to a huge house in a small mining village called Farnsfield. Mother now had big boys to deal with; teenagers from London who were proving difficult to handle in their billets. They were a challenge, but Mother coped very well. The war ended and at last my father was demobbed. He had been called up from day one of the war and we hardly ever saw him at all during all those years, except for a few days leave now and again, as he was stationed abroad all the time.

We all returned to London in 1946. It was good to be home, but to me everything seemed very strange. I had left it as a small girl and now I was almost eleven. I missed the countryside so much and still do.

We had had chickens (that laid strange shaped eggs during air raids) and ducks, rabbits and guinea pigs in Speldhurst and for me the war time has very happy memories. Funny things stick in the memory. I remember my sister who was very glamorous trying to make lipstick by melting down in a tin over the hotplate all the stubs of lipstick that usually are thrown away. She would make sticks by rolling the setting lipstick in cellophane and popping them back into their containers to set hard — it worked too!

We never saw any bananas during the war and mother made mock banana by boiling parsnips then mashing them and when cold added banana essence and sugar. We thought it was delicious.

I returned to Speldhurst last week on a 'nostalgia trip'. It hadn't changed too much. 'Chez Nous' was still there, but houses were now where our garden had been. In the church yard I found some unmarked graves where the German had been buried. I don't know if he is still there or been taken back to Germany.

Also I surprised myself by being able to go directly to the grave of a local lady who had joined the ATS. She was tragically killed in action and I remember her funeral with masses of flowers on her grave. Several of the cards on the wreaths had her actual regimental cap badges attached to them; these had disappeared by the next day and I thought somebody wicked had stolen them. It is more likely that her family had moved them. I know the whole village was very sad on hearing of her death. Her grave now has a headstone engraved with her regimental company and ATS insignia.

I'm happy to say that Rover survived the war and when it ended we were offered him back. He was a very big dog, and in the army he had been well fed. Food was still rationed for us so it was kinder to let him stay in the army, which he did. We were sent a photograph and a certificate with his army number.

Mr Field, a neighbour, takes Eileen, aged seven, for a ride on his motorbike.

249

DEIRDRE WYNNE-HARLEY

The journey from London, begun as a great adventure, ended some twelve hours later when twenty exhausted, cold and hungry children gulped down cups of cocoa and saffron buns in Chacewater village hall.

As we had travelled west, the length of the train dwindled as coaches were uncoupled at towns and villages, until by Truro only two remained. There, the party divided again; some walked off in a crocodile and the rest of us were bundled onto a bus. Excitement and uncertainty grew again and we squabbled, cried and felt sick as the bus rumbled and lurched. Outside was complete blackness; inside, a few heavily masked lights gave a dim blue glow. And then we arrived, stumbling up the steps of the hall, stiff and tired.

Inside we found lovely warm cocoa, bright yellow, sweet-smelling buns — and people. It seemed like hundreds of them, large, red-faced countrymen and women, speaking words we didn't understand. The Cornish dialect and loud voices were so strange; for the first time, I was frightened and can still see my seven year old self squeezing behind a row of chairs, piled with our haversacks, sobbing desperately for home and, above all, Granny. Kind hands found me and lifted me up, voices I still couldn't really understand, belonged to 'Auntie' Gladys and 'Uncle' Russell — I was to be their evacuee.

Deirdre with her host family.

We went out into the country night, clear and starry, full of unfamiliar sounds and smells. Down the hill and into a granite cottage in the village street, darker inside than out. Uncle found matches to light a candle, then a strange lamp on the table; no switches, no electricity! In the next five minutes, the little girl from London learned that water was a precious commodity which had to be carried from the village well and collected in the rainwater butt; that the privy at the bottom of the garden had replaced the familiar flush WCs and that the big black kitchen range cooked and heated all the food and water. Now, we call it culture shock; more discoveries were to come, but none brought more amazement than those first few minutes of country living.

The first morning, I woke in strange surroundings, in a bedroom barely seen in candlelight the night before, with a camp bed and scratchy starched sheets. Uncertain what to do, where I was, I shut my eyes again, and heard noises of dogs, crows, cockerels, cows and horses; only the dogs and horses were really comprehended. More noises, people this time and their different words, just outside the door, then my name. Auntie came in and hugged me and said I would be their little girl, but my Mummy and Daddy would come and see me and write to me. 'I haven't got a Mummy and Daddy,' I said. After hours of sympathy and enquiry, it was sorted out — I was not an orphan, just a child whose parents were Mother and Father!

Face and hands washed in a pretty blue china bowl on a wash-stand — scratchy harsh towel (Auntie starched everything). Dressed in the spare clothes from my haversack (parcels of clothing were to be sent after us when the families knew where we were) I met my first Cornish breakfast: eggs and potato cakes and sausages without skins, huge amounts accompanied by dismay and hurt at my small appetite.

School for us that day was in the village hall; on the way down the street everyone was looking at us, exclaiming at the unhealthy pallor of all these 'little vaccies', telling Auntie that what I needed was good Cornish food.

When our small school in exile was assembled, we had a full age range from five to fourteen and one teacher. Some of the children were billeted on farms well outside the village and that first day had a two or three mile walk, and though a few had been brought in by pony and

Deirdre with her knitted teddy.

251

trap, most arrived with tired, blistered feet. We all wrote postcards saying we were all right and giving our new addresses. For most parents, this card, arriving two or three days after they had waved us goodbye, was the first news of their children. Now, as a parent and grandparent, it is possible for me to understand some of their anguish at sending a child away to a completely unknown destination and, for many, a different world.

We went up the hill to the village school in the afternoon to meet the village children. Playtime saw battle lines established as the locals prepared to protect their territory; somehow I was in the middle of it all and by the end of break had two bleeding knees and a torn dress. From that day, it was decided that we would have half day schooling, alternating morning and afternoon, so that the building could be shared peacefully.

Like most villages, Chacewater was populated by only a comparatively few extended families. 'My' family revolved around 'Granny', Auntie's mother, who lived on a small-holding just outside the village. Every Sunday evening after church, we went up the hill for supper and sometimes, on special occasions, there were songs round the piano. Granny M had lovely old oil lamps of delicately engraved glass which were used for Sunday best. Many vivid memories of her cottage come to mind — linen drying on the gorse bushes around the field; a medlar tree — 'mind you never climb that, or the witches will get you'; headless chickens running in the minutes after slaughter; and she it was who took me to the old woman who charmed away my warts for sixpence.

I adapted quickly, learned the language and the prohibitions, including most importantly which games and activities were permissible on Sunday (cutting your nails and hide-and-seek were not). I learned the routines, trimming the oil lamps (even at seven), making sure there was always a pot of hot water on the range, and carrying a can of water from the well night and morning.

School was wonderful, our half days off were spent roaming the countryside; at first, there were organised nature walks with our teacher, but very soon we were left to ourselves. We learned of country life, the farming seasons, plants and animals. My world held no threat or danger; the talk of war was between adults or on the wireless — until my father was killed.

They tried to tell me gradually, saying first that he was burnt when his plane crashed. I remember my anger and frustration, half understanding this was not true. I wanted my grandmother to come and see me in Cornwall. She came early in 1941, even though it was a long and difficult journey from London in those days.

Many children returned home, some because they had been very unhappy, or because their parents felt this extreme precaution was unnecessary. So, we happy few who remained became the 'village children' when the next wave of evacuees from Bristol, Exeter and Plymouth arrived. We resented their presence and delighted in taunting them as we had been. But it did not last long; the village pantomime broke down all the barriers, written, cast and directed by one of the village in-comers whose acceptance was solely based on her ability to charm and tame the various mobs of village and evacuee children.

The year I remember best, 'The Babes in the Wood' was chosen. I remember being somewhat disapproving because, as a rather literary and literal child, I did not approve of a ploy which had strong elements of 'Cinderella' and 'Jack and the Beanstalk' as well. As usual, I argued, and nearly got sent home!

Once the show was cast, we had rehearsals three times a week. Absolutely everyone in the village had some part in the production. The group of women who used to gather in the Parish rooms to knit socks put all their energy and imagination into creating wonderful costumes. Butterflies wore butter muslin, with flowers cut out of old curtains appliqued on to the wings which were stiffened with finely split sycamore canes, providing which was the job allocated to the verger. Sheets were used for many of the dresses, draped, tied, pinned, and again, lots of coloured bits were added. Some of the local 'gentry' donated old ball dresses which we used to fight to try on, collapsing into fits of giggles at the thought of their previous owners, familiar to us in sensible tweeds, wearing such diaphanous gowns.

Most of the male members of the cast wore riding breeches and wellington boots — the wellies often being painted with a coat of distemper. This was easy to clean off, so did not damage the war effort by unnecessary destruction! Hats were important, and we used to collect feathers and leaves and berries to decorate them.

The scenery was minimal and, as I remember, mostly quite inappropriate. The village hall had just two backcloths, left over from some dim, distant W.I. play. One had a window looking into a farmyard, and the other was Tower Bridge. The year I was a butterfly in 'The Babes in the Wood', I danced to the Blue Danube against a background of the Thames with some large and rather precarious branches placed to cover the bridge.

The day of the performance was always full of drama. Someone was always ill, costumes lost or torn, and, of course, the lamb or pony or whichever was the chosen animal could not be caught. There always had to be an animal, and just once, we were allowed to borrow Dorothy's father's parrot.

One of the problems when everyone is involved in a village panto is that the paying public is thin on the ground, so it was important to pull them in from the surrounding villages. Posters were made, but we did not stop at that. We took a farm cart, decorated like a scene from the show, and toured round, selling tickets as we went. I remember being given lots of mince pies and dried apple rings to eat as people came out to look at us.

It was always great fun and, with hindsight, I can see that it must have done much to brighten some of the darkest days for many local people. There was real co-operation in spite of class differences. In village life, everyone was aware of their own worth.

Family visits took place. I even returned to London for a few days to be a bridesmaid and Auntie Gladys, accompanying me, had her first visit over the Tamar Bridge. Leaving Cornwall is always hard and when we returned, I felt for the first time the excitement of crossing Brunel's bridge back into my adopted country.

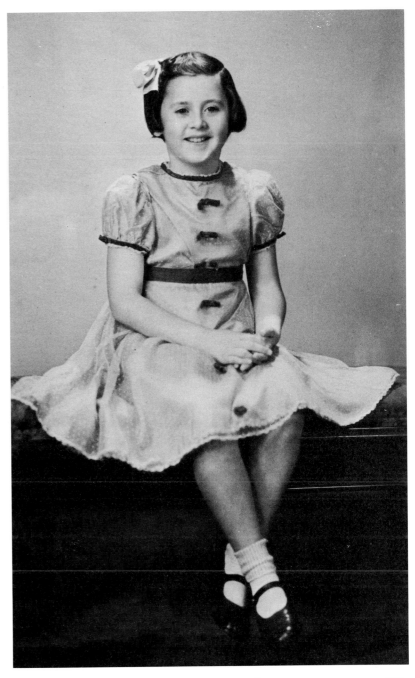

Deirdre in her party dress.

We had blackout and we had ration books — though they did not signify much except for sugar and sweets. Everyone had a relative with poultry, cows for milk and cream, and the occasional pig for slaughter — and no one really felt the war. Except for my father, no-one in the village had family casualties until after 1942. Many of the men were in reserved occupations as ours was a mining as well as agricultural community, so comparatively few were called up.

And then we had the bombs, late one Saturday night. There was a whistling sound, followed by two loud bangs. Everyone knew they were bombs and on Sunday morning, after church or chapel, the whole population walked the mile and a half to view the craters, ideally sited amongst disused mine workings!

We knew there really was a war when the village was encircled by American Army camps. A wondrous source of sweets and illicit cigarettes. For a while, every ten year old carried a pack of Camels, which inevitably made us sick, so we soon gave up.

The village took the Americans to its heart, as it had with us. Every family had Yanks to Sunday tea or supper. The utter strangeness of the black soldiers and their regular attendance at church services made them very popular. My village knew no colour bar, but there were fights sometimes between black and white soldiers, and, once, a knifing. As with the bomb craters, everyone went looking for blood stains.

Suddenly, one day, the Americans were on the move. A seemingly endless, two-day convoy travelled through the village. Unused to traffic, except the daily bus, horses and carts, and the doctor's car, we wondered if we would ever be able to cross the street.

I did well at school. The informal, almost casual education, coupled with a voracious appetite for anything printed, suited me well, and at ten, I did the entrance scholarship exam. The result came on June 6th, 1944. At a very solemn school assembly, the headmaster told us all that this was one of the most significant days in history, and asked if we knew why. 'Please sir,' said I, 'I have a scholarship for the High School.'

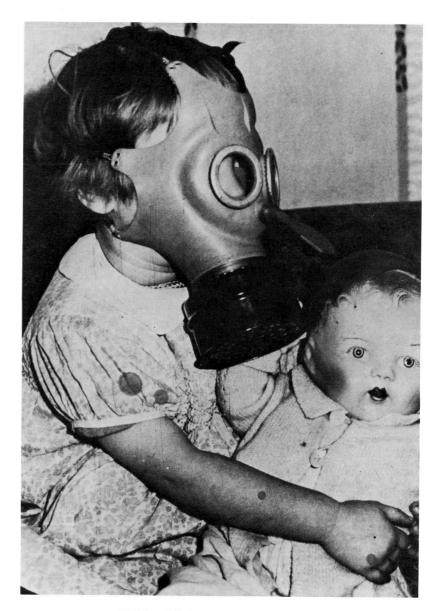

Child in Mickey Mouse gas mask.

AGE EXCHANGE REMINISCENCE BOOKS

Age Exchange is a theatre and publishing company working with London pensioners on shows and books which record their life experience and their current concerns.

It is a feature of all these books that the contributions come from many pensioners, are lively and easy to read, conversational in style, and lavishly illustrated with photographs and line drawings of the time. All the stories are told in the original words, from transcribed tapes, or pensioners' written contributions. The following books are already available:

'On The River': Memories of a Working River. Recollections of older Londoners who have lived by and worked on the River Thames. Their stories recapture the sense of bustle and industry when the river was London's main thoroughfare and a crucial source of livelihood for thousands of families. The book contains over one hundred full page photographs of the river in its heyday. £15.95

'Fifty Years Ago: Memories of the 1930s: a collage of stories and photographs of day-to-day life around 1933. £2.95

'Of Whole Heart Cometh Hope': Centenary memories of the Co-Operative Women's Guild, being the history of the Guild in photos, advertisements and, of course, stories supplied by older women who have had a lifelong involvement in the Co-operative movement. £2.95

'What Did You Do In The War, Mum?': This book of memories, photos and line drawings provides a clear picture of the wide range of jobs which opened up for women in the war years, and of their undoubted skill and ability in these new areas. These individual stories, full of detail and humour, project a positive image of women as flexible and resilient workers. £3.95

'All our Christmases': a book of Christmas memories by Greenwich pensioners. £2.95

'My First Job': Pensioners' memories of starting work in the 1920s and 30s. £2.95

'Can We Afford The Doctor?' was a frequent cry before the days of the NHS. This book examines health and social welfare in the early part of this century when people often had to rely on their own resources and remedies to cope with illness or disability. Childhood diseases, infectious diseases, accidents and more serious illnesses are recalled. Doctors and nurses remember their early years of service and conditions in homes and hospitals. The book has many photographs and illustrations. £3.95

'The Time Of Our Lives', is a compilation of memories of leisure time in the 1920s and 30s. Spare time stories reveal the energy and enterprise of young people who made their own entertainment in the days before television. Pensioners who are now in their seventies recall vividly the comedy of their courting days, the dance, cinema, rambling, cycling and outings of their youth. Generously illustrated with photographs and line drawings, this makes good reading for all ages. £3.95

'Many Happy Retirements': 'For anyone who has sat through conventional pre-retirement courses, being lectured at by experts, relief is at hand. Wisely used, the refreshing new source material in this lovely book from Age Exchange, with its case studies, transcripts and dramatised cameos, is guaranteed to revitalise even the dullest course.' Michael Pilch, Vice President, Pre-Retirement Association. £3.95

'Health Remedies And Healthy Recipes': Reflections by Caribbean elders on the subject of health and diet as remembered in Jamaica and experienced here in Britain. Illustrated with photographs, many donated by the contributors. £3.95

'Lifetimes': A sixty-eight page handbook and sixty Picture Cards, designed to stimulate older people to remember their own lives. The pack is intended for use by people working with the elderly. £20

Posters: Ten of the most evocative Lifetimes pictures are also published as A2 size posters. £10

'Good Morning Children': Memories and photographs of schooldays in the 1920s and 30s. £3.95

'Across the Irish Sea': London Irish pensioners remember their childhood in Ireland and their decision to 'cross the water'. They describe their experience of finding work and homes over here and reflect on their continuing relationship with Ireland. £4.95

'A Place To Stay': memories of pensioners from many lands. Ethnic elders from the Caribbean, the Asian sub-continent, the Far East, Cyprus and Poland tell of their arrival in Britain and their experience of growing old here. The stories are told in English and in the mother tongues. £3.95

There are special prices for OAPs who wish to order any or all of these books.

If you would like to order any of the above titles please write to:

Age Exchange,
11 Blackheath Village,
London SE3 9LA.

If readers are interested in hiring our touring exhibitions of photographs, they should contact us at the above address.

The Age Exchange Reminiscence Centre in Blackheath, South-East London.